Daughter of the Empire State

The Life of **JUDGE JANE BOLIN**

DAUGHTER
OF THE
EMPIRE
STATE

Jacqueline A. McLeod

UNIVERSITY OF ILLINOIS PRESS

Urbana, Chicago, and Springfield

Library of Congress Cataloging-in-Publication Data
McLeod, Jacqueline.
Daughter of the Empire State : the life of Judge Jane Bolin /
Jacqueline A. McLeod.
p.   cm.
Includes bibliographical references and index.
ISBN 978-0-252-03657-6 (cloth : alk. paper)
1. Bolin, Jane M. (Jane Matilda), 1908–2007.
2. African American judges—New York (State)—New York—Biography.
3. Women judges—New York (State)—New York—Biography.
I. Title.
KF373.B554M38   2011
340.092—dc22   2011014505
[B]

Dedicated to Doris Elaine McLeod
and Percival Sinclair McLeod

"I am always impatient with those who say, 'You women have come a long way.' Since I am no gradualist I think to myself that 150 years is too long a time to come 'a long way' in and that those gains we have made were never graciously and generously conceded. We have had to fight every inch of the way—and in the face of sometimes insufferable humiliation."

—Judge Jane Matilda Bolin, 1958

Contents

Illustrations follow page 42

Preface

Several years ago while doing research on Constance Baker Motley, the prominent civil rights attorney and federal judge, I encountered another woman, Judge Jane Matilda Bolin, and discovered what a profound impression she had made on Motley as a black woman in the legal profession. Although Motley had had outstanding mentors such as Thurgood Marshall, it was Jane Bolin whom she heralded as her role model. In Motley's words, it was Judge Bolin who had shown her "how a lady judge should deport herself."[1] This acknowledgement or naming of one black woman professional by another started me on a journey of inquiry and discovery that interrogated Jane Bolin's obscurity in the historical record.[2] Relegated to the vignettes of *firsts,* Bolin had eluded historical inquiry and remained invisible in the scholarship on black female professionalization, politicization, and early civil rights activism.[3] Yet, in the tradition of contemporaries such as Mary McLeod Bethune and Ella Baker, her footprints sketched a life that was fully visible and too remarkable to ignore.

Limited correspondence with Judge Bolin over several years led finally to a memorable meeting in New York City in 2002. On that hot summer day before I set out to meet Judge Bolin, my mother insisted that I change my attire to reflect an image that was, in her estimation, "more ladylike." I could still hear her emphasizing every word with the authority of a Caribbean mother. "Is how you going to meet the first lady judge dressed in pants? You better put on a skirt and blouse and look like a proper lady." I could not muster the gall at that moment to engage her on progressive gender politics. So when I met Jane Bolin I looked like "a proper lady," nicely clad in a skirt and blouse and clutching a bouquet of flowers.

Face to face with the nation's first African American woman judge, I imagined myself a sort of witness to this history. That I am an emigrant from Guyana's shores made the experience even more extraordinary. My mother, like many Caribbean women, had made the trek to the United States several decades earlier in search of economic sponsorship and a chance to secure broader educational opportunities for her children. She was proud and amazed that her sacrifices, which began with her sponsorship as a domestic servant, had made my meeting with Judge Bolin possible. For her, it made defensible every indignity she had ever suffered as a domestic servant, and came to embody every dream she had ever had for her children. My meeting with Judge Bolin was the realization of a dream my mother could not have had, but nonetheless, one she rightfully claimed.

At ninety-four years old, Judge Bolin bore her grace with ease, and her humility seemed to narrow the gulf of wisdom and generation that separated us. I entered the moment riddled with anxiety and convinced I would be tongue-tied in the presence of such history. But almost immediately the lady judge facilitated a dialogue that disarmed all of my anxieties about our meeting. She spoke of things present and of the pleasantries of weather and travel, and seemed genuinely surprised and embarrassed that she would be the subject of historical inquiry. To the extent that she ventured into the past, she recalled, with great fondness, her friendship with judicial peers, judges Hubert Delany and Justine Wise Polier, both of the Family Court of the State of New York. But as reticent as she may have been about foregrounding her importance in the historical record, Jane Bolin had nevertheless evoked a memory of herself as change agent when she recalled Delany and Polier, with whom she was staunchly allied in her crusade for justice. This reinscription of herself, however veiled, had privileged a performative *self* for which she is least remembered over a fixed judicial identity, as the first African American woman judge, for which she is most visible in the historical record.[4] This signification of a fixed judicial identity that was always already racialized and gendered had effectively obscured the discursive realities that constituted a *self* that could no longer be confined within the vignettes of firsts.

My book rescues Bolin from a signification that has limited our understanding of her life. It therefore examines her lived visibility that spans more than half a century and extends beyond the perimeter of the courtroom, because her judicial appointment, although a significant node, is not the only lens through which she can be historicized. When asked to describe her early life, Bolin said in a 1990 interview, "I was born April 11, 1908, in a redbrick, three-story house at the foot of one hill and the top of another in Poughkeepsie, New York."[5] At eighty-two years old, Bolin had framed her life story in terms of status and class. She had positioned herself in what would have been a solid middle-class family in Poughkeepsie, New York, at a time when the majority of black residents were among the class of domestic servants, day laborers, porters, and janitors. Still, her words betrayed a consciousness of the challenges that she confronted as a black woman in the United States in spite of her class standing. Situated as she was at the intersection of the race, class, and gender politics of early twentieth-century U.S. society, Jane Bolin's striving and becoming, no less than her standing and belonging, would come to signify the contours of her educational and professional life.

A broad reading of Michelle Wright's analysis of subject formation as presented in *Becoming Black: Creating Identity in the African Diaspora* is instructive here to an understanding of how Bolin negotiated this space of "inbetweenness," which at times produced her as "other" from within a discourse of race even as it produced her as subject from within a discourse of gender.[6] By contrast, her formative years in Poughkeepsie, although marred by moments of devastating loss within her immediate family, mirrored a self-identity that appeared to transcend the artificial boundaries of race and gender.

A daughter of the Empire State, Jane Bolin was a descendant of a long line of free Dutchess County African American residents who had lived in and around Poughkeepsie for nearly two hundred years.[7] The Bolins were a prominent family steeped in a tradition of public service and activism that reached back to Abram Bolin, her paternal grandfather, who was active in the black convention movement of the nineteenth century. Building on this legacy, Jane Bolin involved herself intimately with the National Association for the Advancement of Colored People (NAACP) from an early age and became a founding member of its Dutchess County branch in 1931. She later rose to prominence in the New York City Branch of the NAACP and remained active in the organization until the internal dynamics of politics and purpose at the national level soured her on the nation's premier civil rights organization. She was an active member in the early years of the National Council of Negro Women (NCNW), heeding the call of founder-president Mary McLeod Bethune to serve with other black women lawyers on legal committees.

Bolin operated just as well beyond the confines of organization. Early in her career she used her influence on the bench to advance and promote the cause of social justice. At a time when it was customary for local white judges to never assign black lawyers to represent indigent white defendants, Bolin challenged the race-specific assignments of probation officers and race-specific placement of children into private child care agencies that routinely accepted children based on racial and ethnic background. Her reformist zeal excited her judicial colleagues and helped to transform the juvenile justice system for the better when the director of the New York City Office of Probation for the Courts was forced to discontinue the practice. She formed alliances across racial and gender lines in her fight against injustice, and at times embarked on a veritable letter-writing campaign to get the job done.

Like other black women lawyers of her generation, Bolin's early practice was tied to the practice of her lawyer-father, Gaius Bolin, and later to her lawyer-husband, Ralph Mizelle. Her preparation and practice foretold success, but "credentialism" was routinely manipulated and therefore not always enough to overcome the marginalization that black women confronted in the legal profession.[8]

Unlike most black women lawyers of her generation, however, she rose relatively quickly through the professional ranks to become a judge just seven years after being admitted to the bar. Bolin negotiated the professional terrain with effective alliances and knew firsthand the benefit of having a well-placed advocate. In Bolin's case, the argument can be made that the influence of well-placed benefactors proved invaluable in overcoming the politics of exclusion and marginalization to realize her success. Eleanor Roosevelt was one such benefactor, who interceded on Bolin's behalf against the muscle of New York City machine politics.

This book engages Jane Matilda Bolin as activist, integrationist, and outspoken public figure, who was a lawyer and the nation's first African American woman judge. The chronological history of black women in the legal profession is not as expansive as it is deep. Still, analyses of black women's particular experiences as insurgent professionals remain few as the study of black women lawyers, until recently, was subsumed by the history of black lawyers and female lawyers, without an understanding of their unique positioning even as they shared "some of the problems and promises of all Blacks, of all women, and of all lawyers."[9] By situating Bolin within an early twentieth-century community, however imagined, of black women lawyers, this book examines the particularity of black women's professionalization in the legal profession, the illusion of credentialism, and the extent to which Bolin's experiences may have deviated from those of her contemporaries. Utilizing an intersectional approach to a race, class, and gender analysis of Bolin's life, this book also explores the dynamics that rendered Bolin an outsider in the national office of the NAACP even as she was constituted as an insider within a community of white women in the La Guardia administration (1934–45).

This book draws heavily on my own primary research but builds on the scholarship on black women lawyers. The papers of Jane Bolin, housed at the Schomburg Center for Research in Black Culture in New York City, provided valuable information on her family life, her father Gaius Bolin, and grandfather Abram Bolin. The transcript of a 1990 interview that Jane Bolin recorded with Jean Rudd was invaluable because it revealed much about Bolin's thoughts on a variety of subjects both personal and professional. NAACP correspondence and Bolin's famed letter of resignation ignited an investigation that led me to closely examine the NAACP national and branch records at the Library of Congress. Materials from the papers of Sadie T. M. Alexander at the University of Pennsylvania Archives and the papers of Eleanor Roosevelt at the Franklin D. Roosevelt Library supported the veracity of claims identified in Bolin's papers. Newspaper articles were mined, as were the records of the NCNW at the Mary McLeod Bethune Council House in Washington, D.C. The growing scholarship on black women greatly enriched my analysis of Bolin, as did the scholarship on women professionals and civil rights organizations.

Understanding the family ties that would have influenced Bolin's early socialization is crucial to an understanding of the choices, both personal and professional, made by the adult Bolin. So, chapter 1, "Her Standing in Poughkeepsie: Family Lineage and Legacy," focuses on the Bolins' lineage and legacy and Jane Bolin's place in it as a biracial child coming of age in early twentieth-century Poughkeepsie, New York. It examines her relationship with her two older sisters, Anna and Ivy, and one older brother, Gaius Jr., and with her father, who became the family's primary caregiver upon their mother's death when Jane was eight years old. This very special relationship between father and youngest daughter was tested and strengthened as Jane Bolin ventured out into the world beyond Poughkeepsie for college and law school. Her experiences at Wellesley College and Yale Law School are captured in Ralph Ellison's reference to being an outsider, which frames chapter 2, "On Her Own: The Years at Wellesley and Yale." On her own and removed from every reference to her standing and belonging, Bolin struggled against the prevailing stereotypes about African Americans and against the invisibility imposed by classmates and instructors alike. It is in this space of ostracism that she literally loses her religion, but also where she finds her own voice. Extrapolating from philosopher Judith Butler's reading of "subjection as both the subordination and becoming of the subject," it would appear that out of the experiences of "subordination" that were her years at Wellesley and Yale, Bolin emerges as a fully constituted subject empowered to challenge the very instruments of her subordination.[10] According to Butler, "A power *exerted on* a subject, subjection is nevertheless a power *assumed by* the subject, an assumption that constitutes the instrument of that subject's becoming."[11]

Chapter 3, "The Politics of Preparation: The Making of the Nation's First African American Woman Judge," and chapter 4, "The Politics of Practice: An African American Women Judge on the Domestic Relations Court," examine Bolin's career in the legal profession and the lived experiences that produced her as the nation's first African American woman judge. A member of a small cohort of black women lawyers, Bolin's early practice mirrored that of other black women lawyers. This second generation of black women lawyers gained entrance, but not full integration, into the legal profession. But in 1939, Bolin's trajectory in the legal profession diverged suddenly from that of her peers when New York City Mayor Fiorello H. La Guardia appointed her to the Domestic Relations Court, making her the nation's first African American woman judge. Bolin was uniquely positioned for this appointment as a lawyer in the Office of the Corporation Counsel who was already assigned to the Domestic Relations Court. Still, some dismissed her appointment as one of La Guardia's political overtures to the city's black residents at a time when many charged his administration with neglect. That she was reappointed to three consecutive ten-year terms by mayors William O'Dwyer, John Lindsay, and Robert Wagner, however, speaks to the quality of her judicial performance.

When La Guardia appointed Bolin to the Domestic Relations Court in 1939, she was emblazoned on the pages of the black press as the nation's first African American woman judge. But what was the substance of this new professional identity? What did it mean to be the first black woman judge? What did she bring to the position? How did she construct the authority of her position? These are only a few of the questions addressed in chapter 5, "Speaking Truth to Power: A View from the Bench." It examines her tenure on the bench and analyzes her public and professional voice against social injustice. A sample of her judicial decisions that were selected for publication because of their usefulness as precedent or importance as a matter of public interest, along with her speeches and letters of communication convey the determination of an ardent integrationist and the immense compassion and intellect that endeared her to La Guardia and her judicial peers.

In 1949, ten years after she was celebrated as the nation's first African American woman judge, Bolin was vilified in the black press. Her ongoing fight for greater democratic participation of the NAACP branches in the policies and function of the national organization provoked internal discord and a power struggle that spilled over onto the pages of the black press. Chapter 6, "Persona Non Grata: Jane Bolin and the NAACP, 1931–50," is therefore concerned with Bolin's service within the NAACP, her relationship with the NAACP's national leadership, and how she became "persona non grata" to an organization with which she was affiliated since childhood.

When women penetrate the walls of male-dominated professions they are usually celebrated. Their intrusion or inclusion is often seen, or expected to be, a challenge to male hegemony. As a result, when Jane Bolin scaled the professional ranks of the legal profession to become the nation's first African American woman judge, her appointment was celebrated. The press boldly inscribed this event onto our collective consciousness as a *first,* not merely because she was a woman but more significantly because she was a black woman and therefore one who was doubly marginalized in the legal profession because of race and gender. But, for decades she remained suspended in the headlines of her appointment, divorced from any analysis of who she was or the nature of her professionalism. An understanding of how or if Bolin challenged male hegemony was therefore obscured by the initial and enduring signification. Furthermore, an eagerness to attack male hegemony may have slighted the record of a woman who functioned in a court identified by a domestic analogy or categorized as being within the "women's sphere" and therefore not truly revolutionary.[12] This book goes beyond the signification of headlines that consigned Bolin to vignettes of firsts. It further moves beyond the prescriptive nature of the judicial appointment to expose how Bolin utilized the authority of her position, and therefore examines her performance as a professional and social justice advocate.

Acknowledgments

My scholarly interest in Jane Bolin began over a decade ago and benefited greatly from the many helpful staff members at the various institutions where I did research: the Library of Congress, the Schlessinger Library, the University of Pennsylvania Archives, the Mary McLeod Bethune Council House, the Franklin D. Roosevelt Library, and the Schomburg Center for Research in Black Culture of the New York City Public Library, where I did most of my work. I owe a special debt of gratitude to Gregory Murray of the Office of Public Affairs, New York State Unified Court System, who was with the project from its inception and graciously helped to coordinate the Unified Court System's celebration of Jane Bolin's life in 2007. I am grateful for the research grants and professional development funding from Western Illinois University and Metropolitan State College of Denver that made visits to several of these institutions possible.

This book matured alongside my daughter and was almost as difficult to release. But the encouragement and support of a community of family and friends allowed me to trust that I had done that which I set out to do. I owe an enormous debt of gratitude to Dr. Darlene Clark Hine who helped me narrow the gulf between earning a PhD and becoming a practicing historian. In her and Dr. Wilma King, who made time when there was no time, I found sincere mentors who never doubted my commitment to complete this work. They therefore never wavered in their support during my moments of suspended productivity. And, although resumption proved to be harder with each succeeding lapse, their gentle nudges did help to keep me on task.

Many thanks to my MSU comrades, especially my friend and brother Felix Armfield, who inspired by example along with Randal Jelks, and never forgot to give thanks for what was already done. Chantalle Verna, who in blind anticipation congratulated me on a book that was yet unfinished, was as inspirational as my soul brother Haynesly Blake, who though military-bound still found time to encourage me. Many thanks also to my friend and colleague Linden Lewis, whose sociological moorings challenged me to consider a broader interpretation of my subject. This book benefited greatly from the valuable comments of the two scholars who read it for the University of Illinois Press, but I am fully responsible for any flaws that remain.

I am eternally grateful for the unconditional love, support, and encouragement of family. Special thanks to Pinky who remained my big sister long after I had grown up. My mother, Doris Elaine McLeod, did not live to see the finished product, but she never left my side. Finally, my heartfelt thanks to Jeuneille, my daughter and best friend, who was my sounding board and staunchest supporter throughout this process. You continue to be a source of much inspiration and happiness in my life.

1. Her Standing in Poughkeepsie

Family Lineage and Legacy

On April 11, 1908—the year Springfield, Illinois, erupted in a race riot that led to the creation of the National Association for the Advancement of Colored People (NAACP)—the woman who would become the nation's first African American woman judge was born in Poughkeepsie, New York. Although a world removed from New York, the injustice that was Springfield and the hope that would become the NAACP easily embodied the motivational forces that would guide Jane Matilda Bolin in service for the rest of her life—a life devoted to social justice. Standing as she was "at the foot of one hill and the top of another,"[1] Jane Matilda Bolin was situated in a lineage that had a legacy of service and community activism in and around Poughkeepsie that she could trace back to her paternal grandfather, Abram Bolin.[2]

Abram Bolin descended from a long line of free Dutchess County black residents who lived in and around Poughkeepsie for nearly two hundred years. The Bolins could most likely count relatives among the freed population that increased between 1799 and 1826 in the Mid-Hudson region (Newburgh, Poughkeepsie, Fishkill Landing, Hudson, Catskill, and Kinderhook) under an act that called for the gradual abolition of slavery. In 1817, New York State declared that after July 4, 1827, the practice of slavery would be abolished; by 1830, only Putnam County in the Mid-Hudson continued the practice under a legal loophole that permitted nonresidents to keep slaves in the state for a period of up to nine months.[3] The freed population also included those who escaped the South through the Underground Railroad (which had station stops in Poughkeepsie and other cities along the Mid-Hudson) where abolitionist Sojourner Truth hid runaway slaves in a cellar in Hurley, New York.

A number of African Americans settled in Poughkeepsie after its incorporation as a city in 1854, particularly during the "city-building" period from the 1860s to the 1880s. Before the city's incorporation the black population was scattered on the outskirts of the central business district (bounded by Washington and Market Streets), an area that was also inhabited by members of the white working class and ethnic groups, especially recently arrived German immigrants. Although most African Americans remained on farms and in rural areas, by 1870, the "Queen City" of the Mid-Hudson, as Poughkeepsie was called, had an overall population of roughly twenty thousand, with a black population of more than five hundred, the largest in the area. The 1869–70 and 1880–81 editions of the Poughkeepsie City Directory for *Colored* persons listed the Bolins and other prominent families such as the Lawrences, Cooleys, Hardens, Du Boises, and Van Dusens among Poughkeepsie's early black residents. Their occupations included laborer, porter, farmer, waiter, carman, basket-maker, cook, and washerwoman. But by the early twentieth century the occupations of their children and grandchildren would include ministers, doctors, teachers, and at least one lawyer. However, many of the descendants of these early families still listed the same street addresses as their foreparents, suggesting a generational pattern of housing within the black community. For example, the Bolin family called 35 North Clinton Street home for several generations.[4]

Abram Bolin was born on February 10, 1826, in Dover Plains, New York, where his father had been a farmer all his life. He grew up among Quakers and was educated in a local country district school. In 1855 he met and married Alice Ann Lawrence, a native Poughkeepsie resident. Lawrence, whom Jane Bolin described as Native American, was most likely a woman of mixed Native American and African American heritage and a member of the Lawrence family identified in the *Colored* directory as one of Poughkeepsie's early black families.[5] She bore thirteen children and reared them at the Clinton Street residence in Poughkeepsie, where the Bolin family lived for nearly one hundred years and where all but two of her children were born.[6] The head of a large family, Abram understood only too well the benefits of self-sufficiency. He was an independent businessman. He worked in the wholesale vegetable business and at various times as a farmer and gardener like his father.[7] But Abram had also been a grocer, a meat-market proprietor, and a livestock salesman, before serving as superintendent of the Poughkeepsie Reservoir at College Hill later in life.[8] His property holdings, economic independence, and government appointment no doubt elevated his standing in his community. But it was his vision as a parent and community leader that distinguished him in the annals of Poughkeepsie history.

A community leader and reformer in his own right, Abram Bolin is remembered as "a man of high principles."[9] He had worked very closely with Reverend

Jacob Thomas in the 1860s to erect the $6,000 edifice that was Poughkeepsie's A.M.E. Zion Church, a vital black parallel institution in a city that practiced de facto segregation. The A.M.E. Zion Church and other local black churches in Poughkeepsie, like black churches elsewhere, were never merely places of worship but served also as essential community centers when other Christian institutions like the YWCA and YMCA denied membership to African Americans, as Poughkeepsie did until after the Second World War. Abram Bolin's success in building the A.M.E. Zion Church encouraged his crusade for a parallel institution of higher learning for African Americans in New York. This, however, proved to be a greater challenge.

African Americans and their white allies had tried several times to establish a black college in or near New York State. In the early 1830s a black national convention proposed to establish a black college in New Haven, Connecticut. In the 1850s Frederick Douglass assisted in the plan to establish an "industrial college" in Rochester or within one hundred miles of Erie, Pennsylvania. In 1859 and 1866 African Americans attempted to transform the abolitionist-oriented New York Central College in McGrawville (near Cortland, New York) into a black college—but none of their initiatives succeeded.[10] Nevertheless, in 1870 Abram Bolin and eight other Hudson Valley black residents embarked on a crusade to found a college for black New Yorkers.[11] These residents were absolutely dissatisfied with the segregated schools available in such Dutchess County cities as Poughkeepsie, Newburgh, Hudson, and Catskill, and utterly discouraged by the racial hostility at such institutions as Eastman Business College and Vassar College in Poughkeepsie. The Mid-Hudson had several public schools but no colleges for African Americans; several colleges in the state had never admitted a black student.[12]

Eastman Business College, located on the Hudson River in Poughkeepsie, refused to admit blacks because, as its president later explained, its many southern students would not like it. According to the *New York Times* and the *New York Freeman,* by 1866 Eastman Business College still excluded blacks. Vassar College, located just blocks from where Jane Bolin grew up, did not admit African Americans either, and as late as 1900 a Vassar administrator explained that the conditions of life at Vassar were such that he strongly advised against the admission of blacks.[13] But the belief among Poughkeepsie's black residents was that an African American girl had passed for white while attending Vassar and was not discovered until her parents showed up for her graduation.[14] It was not until 1934, a full decade after Jane Bolin left Poughkeepsie for Wellesley College and three years after she graduated from Yale Law School, that Vassar College announced its readiness to admit African Americans.[15] Down the Hudson from Poughkeepsie at the West Point Military Academy the first black cadet, James Smith, enrolled in May 1870, but he was persecuted from the day he entered until the day of his premature departure.[16] Perhaps the public debate over Smith's treatment at West Point had motivated the black leaders of the Mid-Hudson region to push even more aggressively for separate institutions of higher learning.

Those people signing the call for a black college wished to establish an institution of higher learning for the residents of their communities because existing institutions did not admit African Americans or admitted them without truly integrating them. Although it could not match the scale of Vassar College with its two-hundred-acre allotment and $800,000 endowment at founding, this endeavor to establish a black college with a fifteen-acre allotment and $300,000 endowment was nevertheless a remarkable feat for farmers, laborers, and janitors.[17] A majority of the all-black board of trustees for the proposed institution came from Poughkeepsie, and Abram Bolin was a leader among them. The proposed institution was called Toussaint L'Ouverture College, in honor of the legendary revolutionary who led the slave revolt that in 1804 gave birth to Haiti, the first black republic and second sovereign nation in the Western hemisphere.[18] As historian Millery Polyné reminds us in *From Douglas to Duvalier,* African Americans had from the nineteenth century continually invoked the Haitian Revolution as a symbol and promise of black empowerment in their struggles against racial inequality. According to Polyné, "References to the Haitian Revolution and its significance to black progress exemplified the purpose of transnational racial uplift."[19] But a name that no doubt evoked honor for some might have symbolized too much radicalism for others, portending the challenge that the endeavor would face.

In early 1871 Bolin and his fellow trustees arranged to have a local Republican assemblyman introduce a bill into the New York Legislature to incorporate the college. A Poughkeepsie Republican newspaper appealed to whites for contributions for the proposed college, stating, "It is to be hoped that our people will give this institution a helping hand, as it will go far toward settling the vexed question of the mixture of the races in our schools and colleges."[20] But the proposal received strong opposition from many in New York's African American community. At the 1871 New York Annual Conference of the A.M.E. Zion Church, the Reverend William Butler of New York City, a former pastor of Poughkeepsie and a most powerful personality at the conference, objected strongly. He was completely opposed to separate schools, and believed that if African Americans stood together and demanded equal access that they would get it. Like many in New York's black community, Butler thought that the Toussaint College would hinder their struggle for integrated schools. The A.M.E. Zion conference refused to endorse the college. Even Abram Bolin's assurance that the college would be open to both blacks and whites was ignored, and at the 1872 New York State black convention held in Troy, there was still no endorsement of the college. Without the support of the major black denominations in the state or the state black convention, the hope for Toussaint College was surely dashed.[21]

By the end of 1872 the campaign for the Toussaint College had collapsed under the weight of entrenched opposition. The belief of both blacks and whites in the viability of educational integration had no doubt helped prevent the creation of Toussaint College and the establishment of any black college in the state.[22] Moreover, the passage of the Fifteenth Amendment to the Constitution of the United States guaranteeing full male suffrage may have provided African Americans in the state with added motivation to push for full access and equal opportunity.[23]

Abram Bolin's efforts failed to create a black college for the benefit of his children and grandchildren, but those efforts certainly helped to energize the struggle for full educational integration at the public school level. In 1873 a state civil rights law allowed New York youth, regardless of race, to enroll in any public school, thereby abolishing separate public schools for Poughkeepsie's black residents, which in the end benefited Abram's children and grandchildren who were subsequently educated in the integrated public schools of Poughkeepsie.[24] Abram Bolin's activism reflected the depth of his racial pride and the strength of his commitment to uplift his community. When he died in April 1910, several community organizations, including the Ebenezer Baptist Church Auxiliary, and fraternal organizations, such as the Grand Court Order of Calanthe, the Grand United Order of Odd Fellows and its sister organization, the Household of Ruth, paid tribute to him. A white Episcopal priest and a black Baptist minister presided at the funeral in his Clinton Street home in a manner befitting a man of his standing in the community.[25]

This commitment to community leadership, inherited or bestowed, was not lost on future generations of Bolins including Jane Bolin and her father, Gaius Bolin. Gaius Bolin once quoted the scriptures about the sins of the fathers being visited upon their children to the third and fourth generations to make the point that heredity played an important role in shaping his character.[26] One of Alice and Abram Bolin's thirteen children, Gaius was born September 10, 1864, and had no other goal than that of becoming a lawyer.[27] Clearly, what the elder Bolin had accomplished with only a country district school education was extraordinary enough to inspire his son to become a man of the professional class and, more importantly, a leader in his community. Gaius Bolin became a lawyer, and by the time Jane Bolin left Poughkeepsie for Wellesley College in 1924 he was prominent in his profession and community.

Gaius Bolin benefited from both his father's activism and the 1873 legislation that ended segregated education for Poughkeepsie blacks. He attended Poughkeepsie's public schools, graduating from the racially integrated Poughkeepsie

High School in June 29, 1883, the only African American in a class of twenty-three students. Gaius Bolin delivered an oration at commencement that inspired the *Poughkeepsie Daily Eagle* to comment favorably on his intelligence and the desirability of integrated education.[28] He considered it an honor to be a graduate of Poughkeepsie High School, whose alumni were embraced as outstanding members of the larger community. Gaius recalled that "they had no trouble obtaining the best jobs to be had in the mercantile world, the banks and as school teachers and in other walks of life, and many of them entered the professions and were successful."[29] However, the prestige of his diploma notwithstanding, it was still necessary for him to study for two additional years in a private school to acquire more Latin and the full two years of Greek required for entrance into college. He therefore enrolled in and, in 1885, graduated from the Professor John R. Leslie's Select Classical School in Poughkeepsie.[30]

At the suggestion of his high school principal, Samuel W. Buck, who had graduated from Williams College, and with the support of his parents, Gaius Bolin applied to Williams College, passed the entrance examination, and entered the freshman class of 1885.[31] In his study *The College Bred Negro*, W. E. B. Du Bois reported that 2,331 blacks had graduated from the nation's colleges and universities between 1826 and 1899. The majority of these graduates, according to Du Bois, had earned their baccalaureate degrees after 1865 from such black institutions as Lincoln, Fisk, Wilberforce, and Howard. However, approximately 390 of these graduates or a full 16 percent had received their education at a variety of predominantly white colleges and universities including Amherst, Bowdoin, Yale, and Oberlin.[32] In 1885 Williams College followed the precedent set by these institutions and admitted its first black student when it admitted Gaius Charles Bolin. Gaius recalled having "four beautiful years" at Williams where he played football and formed lasting friendships with his white classmates, an experience that was diametrically opposed to his daughter's experience at Wellesley College four decades later. To his classmates he was "Old Charlie Bole"; fifty years after his graduation from Williams he could still recall the names of the many classmates "who made a rendezvous" of his room and "the glorious times" they had there.[33]

Upon graduation in June 1889, Gaius Bolin returned to Poughkeepsie armed with his Bachelor of Arts degree but no comparable job prospects. Poughkeepsie had integrated its public schools, but had no equal access when it came to employment. In late nineteenth-century Poughkeepsie, the most common type of employment for black women was as domestic servants, while the majority of black men worked as day laborers on the Hudson River boats, the lumber yard, the glass and cigar factories, or as porters and janitors in local hotels and restaurants. A few worked as chauffeurs and servants for wealthy white families in the area, or independently as barbers, grocers, plumbers, and milliners. But besides the clergy, the black professional class was almost nonexistent with only one doctor and a dentist. So, for a year after his return to Poughkeepsie, Gaius worked in his father's produce business. He never gave up his lifelong ambition to become a lawyer, however, and in 1890 Fred E. Ackerman, a local white attorney, gave him the opportunity to fulfill his ambition. Gaius read the law with Ackerman for two years, passed the bar, and in 1892 was admitted to the General Term of the Supreme Court in Brooklyn, New York, to practice law. He became the first black lawyer in Poughkeepsie and the only black member of the Dutchess County Bar Association. He continued to work with Ackerman for the next three years, gaining the necessary experience before establishing his own law practice in 1895.[34]

Gaius Bolin had only been in private practice for two years when an important biographical directory of prominent Dutchess County residents listed him as "a talented and enterprising young lawyer" who had gained a reputation for "fair dealing" and "devotion to the interests of his clients."[35] His reputation as a community leader was just as impressive, so it was no surprise when in April 1899, New York Republican governor Theodore Roosevelt appointed him a commissioner of the Pan-American Exposition that was held in Buffalo in 1901.[36] Bolin was appointed to serve as a member of the board of general managers for the selection of the site of the New York State Building at the exposition, which subsequently became the home of the Buffalo and Erie County Historical Society.

With his nomination confirmed by the state senate, Bolin became the only African American commissioner of the Pan-American Exposition. He was no token member but very active in the proceedings of the general managers, being present at all informal board meetings that had been held in Buffalo and at all formal board meetings beginning with the first one held pursuant to a call from the governor in Albany on March 7, 1900. This appointment, considered by Roosevelt to be a "position of high trust and honor," politically empowered Bolin, who became a staunch supporter of the Republican governor, which in turn kept him plugged in to the pulse of local politics.[37] When, at an Assembly District Convention in April 1900, local party bosses proposed a resolution that offered only lukewarm support of Roosevelt's renomination as governor but an overwhelming endorsement of the reelection of William McKinley as president, Gaius Bolin alerted the governor within days. In a letter to the governor Bolin stated that "there was an incident which occurred in connection with the offering of the usual resolutions of endorsement and commendation of the President and the Governor which *shows very plainly the attitude of the so called leaders and those in control of the Republican organization in this county toward your renomination for Governor*" (emphasis added). Bolin indicated to the governor that those who controlled the Republican organization "the same as a man would control a lot of dogs, by threats and curses," were ready to do everything "to embarras and defeat you." Bolin could not have known that

shortly thereafter McKinley would choose Roosevelt as his vice presidential running mate nor that Roosevelt, less than a year after being elected vice president,
would assume the presidency upon McKinley's assassination. In the same letter
Bolin also informed the governor of the underground dealings of these same party
bosses, who were attaching amendments to Poughkeepsie's new city charter that
would personally benefit the school superintendent but go against the wishes of
the people of Poughkeepsie. He assured the governor "and your honest friends
here, not only for the good of the city but for your interest as well, hope and trust
that you will not put your name to this bill." The city charter was purged of the
objectionable parts before Roosevelt signed it, but he still respectfully requested
that Bolin review the revised city charter to ensure its acceptability. Roosevelt was
certain that he did "not wish to sign any bill to which the majority of the decent
citizens of Poughkeepsie object."[38]

    As a prominent lawyer, Gaius Bolin served Poughkeepsie and its surrounding
communities for over half a century and assumed the presidency of the Dutchess
County Bar Association the year before his death in 1946. His profession was
his passion. He recalled in later years that "nobody ever enjoyed making a living,
either with his hands or his head, more than I've enjoyed practicing law in the
city of Poughkeepsie."[39] Although Gaius modestly described his general practice
as "the usual experience of a country lawyer," it was quite unusual. He handled
individual and corporate cases of every stripe, criminal cases including homicide, and often worked as co-counsel with white lawyers throughout Dutchess
County. His reputation as a lawyer seemed to transcend the usual racial barriers
so prevalent at the time. The vast majority of his clients were whites, and his son
Gaius Charles Jr. calculated that roughly 5 percent of his father's clients were
African Americans.[40]

    But the fact that Gaius Bolin counted a majority of whites among his clientele
was not suggestive of pervasive social equality in Poughkeepsie. Furthermore,
that whites may have enlisted the expertise of Gaius Bolin did not necessarily
liberate them from their racial prejudice. Clients would simply redraw their
circle of acceptability to make their attorney, Gaius Bolin, an exception to their
racial assumptions, without fundamentally altering the irrationality of their racial
biases. One such client, who worked in the beauty parlor of one of Poughkeepsie's
leading department stores, refused service to young Jane Bolin because the salon
did not cut "colored" people's hair. As a consequence, until she left Poughkeepsie,
Jane Bolin had her hair cut at a local barber shop run by a recently arrived Ital-
ian immigrant. Suggesting that her father had gotten rid of the hairdresser as a
client, Jane later recalled, "I don't know after that incident with me how long
he permitted her to be his client."[41] Gaius Bolin clearly did not let professional
pragmatism compromise his commitment to social justice.

Gaius Bolin had always been an advocate "actively protesting racial prejudice and advancing the rights of Blacks" without much concern for how such activism would affect his legal practice.[42] When Vassar's president Henry Noble Mac-Cracken told a "darkie joke" while addressing Anna Bolin's high school assembly in Poughkeepsie, Gaius Bolin wasted no time in denouncing the blatant disrespect for Poughkeepsie's black residents.[43] Decades later this same kind of outspokenness would become a hallmark of Jane Bolin's life. In 1931 Gaius Bolin was one of seven Poughkeepsie residents who founded the local branch of the NAACP; he was also active countywide in the NAACP and served in 1932 on the executive committee of the Dutchess County branch. He was very vocal against the discriminatory practices of the Poughkeepsie YMCA and YWCA, and Poughkeepsie's employment discrimination in the public schools and other government agencies such as the post office and police agencies.[44] His negotiation through this labyrinth of racial custom and professional ethics, magnified as it was in this small, predominantly white city, exposed the precarious position of any black professional whose practice was not confined to the black community—no doubt a motivating factor in Jane Bolin's impatience with the city once she returned as a professional in 1931. It may further explain why the leaders of the black community chose the "quiet way" of negotiating for social change and not agitation.

Poughkeepsie was not unlike other northern cities during the first half of the twentieth century. It did not practice the de jure segregation of the South but it was no racial utopia either. Many prominent African Americans believed that "Poughkeepsie was a good place for Negro people." Yet the evidence reveals a pattern of racial discrimination not limited to the behavior of the local beauty parlor. Prior to World War II the many boarding houses, hotels, restaurants, and community organizations in Poughkeepsie (including the Nelson House, Smith Brothers Restaurant, the YMCA and YWCA) routinely discriminated against African Americans. Perhaps many in this elite class of African Americans who thought that "Poughkeepsie was a good place for Negro people" were spared the indignities of the de facto segregation practices of restaurants, hotels, and other public accommodations precisely because of their status.[45] Quite possibly, the establishment of parallel institutions within the black community routinely shielded many of them from discrimination in housing and employment. But those institutions would not have shielded the young Jane Bolin, who was denied service at a beauty parlor that was willing to serve a white woman but not her racially mixed child. Her mother was considered a suitable client because of racial classification, but as a mother she could not escape the sting of prejudice that was reserved for her young daughter.

Interestingly, this elite group of longtime black Poughkeepsie residents and their professional class of doctors, lawyers, dentists, and teachers that existed into the post–World War II era believed in a "quiet way" of working for social change. They used their status and respect in the black and white communities to negotiate for employment at local hospitals and factories for lesser-situated blacks. Their "polite protest" for social change, to use historian Richard Pierce's terminology, preempted any attempt at mass mobilization, because as he shows in the case of Indianapolis, "African Americans worked within the system primarily because they were reluctant to jeopardize their gains through active, disruptive, civil disturbances."[46] It might also explain why the Poughkeepsie NAACP chapter that was founded in 1931 was defunct by 1935, leaving only its Junior Division operational in Dutchess County. In a letter to Ivy Bolin, who was head of the Junior Division, the NAACP national office even cajoled her "to stimulate interest in organizing a regular branch."[47] The younger generation was clearly veering away from a quiet way of addressing their concerns—a perspective that was held by Jane Bolin, who was eager to leave Poughkeepsie as a young professional and equally eager to return to shame the city fathers for what she saw as a backward climate of racial exclusion.

Gaius Bolin understood his good fortune and the role of well-positioned benefactors in his life. Consequently, he never used his own success to gauge black progress. Instead he used his success and visibility to bring attention and resolution to the plight of blacks who were less politically connected. Gaius Bolin left an impressive legacy that remained a model for both his children and the larger community. When he died in April 1946, at the age of eighty-one, a Poughkeepsie newspaper praised him for his devotion "to the Negro race." He was "fearless," the article said, "in advancing their cause and protecting their rights."[48] In his death, explained another newspaper, "the city loses a respected member of an old Poughkeepsie family and an outstanding citizen," who "can take with him a large share of credit for the progress that has been made, on the local scene."[49] A year before his death, African Americans were still not visible in the government or economy of Poughkeepsie. The semblance of integration quietly negotiated by Gaius Bolin and other African American leaders, however, was seen as progress in the eyes of white Poughkeepsie.

Jane Bolin had a very comfortable childhood in Poughkeepsie growing up in the glow of her father's prominence. Jennie, as she was fondly called by her family, was the youngest of four children born to Matilda Ingram Emery Bolin and Gaius Charles Bolin, who were married on September 14, 1899, four years after Gaius had launched his private practice. Matilda Emery had immigrated to the United States with her parents from Ennis Killem, Northern Ireland, and settled in Poughkeepsie when she was a child. Described by her youngest child as "English Episcopalian," Matilda was educated in the public schools of Troy, New York, before she married into the Bolin clan in 1899. Their eldest child,

Anna May, was born the following year, followed in 1902 by their first son, Gaius Charles Jr., who was named for his father. In 1904 the couple welcomed their third child, Ivy Rosalind, four years before Jane was born. Gaius and Matilda were building a new home, more spacious than the "three-story house" in which they lived, to accommodate their growing family, when, in 1917, Matilda died after a prolonged illness—never having lived to occupy the home that she had designed for her family.[50]

Jane was eight years old when her mother died, and so physically sick and emotionally distraught from the loss that she spent much time immediately thereafter with her Aunt Jane, the wife of her father's older brother Albert, and the woman after whom she was named. Aunt Jane became her surrogate mother. But, being the youngest, it was no surprise that young Jane was showered with attention, and by her own admission, thoroughly pampered. Her father assumed the responsibility of primary caregiver and from all accounts cared for his four children with unselfish devotion. Gaius Bolin never remarried, choosing instead to dedicate his life to rearing his children, a sacrifice that Jane Bolin would not fully appreciate until she herself was widowed and a parent.[51] She recalled that apart from work, her father seldom went out, and that he essentially stayed at home with them all the time, except for those times when he scheduled major outings for the children to the "Trotting Races" and the annual Labor Day weekend trip to visit his brother Livingsworth in New York City.[52]

Gaius's unselfish devotion as a parent created a very special bond between him and Jane. "As the youngest child and motherless from the age of eight," she said, "I was always very close to my father and I guess spoiled by him."[53] But that same devotion may have been perceived as overprotectiveness by his older daughters and may have driven a wedge between him and Anna and Ivy, who were seventeen and thirteen respectively when their mother died. As the eldest daughter, Anna had taken on additional chores after her mother's death, including the daily cooking and cleaning, which may have foiled her interest in educational pursuits. Anna did not pursue schooling beyond high school and eloped when very young to marry Harold Halloway, leaving sister Ivy, who never married or pursued studies beyond high school, to take care of the house, cook the meals, and shop for the household. Gaius Bolin was very disappointed in Anna. He dismissed her husband Halloway as an unsuitable man and disapproved of the marriage. Anna's relationship with her father was clearly estranged as was her relationship with her husband, who turned out to be all that her father had warned of. Still, Gaius opened his home to Anna's son who was an infant when Anna died and completely abandoned by his own father. Gaius Bolin cared for the boy until he died of cancer at age sixteen.[54]

Whether doting father or overprotective parent, Gaius Bolin was a strict disciplinarian who had very definite ideas about how young men and women should conduct themselves. For the transgression of wearing face powder and lipstick, Ivy—who was in high school at the time—suffered the wrath of her father who apparently thought that "decent women . . . girls . . . didn't use cosmetics."[55] His daughters were expected to be at home before dark, but all the children were expected to be in the house for supper and afterward. The children were brought up in the Episcopalian faith and all went to Sunday school at St. Paul's Episcopal Church. Jane Bolin speculated that she might have been the most religious of the four children, having attended Sunday school regularly from the time she was a little girl until she went away to college, and being the only one of the Bolin children who was baptized and confirmed in the religion.[56]

Gaius Bolin was a man of high principles, and like most parents he admonished his children about lying. Jane recalled the day her brother did not come home for lunch but had instead gone to the local pool hall, where "characters that played pool there, stayed around there all day instead of working."[57] She remembered that someone had telephoned her father and tipped him off about her brother's whereabouts, whereupon her father, in her words, "rushed down to the pool room and snatched my brother out by the back of his neck." As she recalled, the humiliation remained so fresh for her brother that even as an adult he never passed a poolroom without thinking about the incident.[58] One could argue that Gaius Bolin's hold over his children was born of his overwhelming desire to protect them from the hard lessons of life.

Jane Bolin grew up in a community where interracial families were not unusual. Nor were Jane's parents the only interracial couple in Jane's immediate social circle in Poughkeepsie. Besides her parents, Uncle Albert and Aunt Jane were another interracial couple in her immediate family. But harboring no illusions about how his daughter would be racialized in the wider American society, Gaius Bolin nurtured her racial identity as African American. So, Jane Bolin was socialized as African American although she was an interracial child of a white mother and an African American father. This socialization privileged the culture and consciousness of her father over that of her mother, and was probably facilitated by Matilda Bolin's death before Jane had come of age. (Perhaps this socialization was also facilitated by her maternal grandmother, aunt, and uncle cutting all ties with the Bolins upon her mother's death—their annual visits from Hoboken, New Jersey, to Poughkeepsie ceased altogether.)

As a child, Jane had never thought about the racial identities of her parents. To her, "My mother was my mother and my father was my father." But at the tender age of seven or eight, a routine play date with a cousin who had come from across town ended in name-calling that shattered Jane's innocence about race and difference. Lashing out in anger at Jane over the outcome of a game, the child blurted out, "You're just a half-white nigger." Jane recalled that she was hurt by the words because "my cousin had made it sound as though it were something dirty to have a white mother." However, she grew up with no confusion about her racial identity. She was fully aware that her mother was white and that she was African American.[59] Although she self-identified as "African American" before it was in common usage, she acknowledged that if she were to claim her whole background to account for heritage, she would have to say, "African-Caucasian-Native American-American." Though she must have grown up using the word "Negro," she began identifying as "African American" at some point in her adult life. It was clear that she would never have used the term "colored," which she detested, "as if you weren't naturally the color you are."[60]

Gaius Bolin created a literate environment for his children. He stocked their home with books and subscribed to two Poughkeepsie newspapers and the *New York Herald Tribune,* in addition to the *Crisis* of the NAACP, the *Chicago Defender,* the *Pittsburgh Courier,* and the *Baltimore Afro-American.* Jane and her siblings were socialized to be keenly aware of current events and the unique issues and challenges confronting African Americans.[61] She remembered seeing a picture and reading about lynching when she was very young, probably between ten and twelve years of age, and "the brutality of it, the bestiality of it," never left her.[62] Years later she surmised, "It is easy to imagine how a young, protected child who sees portrayals of brutality is forever scarred and becomes determined to contribute in her own small way to racial justice."[63]

Jane loved to read, and was encouraged to do so from an early age. There were no children in the new neighborhood to which they moved, so she spent the bulk of her time reading and studying. Before she was old enough to attend kindergarten she learned to read with the help of her sister Ivy, who would borrow books from the local library for her. She also read the newspapers to her mother who was resigned to her bed during a prolonged illness.[64] As a young girl Jane had always enjoyed the stimulating conversations that filled her home, and sometimes entered into the debates surrounding the "Negro Question." At the height of the intense debate over liberal arts education versus industrial education that came to focus on W. E. B. Du Bois and Booker T. Washington with their divergent approaches to the advancement of African Americans, Jane Bolin recalled "that he [Father] reminded me that it was W. E. B. Du Bois and not Booker T. Washington we had admired in our home and that I was never to hesitate to try to achieve any ambition because of my color."[65] It was clear which side of the educational divide her family stood and portended where she was headed.

Before entering the Poughkeepsie Public School system, Jane Bolin attended the Kindergarten Morse School (named for S. F. B. Morse, who invented the telegraph). She was an honor student at Morse, and with great pride, she professed, "I was an 'A' student all the way through high school—used to be on the A honor roll, which was published in the Poughkeepsie newspapers every month."[66] School was a mile away from her home, and since there was no school lunch program at the time, she went home for lunch. She walked a total of four miles each day for school, and was often accompanied each way by her fox terrier, Prince, who waited for her outside school at twelve noon and three o'clock each day. At age sixteen Jane graduated with an academic diploma in classical subjects from Poughkeepsie High School in 1924. In high school she enjoyed Latin and English, but her dearest memory was of her relationship with her English teacher, Lucy E. Jackson. Mrs. Jackson encouraged Jane's penchant for reading. She shared her personal collection of books with Jane and suggested books to read from Gaius Bolin's library.[67]

There was no question in Jane's or her father's mind that she would attend college. She was, after all, the youngest in this professional household where education was celebrated. Her brother, Gaius Charles Jr., had by then begun his studies at New York University Law School, and her sister Ivy, who had completed high school, had become a teacher. Jane chose Wellesley College in Massachusetts over Vassar College, which was two blocks from her home, for what she considered obvious reasons: "One because it was near home and [two] the president was a Southerner." Jane had not forgotten that years earlier President MacCracken of Vassar College had made a "darkie" joke at Anna's school assembly that elicited a scathing letter of reprimand from her father. She felt that she could not in good conscience be affiliated with such an institution.

But MacCracken's comments notwithstanding, Jane Bolin could not have attended Vassar College in 1924 because the school's unofficial policies barred the admission of African American students. Because Jane always expected to attend college, she had sent away for catalogs from several women's colleges, but decided that Wellesley was for her and applied to only Wellesley. She was accepted and, at "sixteen years old, sensitive and idealistic, first time away from the family, one of two Black freshman who were the first Black students for some years," she reminisced, "this was I in 1924."[68]

2. On Her Own

The Years at Wellesley and Yale

In *Invisible Man,* Ralph Ellison reminds us that "outside the Brotherhood we were outside history; but inside of it they didn't see us."[1] These words capture fully Jane Bolin's experiences at Wellesley College, where an educational institution for women offered no more community than an educational institution intended for white men. Bolin's years at Wellesley and Yale Law School therefore reveal the degree to which her experiences were framed by the historical, social, and political construction of race.

In 1924 Jane Bolin entered Wellesley College, the small New England women's college, where she and another black woman were the first black students admitted in several years. Two African American transferees from other schools arrived during her junior year, but no cohort of black students existed at Wellesley when she first arrived.[2] But Jane would have had no illusions about the racial makeup of the student body at Wellesley when she applied, and would not have anticipated any problems making the transition into Wellesley since she had always attended integrated public schools in predominantly white Poughkeepsie. Furthermore, at sixteen, "sensitive and idealistic," she would have been persuaded by the mission of Wellesley College, which was founded in response to the need for improved education for women, specifically an "education for more than carrying out housewifely duties."[3] Chartered in 1870 as the Wellesley Female Seminary and opened as Wellesley College in 1875, the institution was founded by Henry and Pauline Durant, who were committed to the Christian education of women but believed that the true meaning of the higher education of women was "revolt."[4] Understandably, Wellesley College had been Jane Bolin's first and only choice out of the many women's colleges she considered. "I didn't apply to any but one," she said, "and that was Wellesley."[5]

Her father supported her decision to attend Wellesley, although he would have preferred if she had chosen a college closer to home. Although Vassar College was two blocks from the Bolin home in Poughkeepsie, it had never been an option for Jane. By 1924, Vassar had never knowingly admitted an African American student, and had earlier advised that none apply because the climate at the college was such that they would not feel welcome.[6] Jane Bolin was not interested in testing Vassar's admission policies because she was certain that it was a school with which she could not, in good conscience, be affiliated. Upon application, Wellesley College would therefore have represented for Jane a degree of progress lacking at Vassar. Jane may have known of the other African American women who attended Wellesley. She may even have known that Portia Washington, daughter of Booker T. Washington, the founder of Tuskegee Normal and Industrial Institute and the most prominent African American in the nation at the time, had attended Wellesley for one year in 1901.[7] Nevertheless, her idealism was dashed upon enrollment—which set the stage for her four years at Wellesley.

Her father and brother had driven her to Wellesley, and she remembered how she clung to her father and cried when it was time for him to leave because she could not imagine being without him.[8] Jane was extremely close to her father, and as the youngest child had enjoyed a very special relationship with him. He was equally as anxious about leaving his sixteen-year-old daughter. She remembered that he also had tears in his eyes.[9] Might Gaius, his experience at Williams College notwithstanding, have anticipated how unpleasant Jane's experience at Wellesley would be?

As one of the only two African American students, Jane Bolin was assigned to room with the other African American student. The policy at Wellesley was no different than those of other New England liberal arts colleges for women. For example, when Portia Washington applied for admission as a transfer student to Wheaton College in 1902, the president was concerned that the admission of an African American student would give rise to "some practical difficulties, and might seriously disturb a portion of the patronage of this school."[10] Her application had raised concerns about "finding an appropriate residence for Portia off-campus, so that no white students would have to share living quarters with her, and finding a second African-American student to attend Wheaton so that Portia would not be totally isolated from the community, since it was possible that none of the white students would socialize with her."[11]

At Wellesley, Bolin and the other African American student were assigned the same room in a family's apartment in the village of Wellesley, away from the school dormitories that housed the white students. Though Wellesley had addressed the issue of housing for its African American students, it could not guarantee that their matriculation would not "disturb a portion of the patronage" of their school, specifically their Southern students. Bolin admitted that she was not very compatible with her roommate, which resulted in each girl moving into separate dormitories after the first year and therefore into closer social contact with their white classmates.[12] Almost a half-century after graduating from Wellesley, Bolin was still "saddened and maddened" to recall many of her Wellesley experiences as she recounted a representative experience of bigotry for each of her four years at Wellesley.

Bolin characterized her college years at Wellesley as sad years where she was essentially ignored outside of the classroom. As a female student she was allowed into the academic life of Wellesley, but as a black woman she was effectively excluded from its social life. "I felt largely ignored," she said, "although I had an excellent education, I felt ignored socially."[13] Historian Evelyn Brooks Higginbotham reminds us that "in societies where racial demarcation is endemic to their socio-cultural fabric and heritage—to their laws and economy, to their institutionalized structures and discourses, and to their epistemologies and everyday customs—gender identity is inextricably linked to and even determined by racial identity."[14] Wellesley was theoretically committed to the education of women, but routine "racial demarcation" served to exclude black women from full participation in its community of women. A sisterhood that was common among Wellesley students who generally shared the moral standards and cultural values in the middle-class tradition was hijacked by ingrained prejudice that further exposed the gulf between the rhetoric and reality of Wellesley's commitment to the education of women.[15]

Although secluded in living quarters away from the rest of the student body, Bolin and her roommate were allowed to have meals in the college dining room with other first-year students. But even this most routine activity was problematic. Students were usually assigned to tables at dinner but were allowed to choose their seats at all other meals, provided a table was filled before another table was started. What seemed like a reasonable institutional initiative to foster socializing among its first-year students proved to be socially isolating for its two black students because if either one was sitting at an unfilled table, "the Southern students would come in the dining room, see this and ostentatiously walk out and stand outside the door peeking in until our table was filled."[16] Bolin was amazed at the inconvenience her presence caused the "Southern students," but she was shocked by the fact that "no one in authority, though observing this, interceded in any way."[17] Such indifference ran counter to the accountability that Bolin had come to expect from those in authority from the example set by her father, who took Vassar's President MacCracken to task for inconsiderate remarks made before Anna's school assembly.

Sometimes the indifference of those in authority manifested itself as blatant bigotry that distorted the image and meaning of black history and culture. But Jane Bolin had entered Wellesley a self-assured, racially conscious sixteen-year-old who was already radicalized by her socialization at home. At age fifteen, she wrote a letter to a Poughkeepsie daily newspaper protesting the designation "Negro" in its reporting of African Americans when there were no racial or ethnic designations of others. She also protested the newspaper's use of a southern dialect in all such reporting, and pointed out its ignorance in not capitalizing the word "Negro." Although the public protestations of a fifteen-year-old did not stop the racializing that was reserved for African Americans, her letter was printed and Negro was capitalized.[18]

The horror of lynching was already emblazoned onto her memory and convenient silence in the face of injustice was not a lesson she had learned. Therefore, when a French teacher asked Bolin's roommate to play the role of Aunt Jemima, "bandanna too!" in a charity fundraising skit, it was Jane who challenged the utility of this stereotypical image depicting the black woman in perpetual servility.[19] As passive, longsuffering, and submissive, Aunt Jemima, like Mammy before her, had come to symbolize for whites a prototype of "acceptable black womanhood."[20] The assignment fit squarely within what historian Micki McElya calls the "narrative of the faithful slave" that pervades the popular imagination on race and "blurs the lines between myth and memory, guilt and justice, stereotype and individuality, commodity and humanity."[21] Discerning no redeeming academic value in the French teacher's request, Jane Bolin confronted her and "remonstrated vociferously" on her roommate's behalf.[22] Though the teacher was not hers and the request was not made of her, Bolin still felt responsible to stand up for what was right and against that which assaulted and distorted the image of the black woman. As a result, the request for an Aunt Jemima character was withdrawn, but as she later recalled, it was impossible to withdraw the deep feelings of hurt brought on by such "insensitive protestations and wondrous lack of understanding by a teacher of young people."[23]

Bolin's junior year at Wellesley brought her into closer living quarters with her white classmates, but it did nothing to improve their social interaction with her. She was an honor student, yet was rejected for membership in one of the college societies interested in social problems. The irony of the rejection of membership could not have been lost on the members who informed her "by an unsigned notice surreptitiously slipped under my door during the night."[24] Bolin, however, found a way to address social problems directly by doing volunteer social work three afternoons every week in Boston, which was also her venue for social activities. Because of the social isolation and lack of community at Wellesley, Bolin would travel to Boston with other black students from Harvard, Dartmouth, Amherst, and Williams for some semblance of a social life.

However, since parental permission was required by the college, and none was forthcoming from her father, she spent her entire freshman year on campus.[25]

Gaius Bolin was particularly strict with Jane, and obviously feeling some angst about her being so far away from home at such a tender age, he simply forbade her to leave Wellesley College campus for any type of socializing. As a result, when Jane sought her father's approval of two African American women from Boston to serve as her chaperones should she want to go to Boston (which was about sixteen miles from Wellesley), he promptly disapproved. The fact that the proposed chaperones were two respectable Christian ladies who had reached out to ease the loneliness they knew Jane was suffering was irrelevant and meant nothing to her father. In a very stern letter Gaius informed Jane that he did not send her to college for a social life but to study. Her sister Ivy, older and much more independent-minded as she recalled, wrote her a letter reminding her that she was a big girl and encouraging her to "go anyway, go anyplace you want anyway," but Jane felt that she could not defy her father, even in his absence. As she recalled, "I never went into Boston for any parties or any social life or even to go to the symphony until my sophomore year, and after which at that time, we were not required to have chaperones."[26]

Even in Boston, Bolin did not always escape the tentacles of Wellesley's discrimination. The first time she made a reservation to spend the weekend at the Wellesley Club in the city became the only time she made such a reservation because of the pain she felt when she was ushered into an attic room, the only room on that level. As she saw it, the club reasoned there would be "no contamination there!"[27]

It was in the context of this viciousness that Jane Bolin literally lost her religion. She grew up an observant Episcopalian, and while at Wellesley continued her custom of attending an early morning service at a local church. However, she soon realized that the local church offered no more community than Wellesley College. One morning while she knelt at the communion rail waiting to partake in the sacrament, the priest bypassed her while serving the wafer and went back to serve the wine. But when she did not excuse herself, the priest made a big production of wiping all around the rim of the silver chalice for several seconds with his napkin, clearly in an attempt to indulge the prejudice of the other communicants. That marked the end of her church attendance, not only while she was at Wellesley, but for the rest of her life. "If that was Christianity," she thought, "the practice of Christianity, it was not for me."[28]

Jane Bolin's "sharpest and ugliest memory" of her Wellesley years occurred during her senior year, when all students were required to meet with a guidance counselor to discuss their postgraduation plans. What started out as a routine counseling session with Jane laying out her plans for a career in law quickly deteriorated into a misguided lecture from her counselor about the futility of her plans. Jane recalled that the guidance counselor exhibited obvious physical shock when told of her plans to study law. The counselor, according to Jane, "threw up her hands in disbelief," and said that "there was little opportunity for women in law and absolutely none for a 'colored' one," and suggested that she consider teaching.[29]

Despite the counselor's obvious insensitivity to Bolin's genuine aspirations, her response might have been informed by the reality that by the second decade of the twentieth century the legal profession, from preparation to practice, was still very much a white male domain. In 1910, of the 558 women lawyers in the United States, two were African American.[30] By 1930 there were 22 black women lawyers;[31] by the 1940s there were only 57 black women lawyers in the entire United States.[32] It was indeed a very bleak picture for black women wanting to enter the legal profession, a picture that did not change much by 1950, when of the 6,271 woman lawyers in the United States only 83 were African American.[33] Teaching was virtually the only profession open to black women well into the twentieth century, and most black women in the professional world were teachers. But, writing in the *Opportunity* in 1923, Eva Bowles, the first black woman on the staff of the YWCA, noticed that although "most of the 30,074 Negro women in the professional world are teachers, there is an ever increasing group entering the world of law, medicine, nursing and business," and warned against the "prescribed limitations" that were being placed on black women, "especially in pursuits other than teaching."[34]

Gaius Bolin was not happy about his daughter's plans to pursue a career in law. He was clearly oblivious to his own influence on her and the impact of her daily after-school visits to his law office. She recalled that "being surrounded by those shelves and shelves of law books—those great big law books that he had and hearing him talk—I think that must have been really why I wanted to become a lawyer." Gaius always thought that Jane would become a teacher like her sister Ivy. "I don't like you becoming a lawyer," he told her, "because lawyers have to hear such dirty things sometimes and a woman shouldn't have to hear some of the things a lawyer hears."[35] He found the law too indelicate a profession for his daughter, subscribing to the belief that teaching was the more acceptable profession.[36] Jane later recalled that she had to convince her father that he was showing prejudice of another kind.

"Realizing I was not to be deterred by my sex," she said her father then dealt with the matter of her race.[37] He was incensed that the counselor would try to discourage his daughter's career plans. Jane remembered that "after disposing of the vocational guidance counselor with a few forceful words concerning the desirability of her residence in a warmer place than Massachusetts,"[38] her father reminded her "that as long as he was paying for my education it was solely our business what education he provided for me."[39] He let her know that he still did not approve of women lawyers, but if she was sure she wanted to be a lawyer she should apply to the finest law school that admitted women.[40]

(Unbeknownst to her father and guidance counselor, Jane had already applied to and interviewed at Yale Law School. She planned to tell her father only after she was accepted because she knew that he would not approve. Gaius Bolin may have opposed the idea of women becoming lawyers, but when it came to his daughter, he conceded, however reservedly, and offered the full force of his support behind her. At that moment, Jane informed her father that she had been accepted to Yale Law School, and just as he had always done, he agreed to finance her education.)[41]

In advising Bolin about her career plans, the counselor had ignored the particular circumstances of her status, coming as she did from a professional household with a father who was a prominent lawyer and a brother who was at the time enrolled in law school—circumstances that may have predisposed her to the study of law and in the end advanced her practice in the legal profession.[42] Jane had never framed her aspirations in terms of the restrictions placed on African Americans or women, but rather on the possibilities lived by her father. Growing up, she spent lots of time in her father's office, and knew from a very young age that she wanted to be like him.[43] Using her father's prominence as a point of reference, she informed her counselor that she expected the same future that any other aspiring lawyer might.

At the time of her meeting with her guidance counselor, Bolin had already begun researching possible law schools in the region. University of Michigan Law School accepted women, and of course Howard Law School had always been open to women since Mary Ann Shadd Cary and Charlotte E. Ray enrolled in 1869.[44] Yale and Columbia were the two law schools in the broader metropolitan area that were open to women at the time. Bolin chose Yale because she did not want to go to school in New York City.

Jane's insistence on a career in the law, as opposed to one in teaching, articulated her own reconfiguring of the black woman's public space. It also demonstrated the complexity of the black woman's consciousness—for in the third decade of twentieth century not all black women aspired to become teachers, and not all black women became teachers. Bolin dared to transgress the script of black women's professional space at that time, not because of an indifference to a mission of "racial uplift" that was so tied to teaching, but precisely because of it.[45] She confirmed this in her 1937 appointment to the Office of the Corporation Counsel of New York Law Department when she said, "My main interest has always been the uplift of our race."[46]

Wellesley had provided Jane Bolin with a lifetime of discouraging experiences. As such, she should not have been surprised by the school's indifference when on the occasion of her 1939 judicial appointment she received "not a single note from teacher, president, dean, house mother or anyone. . . . who was at Wellesley during my four years."[47] But she was surprised, because the publicity of her appointment had generated hundreds of letters and telegrams from people, mostly strangers, from all over the world, including her law school, high school, and even grade school teachers. She was surprised also because the press had implicitly credited Wellesley for having contributed to the woman she had become. And, in a perverse way, it had. She had come to believe that "these experiences perhaps were partly responsible for my lifelong interest in the social problems, poverty and racial discrimination rampant in our country."[48]

In 1974, Bolin graciously accepted an invitation to submit a memoir for Wellesley's centennial. It had been almost half a century since she graduated from Wellesley. Still, remarkably she was "saddened and maddened" to recall many of her college experiences. The resulting memoir was a scathing account of the racism that she felt was "part of Wellesley's history" and that "should be recorded fully, if only as a benighted pattern to which determinedly it will never return and, also as a measure of its progress."[49] Bolin was so intent on her words remaining intact that on several occasions she informed the editor she would not approve anything other than her complete submission despite the editor's apparent concern about the length of her essay (it was two pages long).[50]

It took this painful reliving, this exposure, to prick the conscience of one of those "in authority" who had sat idly by while Jane endured the misery that was her college years at Wellesley. After reading the memoir, Louise Overacker, one of Bolin's former professors at Wellesley, confided to Bolin, "What I never suspected were the slights to which you were subjected and the loneliness that lay beneath that composed, self-reliant exterior."[51]

What this professor never suspected was the degree to which Bolin's composed, self-reliant exterior was just that—an exterior, and one consciously constructed by Bolin to protect her *self*. Historian Darlene Clark Hine suggests that "black women as a rule developed a politics of dissemblance, to protect the sanctity of the inner aspects of their lives." This "culture of dissemblance," which creates the appearance of openness without full disclosure, although discussed within the context of rape or the threat of rape, is instructive here because as Hine has suggested and as Bolin has demonstrated, dissemblance does facilitate mental survival in a hostile environment.[52] Had Bolin's professor been more aware of the only two black first-year students, she might have understood why in the intervening years Bolin never accepted invitations to return to Wellesley. Moreover, had she truly *seen* them while they were matriculating at Wellesley, she might have recognized what they had—that like Ralph Ellison's invisible man they were outside history when outside the sisterhood, but invisible when inside.[53]

During the 1890s the law school was replacing the law office as the primary locus of legal training. As such, practitioners lost direct control over entrance into the profession, and African Americans found it almost impossible to obtain a law school education at a time when that became mandatory for the practice of law.[54] Howard University School of Law met the responsibility of training a significant percentage of black lawyers during an era of tokenism in the North and complete exclusion in the South. Established in 1869 to provide legal education for Americans traditionally excluded from the profession, especially African Americans, it had become in the twentieth century the epicenter of legal activism in the black freedom struggle. The "Harvard Model" of legal education, instituted in 1869, emerged as the rule requiring the traditional three-year course of study instead of the earlier one-year course of study.[55]

By the turn of the twentieth century, law schools were primarily responsible for training lawyers, and had begun to ally themselves with prestigious law firms and bar leaders.[56] As such, it was not sufficient for aspiring lawyers to attend law school only, because quite often where they went to school determined the advantages they would have. Sociologist Cynthia Fuchs Epstein contends that so long as women were not part of the educational elite, their chances of being Brahmins of the legal profession were that much diminished. She observes that "restrictions or quotas on their entrance meant that channels to the larger firms served by Columbia, Yale and Harvard were cut off, and channels to the other firms that comprised the country's principal legal community and to posts in government and leading corporations were also severely limited."[57] Of course Epstein's reference to women does not address the issue of status anguish felt by black women like Jane Bolin, who were part of the educational elite but without access to the opportunities of the educational elite because race remained a medium through which her class was lived and her status ignored.[58]

J. Clay Smith Jr. observes that the experiences of early black law graduates of Yale remain a mystery, although it is reasonable to imagine that they were no better. Smith finds that Yale's admission policy was quite favorable to African Americans. In 1878, Yale admitted its first black law student, Edwin Archer Randolph, and in 1910, the first black deaf-mute law student, Roger Demosthenes O'Kelly. According to Smith, in 1915 when Nathan B. Young, another black law student, entered Yale, there were two other black law students enrolled and not "much prejudice."[59] However, even as the evidence of "firsts" suggests an unraveling of one form of prejudice, it does very little to enlighten about the real climate and gender dynamics of prejudice at these institutions. For example, as an African American woman at Wellesley and Yale, Bolin's experiences were diametrically opposed to those of her father, who attended Williams College in the late nineteenth century, and the black men of Yale mentioned above.

In 1928, after graduating from Wellesley College, Bolin entered Yale Law School, one of four women enrolled there that year, and the first and only African American. The other women were white. Two were in her class and one was in the third-year class. Thought it had been exactly ten years since the University Corporation at Yale voted to admit women for legal education, the climate was no more welcoming of women than it had been before this decision, and doubly hostile for black women. As lawyer and lay historian Karen Berger Morello points out, no matter when the change occurred to accept women, those women who were determined to get an Ivy League education inevitably faced long periods of resistance, resentment, and grudging accommodation.[60]

The university had no dormitories for women at that time because so few women were law students. So they all had to live in private homes. Bolin remembered that there were many Southern students and Southern professors. Although she did not detail her years at Yale in a memoir, one account makes it reasonable to infer that events there were somewhat reminiscent of her experiences at Wellesley. Yale, not unlike Wellesley, seemed to have accommodated the sensibilities of their Southern students. Bolin recalled that "a few Southerners" at the law school had taken pleasure in letting the swinging classroom doors hit her in the face.[61] The affront was sufficiently cruel that many years later when one of these Southerners became active in the American Bar Association (ABA) and invited Bolin to appear before the ABA's group in Texas, she declined without hesitation. It is not clear whether her former classmate remembered his actions, but if he did, maybe he hoped that she had forgotten.[62]

While at Yale, she was made to feel invisible when she was not the object of racial slights. She remembered having two Southern professors during her three years at Yale, neither of whom ever called on her in class. One of them, who never acknowledged her whether he encountered her on campus or on the streets, was forced to acknowledge her one morning while conversing with Dean Charles Clark in the hallway. Clark acknowledged Bolin with a "Good morning," but the professor did as he had always done, and completely ignored her when she said good morning. Clark, who later went on to become a federal judge, punctured the façade of invisibility when he asked the professor if he had not heard Miss Bolin say good morning. Bolin remembered that at that moment the professor was forced to acknowledge her and "sotto voce mentioned, mumbled 'good morning'"[63]

During her first year at Yale she met the man who would become her life partner. She and Ralph Mizelle met at a social gathering following a Yale-Harvard football game. They had both been invited to the party that was hosted by a prominent African American dentist and his wife in New Haven, Connecticut. Much like the church women from Boston who reached out to her once aware that she was a student at Wellesley and most likely isolated, this couple likely provided a social space for Yale's black students knowing there was no real community for them at the university. Mizelle, who was almost fifteen years Bolin's senior, was practicing law in New York City at the time. Although her sister Ivy thought that she was attracted to Mizelle because he was somehow a substitute for her father, Jane thought only that "he was a very attractive man, physically," who had a flair for life. She never alluded to it being love at first sight, but she and Mizelle were engaged a year after she graduated from Yale and married in 1933. His graduation present to her was a Ford automobile, the first car that she owned.[64]

In 1931 Jane Bolin graduated from Yale, the first black woman law graduate. She shared the celebration with her father and brother who attended her graduation. Others in the family wanted to be present, but graduates were limited to two tickets. Jane had survived an atmosphere of prejudiced professors and resentful students who may have hoped that they could make it impossible for her to continue. According to Morello, "Their behavior had the opposite effect—it toughened women students and taught them how to survive the hostile environments they would find in government and industry."[65] The experience, however painful, provided a valuable lesson for what was to come in the profession. Bolin found that being part of the educational elite was not the passport it was for white men and many white women. She was credentialed in 1931 from an Ivy League law school, yet she had no access to the major law firms that remained all white and for the most part, all male.

For African American lawyers and more specifically African American women lawyers, being "credentialed" did not readily overcome the barriers set up by the dominant model of preparation and practice. It was therefore not an easy predictor of professional success for African Americans. Understanding how Bolin negotiated the myth of "credentialism" is therefore essential to an understanding of her early successes in the legal profession. This is examined within the politics of preparation that is addressed in the following chapter.[66]

3. Politics of Preparation

The Making of the Nation's First
African American Woman Judge

Jane Bolin's graduation from Yale University Law School in 1931 signaled the beginning of a series of remarkable firsts in the legal profession. As the first black woman graduate from Yale, she pioneered in a profession that was virtually all white and all male. Six years later she was appointed assistant corporation counsel of the City of New York, becoming the first black woman to occupy that position. When New York Mayor Fiorello La Guardia appointed her to the Domestic Relations Court of the City of New York in 1939, she became the nation's first black woman judge. In 1943 she was the first African American woman elected to membership in the Association of the Bar of the City of New York (ABCNY), an honor that coincided with the organization's investigation of charges that the American Bar Association (ABA) still refused membership to African Americans.[1]

Her strides in the legal profession from 1931 to 1939 were made relatively quickly, suggesting perhaps a tale of easy access and an unobstructed path in the legal profession. Yet, for Jane Bolin, being a member of the educational elite had not been the passport to success it was for her predominantly white and male Yale classmates. An examination of her professional life beyond the pioneering peaks reveals the pervasive discrimination that she overcame, and unravels the threads of gender, class, race, credentialism, and politics that colored the fabric of her professional life. Moreover, it shows how African Americans and African American women in particular negotiated the professional terrain to cultivate a meaningful practice as lawyers.

Political scientist Beverly Blair Cook suggests that if society provided the same material and psychic supports and the same opportunities for all its citizens, then the population proportion of each group would predict the proportionality of its political representation.[2] However, American society had not always provided the same material supports and the same opportunities for all of its citizens across sex, race, and economic lines; the necessary amendments to the Constitution of the United States and the several civil rights acts of the 1950s and 1960s expose the extent to which it had not.[3] Furthermore, since the legal profession inherited its legitimacy from the culture and the social institutions that made it objection-able for over half of its citizens (women and men) to be full participants,[4] the result has been, according to Cynthia Fuchs Epstein, an undistorted reflection of the society's social irresponsibility.[5] The exclusionary practices of the ABA were therefore right in line with the racially segregated society from which it gained its legitimacy. Leaders of the ABA could not conceive of African Americans as lawyers and therefore never anticipated that they would apply for membership in the asso-ciation. Consequently, the inadvertent election of three African American lawyers to the ABA in 1912 resulted in an ABA resolution requiring all future applicants to disclose their race, because as its Executive Committee stated, "The settled practice of the Association has been to elect only white men to membership."[6]

Faced with such structural resistance to their professional opportunities and development, black lawyers founded the National Bar Association (NBA) in 1925 and agreed that its objectives would be the following:

> The advancement of the science of jurisprudence, and in addition to form a na-tionwide organization of practicing attorneys of the Negro race in an endeavor to strengthen and elevate the Negro lawyer in his profession and in his relationship to his people; to improve his standing at the bar of the country, and to stress the ethics of his practice and conduct, to condemn actions that have a tendency to lessen respect for the lawyer and to create a bond of true fellowship among the colored members of the Bar of America for their general uplift and advancement and for the encouragement of the Negro youth of America who will follow their choice of this profession.[7]

The NBA complemented and later replaced local black associations such as the John M. Harlan Law Club of Ohio and the Cook County Bar Association of Illinois, which provided the professional support not forthcoming from local and national white law associations. In 1943 the ABA opened its membership to African Americans—or, more accurately, by 1943 the doors of the ABA gave way to external pressure, when assistant district attorney and Harlem community leader Francis Ellis Rivers's ABA application took center stage in the ABCNY's investigation of charges that the ABA still refused to admit African Americans. In a newspaper interview, Jane Bolin publicly denounced the discriminatory practices of the ABA as a "great shame."[8]

The dismantling of the ABA's racial barriers notwithstanding, overt discrimi-nation in hiring practices remained common at every level of the profession.

Epstein finds this to be a contradiction of the ideology of even-handed fairness on which the law is based, and maintains that by the canons of its own logic the law should welcome to its practice all those who qualify by reason of intelligence and facility.[9] Nevertheless, African Americans in general, and African American women in particular, were drastically underrepresented on the bench and as lawyers relative to their numbers in the larger society.[10]

Ever since Charlotte E. Ray graduated from Howard Law School and was admitted to the District of Columbia Bar in 1872, becoming the first black woman lawyer in the United States, black women had entered the legal profession albeit tentatively, with few practicing law fulltime before the 1920s.[11] By the 1940s more than fifty black women were practicing law full time; a number of these black women lawyers had distinguished themselves in the legal profession.[12] Among them were Sadie Tanner Mossell Alexander, a well-respected practitioner of probate and domestic relations law in the prestigious law firm founded in 1923 by her husband, Raymond Pace Alexander;[13] Eunice Hunton Carter, who became chief district attorney of the Special Sessions Bureau of New York County after engineering the biggest organized crime prosecution in the nation's history while handling low-level prosecutions in the city's magistrate's court;[14] and of course, Jane Matilda Bolin, who by 1949 would have completed her first ten-year judicial term on the Domestic Relations Court of the City of New York and been reappointed for a second ten-year term by Mayor William O'Dwyer, remaining the nation's only black woman judge into the 1950s.[15] In 1950, out of the 1,275 female lawyers in New York, a mere nineteen were African American.[16]

However, when Bolin graduated from Yale Law School in 1931, these accolades were not yet a certainty. White law firms hired few women or African American lawyers, and when they did, they were restricted to specific areas of practice.[17] Karen Berger Morello found that "since the nineteenth century, women have been trying to break down the barriers at these large corporate law firms, but except in the limited areas of trusts and estates . . . they have met with little success."[18] These firms sometimes rationalized excluding black lawyers by placing the blame squarely at the feet of their influential clients who, they argued, refused to deal with black lawyers, "particularly where the clients had to depend heavily on the attorney's skill and expertise."[19]

In actuality, the skill and expertise so integral to the professional development of the lawyer were acquired primarily on the job—which made restrictive hiring all the more burdensome for black lawyers who, as a consequence, possessed limited opportunities for professional development and growth, and often, low professional esteem. Almost by design, the legal profession, like many other professions, limited access to training to a select membership, then resorted to the circuitous argument that the excluded group of professionals was not hired because of a lack of training. Virtually isolated in the profession, black lawyers turned inward to the black community, which did not always help to bolster their self-esteem, preferring as it did to retain white lawyers for fear that black lawyers would be unsuccessful against a white lawyer and before a white judge, regardless of their ability or quality of performance.[20]

The black community, nevertheless, was still the first employer of black lawyers, many of whom could not even secure employment in government agencies such as the district attorney's office, where black lawyers had held positions from the early years of the twentieth century.[21] Whether these black lawyers joined a friend or associate in a partnership or a space-sharing arrangement, the vast majority of black lawyers concentrated in the least desirable and remunerative areas of practice, such as criminal offenses, domestic relations, and small claims.[22]

The network of support that existed within the black bar is therefore instructive of the early professionalization of the black lawyer in the first half of the twentieth century when the black bar was most beset by professional segregation. Hine speaks of this professionalization in reference to the consolidation of the black bar as social engineers during the first phase of the modern civil rights movement.[23] This early period of the 1930s and 1940s represented for the black bar more than the specialization and practice of civil rights law. It also accounted for the reality of the black bar and the black community as the major first employers of the black lawyer.

However, to the extent that the judicial system remained an integral part of the profession, this parallel construction of opportunity would always be limited. To be sure, African Americans did establish their own law schools, law firms, local bar associations, a national bar association (all institutions central to the profession), and opportunities for active practice. But they could not create a parallel judicial tribunal for the practice of law, nor was there some "extra-judicial" tribunal in which to operate. The Constitution stood as the paramount law of the land and its judicial institution as the single tribunal for determining what the law was and was not. Although experience had taught generations of African Americans that there existed two distinct systems of justice, one for blacks and one for whites, the reality was that there was a single judiciary and therefore no option for a parallel court system. For all of their success in self-training, self-employment, and self-association, black lawyers still had to acquit themselves before a judicial system that did not always provide for their equality under the law or their participation in the legal profession.[24]

Two years into the Great Depression, society in 1931 was reeling from an economic crisis and the attendant competition over resources and opportunities. Upon her graduation from Yale Law School, having no job prospects in the new corporate law firms or government agencies, it made sense that Jane Bolin would return to Poughkeepsie. In 1930 there were only three African American women lawyers in all of New York State.[25] But, in Poughkeepsie, Jane's father had built a successful legal practice that by 1931 included her brother, Gaius Charles Jr., who had graduated from New York University Law School in 1927.[26] She was therefore more fortunate than most black women trying to jump-start their careers in the legal profession. Of Charlotte E. Ray it was reported that "although a lawyer of decided ability, on account of prejudice, [she] was not able to obtain sufficient legal business and had to give up active practice" and return to being a teacher.[27] Many other black women since Ray experienced a similar fate, but a few like Bolin had lawyer-fathers or lawyer-husbands with practices that they could join. After Sadie Alexander graduated from the University of Pennsylvania Law School in 1927, she joined her husband's law firm and enjoyed an active practice with the firm for several decades.[28]

In Poughkeepsie, Jane Bolin clerked in her father's law office for the state-required six months before she took and passed the New York State Bar Examination in March 1932. She recalled how proud she was to have her name added to the door of her father's law office, where she actively practiced until she relocated to New York City. There she engaged in general private practice as a partner with her husband Ralph Mizelle in the firm of Mizelle and Bolin until 1937. Though a member of her father's practice, she did not have a clientele of her own. She searched titles for her father, and at his insistence, spent a great deal of time observing trials in the State Supreme Court. She also shared her father's clients and carried a diverse caseload that included many criminal cases. One such case involved girls from the Wassaic State School, a school for mentally challenged children, whom she successfully defended against charges of assault and property damage. Motivated by both parental pride and professional praxis, her father proved to be an invaluable first employer and mentor. Trading on his reputation as a prominent and well-respected lawyer, he also made sure that Jane met all the judges with whom he worked.[29]

Jane Bolin's first year out of law school spent in practice with her father was a very practical decision that afforded her valuable opportunities for professional growth that many black women lawyers did not have. Consequently, her return to Poughkeepsie in 1931 was not tied to any illusion of building a practice with her father and brother there, although they had built a very lucrative practice that served a mostly white clientele throughout Dutchess County. That year clarified for her the degree to which she needed to step out of her father's shadow if she was going to construct an independent professional identity. Years later, while assistant corporation counsel assigned a case in Dutchess County, she argued before a judge of the Dutchess County Supreme Court, when to her embarrassment, he said, "I'm going to tell you what your father would tell you: 'Stop when you're ahead.'"[30] Though not reserved for black women lawyers, this brand of paternalism was routinely showered on black women. Lucia Thomas of Chicago, one of few black women lawyers approved to practice before the U. S. Supreme Court, recounted the "embarrassing gallantry" of a judge who once interrupted her during a prosecution to say, "Young lady, you're acquitting yourself *very* well!" Judicial paternalism notwithstanding, Jane Bolin must have imagined that had she remained in Poughkeepsie she would forever be seen as Gaius Bolin's little girl, even as her brother is ushered in as a junior partner or "rightful successor" some day to his father.[31]

Furthermore, Bolin had no illusions about the opportunities for her own success in Poughkeepsie, a town she found too provincial. Years later, she explained, "I did not see the opportunity in Poughkeepsie to bring to fruition the aspirations and ambitions and dreams I have had from my childhood."[32] Whether she wanted to ultimately create a professional space beyond her father's influence or live and work in a more cosmopolitan area, it was clear to her that opportunities for African Americans in Poughkeepsie had not improved much since she left for college in 1924. The pervasive marginalization that plagued the majority of African Americans in Poughkeepsie might have escaped her as a member of the Bolin clan, but she was sure it was a climate in which she could not thrive. As a result, in 1932 Jane left "the comfortable security of my father's home to start practicing law in New York."[33] Her choice of words betrays a conflation of her "father's home" with her "father's practice," and an awareness that may have confirmed her need to carve out a professional space beyond her father's prominence. She may have also chosen New York City because it was where her fiancé, Ralph Mizelle, lived and practiced as a lawyer.

The same year that Bolin relocated to New York City, James "Jimmy" Walker resigned as mayor of New York City. His departure in 1932 came on the heels of the Seabury investigation that exposed the pervasive corruption of his administration. New York City was mired in the machine politics of Tammany Hall, the city's Democratic Party organization. It grew out of inept urban management that coupled public accomplishments with personal gain, making graft the highest form of gratitude.[34] Although Bolin would have been aware of the sweeping political changes taking place in New York City, she could not have imagined that the anti-Tammany campaigner and next elected mayor, Fiorello La Guardia, would play such an important role in the trajectory of her career. La Guardia became mayor in 1933 having won on the Republican and city Fusion tickets in a mayoral race he called "a citizens movement for the salvation of the city."[35]

In 1932 New York City was home to the national offices of the NAACP, which remained in the forefront of the African American fight for full citizenship, and the Urban League, which continued to fight for greater economic opportunities for African Americans. New York City also had a vibrant black community that boasted institutions such as the Abyssinian Baptist Church; an informed black press with dailies such as the *Amsterdam News* and the *New York Age;* and nationally renowned activist-leaders including Reverend Adam Clayton Powell Jr., A. Philip Randolph, and W. E. B. Du Bois. On many fronts the 1930s marked the end of one era and the beginning of another. The Harlem Renaissance was waning but the "New Negro" of that era had matured politically and stood ready to demand increased participation in the politics and economy of the city that, like the rest of the nation, was in the midst of a great economic disaster.[36]

However, being a graduate of Yale Law School and equipped with a full year of active practice that included trials were still not enough to land Jane Bolin employment in New York City. During her first year there she applied to a few local law firms, but found the climate frosty and dismissive—the reception was usually very businesslike, but she was disposed of rather quickly without an invitation to interview.[37] In 1933 in the absence of independent opportunities, she joined forces with Ralph E. Mizelle in private practice, "and with him for the next four years as wife and business partner after their marriage in the same year,"[38] just as many of her sisters at the black bar had done in the 1930s and 1940s. Among the black women lawyers of this period who took advantage of the opportunity to practice law with their lawyer-husbands were Marjorie MacKenzie Lawson of Washington, D.C.; Elizabeth F. Allen of South Bend, Indiana; Margaret B. Wilson of St. Louis; Alice Huggins and Jewel Stradford Rogers of Chicago; and Sadie Alexander of Philadelphia.[39]

Although the first years of practice in the firm of Mizelle and Bolin were "decidedly precarious," Jane endured because she had come to New York City intent on a career in law.[40] She was more fortunate than many black women lawyers who, without benefit of a lawyer-husband, were forced to quit the practice of law altogether for more secure occupations. A 1947 article in *Ebony* reported that "over 50 percent of today's lady lawyers work in government agencies, social service or civil liberties organizations," because "perhaps steady jobs offer greater security . . . [or] maybe sex and color discrimination make actual practice too difficult." The same article explained that although color was indisputably a barrier to lawyers of both sexes, "most colored Portias agree that their sex is a far greater barrier than color to successful law careers."[41]

The precariousness that black lawyers had come to expect in the legal profession was further compounded by the Great Depression; early successes were often lost during the Depression years when across-the-board earnings were reduced or nonexistent. The early success of black lawyers like Gaius Bolin Sr. and his son (who later joined the practice) was therefore uncommon. The fact that the Bolins were a prominent family in Poughkeepsie for several generations clearly enabled both Gaius Senior and Junior to avail themselves of a majority of white clients, which further enabled them to sustain a lucrative practice.[42] An equal degree of prominence also enabled Sadie Alexander and her husband, Raymond Pace Alexander, to sustain a lucrative practice.[43] Nevertheless, most black firms formed during the first half of the twentieth century were typically small, financially unstable, and short-lived because few could attract the clients needed to sustain a steady practice—they had few white clients and competed with white lawyers for available black clients.[44]

By 1937 the financial strain of private practice had thrust Jane Bolin and her husband back into the job market. The firm of Mizelle and Bolin had dissolved, and Mizelle joined the Solicitor's Office of the United States Postal Service in Washington, D.C., beginning what would become an early commuter marriage for the newlyweds.[45] Bolin applied for a position in the New York Office of the Corporation Counsel and was granted an interview with the first assistant corporation counsel, a man she described as being "from the south of the United States."[46] As she recalled, "He was making short shrift of me by telling me there were no vacancies."

Fortunately, her exit was interrupted when Paul Windels, the corporation counsel himself, just happened to come into the office. She remembered that Windels treated her very cordially. He told her that he was aware of her interest in the position on his staff, when he was interrupted by the assistant who said, "But we have no line for her in the budget." Whereupon Windels said, "But we do," then shook her hand and welcomed her to his staff.[47] It is reasonable to imagine that Windels would have seen Bolin's résumé before she showed up for an interview with his assistant, and might even have recommended the interview, which would suggest his early consideration of her as a viable candidate for a position in his office. That the assistant resorted to a fictitious budgetary reason for denying Bolin employment also suggests, as has already been stated, that she was more than qualified for such a position.

Paul Windels was a close political advisor to La Guardia. He had been one of his campaign managers in 1933,[48] and had been named corporation counsel during La Guardia's second mayoral term (1937–41).[49] Described as "impeccably credentialed," Windels was an astute politician who demanded assurances of exclusive control over his department before accepting the mayor's offer and challenge to create the best law department in the country.[50] Within a year of his appointment, Windels had, reportedly, converted a department that habitually retained expensive outside counsel for every nonroutine matter into one of the best legal staffs in the country.[51]

That Windels counted Bolin among his elite legal staff speaks volumes of her qualifications, but also suggests something about the politics of preparation and appointment. In 1937, another African American woman lawyer, New York City

Assistant District Attorney Eunice Hunton Carter, was appointed chief of Special Sessions Bureau by District Attorney Thomas Dewey. Carter had earlier made a name for herself as a member of then Special Prosecutor Thomas Dewey's "twenty against the underworld," as the prosecution team was later called.[52] In 1935, as an assistant district attorney in the city's magistrate's court, Carter had single-handedly uncovered what led to an unraveling of one of the biggest organized crime rackets that reportedly grossed $12 million annually on prostitution during the Depression years.[53] In a letter of inquiry regarding the status of African American women lawyers two years later, Sadie Alexander first congratulated Carter on the fine work that she was doing in the district attorney's office, then stated, "I cannot say too much for the ability that you have shown as well as the *diplomacy* which you must have exercised to have obtained such a position."[54]

In 1936, the year before Bolin interviewed with the corporation counsel, she tried her luck with politics. She ran on the Republican ticket for the Nineteenth Assembly District of New York County. In 1929 African American activist and Republican politician Francis E. Rivers had won a seat in the New York Legislature for the same assembly district. Furthermore, in 1934, Eunice Carter had run on the Republican ticket for the same seat and although unsuccessful, had lost by only a slim margin of votes.[55] Therefore, when Jane Bolin was prevailed upon to run on the Republican ticket in 1936 in the absence of any other candidate, she was perhaps encouraged by this history and by what Rivers described as "a showing of awakened political consciousness and particularly Republican power in a city which had on the whole gone Democratic.[56]

However, New York Democrat James E. Stephens held the seat after Rivers (1931–35). Moreover, 1936 was the same year that moderately conservative Republican Party stalwart and governor of Kansas Alfred Landon had run against President Franklin D. Roosevelt and was crushed. The presidential election that year was a referendum on Roosevelt and the New Deal—and New York City had fared relatively well under the New Deal thanks to Mayor La Guardia's access to Roosevelt. Therefore, not unlike Landon, Bolin was also crushed at the polls, with a meager 4,572 votes compared to the 18,557 votes cast for the Democratic candidate Robert W. Justice.[57]

Though unsuccessful at the polls, Bolin's candidacy had given her the public orientation that was important to women's eligibility in the pool from which lawyers are so often recruited for the legal hierarchy.[58] Scholars argue that since the selection of judges is embedded in the political process, eligibility requires more than legal experience. Therefore, a viable female candidate—even more so than a viable male candidate—would have to have political credentials in her state and locality and understand the formal and informal steps to the bench.

As latecomers to the profession and its politics, women would therefore require much more visibility to increase their viability.[59] La Guardia biographer Thomas Kessner writes that it was customary in New York politics during the reign of Tammany Hall for Republicans to regularly concede a particular district seat to the Democrats, thus nominating a candidate who was usually a loyal party supporter or, according to Kessner, "some obscure men [or women] of local stature to collect the ceremonial honors and go down in defeat."[60] In 1936 Bolin may have been the designated candidate, who was "prevailed on, for derth [*sic*] of another candidate" to run on the Republican ticket for the Nineteenth Assembly District of New York County.[61]

Like a majority of African Americans in 1936, Bolin supported President Roosevelt, but did not fully identify with the Democrats. On the outside of Tammany machine politics in New York City, Bolin remained a loyal supporter of the party of Lincoln, having lived Republican politics through the recollections of her father, who was known around Dutchess County as the eyes and ears of Theodore Roosevelt.[62] That Jane Bolin, at age twenty-eight, received the Republican nomination to run for the Nineteenth Assembly District seat confirms not just her involvement in local party politics and her loyalty to the party, but also her own political ambitions. Some might argue that she simply played the role of "scripted loser," running as she did on a ticket slated to lose. Indeed, Fiorello La Guardia, the very politician who would a year later appoint her to the bench, had in the early years of his political career played the role of "scripted loser," a role that many argue did not hurt his political career or her legal career.[63]

Unsuccessful as Bolin's candidacy for the assembly was, the party's nomination might have had far-reaching political currency. Her political acumen might have imagined that there would be political awards, including, but not limited to, a patronage appointment. Rivers was no doubt referring to the likes of Bolin when he said, "The New York Negro has learned to play the game [of politics] in a realistic fashion."[64] Paul Windels's appointment of Bolin to the Office of the Corporation Counsel was laced with political meanings. Surely an appointment by Windels would by extension be counted as an appointment by La Guardia. That it was an appointment to the law department, which had achieved national respect because of the vision of the man whom the mayor had handpicked as corporation counsel, meant that La Guardia could count Bolin among the few African Americans in his administration.

In 1934 when La Guardia first took office as mayor of New York City, he assembled a cabinet of all men who represented a cross section of every ethnic group in the city except the African American and Puerto Rican.[65] He appointed Myles A. Paige as magistrate in the court of special sessions, and Hubert T. Delany as tax commissioner of New York City, making them both the first African Americans in such positions. Delany served as an unofficial ombudsman in Harlem, but the overall hue of La Guardia's administration remained the same.[66]

In 1937 the mayor summoned Jane Bolin to his office but never revealed the exact reason for their meeting. She recalled that as she was leaving his office, he said only "that I was too young for the position he had in mind."[67] She was twenty-nine years old at the time. Bolin later found out Domestic Relations Court Justice Rosalie Whitney, one of La Guardia's few female appointees and a judge before whom Bolin had practiced in the Family Court as assistant corporation counsel, had recommended her to the mayor for a judgeship. But he considered her at twenty-nine to be too young for the position. It was no coincidence then that Windels's appointment of Bolin to his elite legal staff and La Guardia's consideration of her for a judicial appointment followed closely on the heels of her unsuccessful bid for the state assembly in 1936. La Guardia had told New Yorkers, "I have sought high and low for men who could effectively do the job." In Bolin, he had found a woman who could effectively do the job in his administration, and one who had paid her political dues.[68]

The lack of a more immediate and direct reward is probably related to what historian Gilbert Osofsky identifies as "the cynical and apathetic attitudes" of white politicians who did not see African Americans as a major political force.[69] An almost religious adherence to the Republican Party may have weakened the political position of African Americans in New York City, but their geographical concentration in Harlem may have afforded them a little more political clout.[70] There would not be a patronage appointment in the form of a judgeship just then for Bolin—but what better consolation than an appointment to the nation's finest law department.

As assistant corporation counsel, Bolin was assigned as trial counsel in the Court of Domestic Relations of New York County. Established in 1933, the court was composed of two parts, the Family Court Division and the Children's Court Division. One assistant corporation counsel was assigned as trial counsel in the Court of Domestic Relations in each of the five counties comprising New York City. In addition to trying cases, Bolin was responsible for preparing her own briefs and memoranda of law, all filings to oppose applications in the Supreme Court for writs of prohibition or for injunctions against the court, and all motions to consolidate actions pending in the court with actions pending in the Supreme Court. In addition, she had to represent the Domestic Relations Court in the Supreme Court in habeas corpus proceedings (which usually arose after a child had been committed to an institution by the Domestic Relations Court). Since the Domestic Relations Court was a newly established court, Bolin found herself at the forefront of domestic relations jurisprudence as she resolved issues involving the court's jurisdiction and the interpretation of the act under which it operated.

Her work in the Domestic Relations Court was timely and important for the black community, which three years earlier had been made the subject of a study commissioned by the court's presiding justice, Edward Boyle. Supposedly alarmed by the disproportionate presence of black children in the court system, Justice Boyle commissioned the study of *The Negro Problem as Reflected in the Functioning of the Domestic Relations Court of the City of New York.*[71] Among other findings, the 1934 report stated that childhood crime among blacks had risen over the past thirteen years by more than 240 percent; that in Manhattan fully 25 percent of all juveniles arraigned in Children's Court were African Americans; that more than one-fourth of all nonsupport cases in the city involved black families. The report contained the alarming conclusion that "the court has not been able for some years satisfactorily to function in cases involving Negro children."[72]

But as thorough as the study purported to be, it neglected to address the real circumstances of life for African Americans in New York City in the 1930s that gave rise to the disproportionate presence of black children in the court system. The Depression had made a poor situation worse in Harlem; the national economic crisis had sent the already depressed ghetto economy into a tailspin. As the last hired and first fired, African Americans suffered from a level of unemployment two to three times the rate of whites. Many men, unable to secure jobs, abandoned their families, while women forced to work outside of the home left young children to sometimes fend for themselves. Moreover, New Deal programs established to assist the needy openly discriminated against African Americans.[73]

In March 1935 Harlem erupted in a riot, ignited when rumors that the police had beaten a black youth to death angered an already frustrated black community that felt overpoliced and underserved by city government. African Americans took out their frustration on white-owned property in the area, destroying what they saw as the instruments of their economic disempowerment so effectively that the all-white Harlem Merchants' Association demanded unsuccessfully that Governor Herbert H. Lehman send in troops to protect their property. The total damage was estimated at more than $2 million. Hundreds of people were injured and the three killed were African American.[74]

Days after Harlem exploded, La Guardia established an eleven-member biracial committee (six African Americans and five whites) to study the causes of the rage underlying the riot of 1935, and for the first time to ask African Americans themselves about the living conditions in Harlem.[75] He declared publicly, "I am appointing a committee of representative citizens to check all official reports and to make a thorough investigation of the causes of the disorder and a study of necessary plans to prevent a repetition of the spreading of malicious rumors,

racial animosities and the inciting of disorder."[76] Eunice Carter was appointed
secretary, and the committee was chaired by Charles Roberts, a black dentist.
Other African American members included Hubert Delany, A. Philip Randolph,
and Justice Charles E. Toney. The actual research was done by famed black sociologist E. Franklin Frazier.

The committee held twenty-five hearings, collected testimony from over 160
witnesses, and more than a year later, issued *The Negro in Harlem: A Report on
Social and Economic Conditions Responsible for the Outbreak of March 19, 1935.* The
committee described the riot as Harlem's "inarticulate response" to racism and
unemployment, and called for sweeping reform in health care, housing, police
practice, and schools. Precisely because the recommendations were so sweeping
and critical of city government, Mayor La Guardia did not act immediately, but
presented the report to Howard University professor Alain Locke (known for
his study of the "New Negro") for further review. Locke agreed with the report's
initial conclusions and urged the mayor to publish the document so that it could
become the basis for a new program of sweeping reform in Harlem. However,
the mayor was not prepared to place Harlem at the center of his agenda as Locke
and the committee demanded.[77]

La Guardia's administration had inherited these concerns, but even with a full
term under his belt, the mayor had not resolved all that plagued the black community. He had tackled long-standing prejudices, integrating the all-white staffs
of city hospitals and expanding civil service opportunities for African Americans.
Yet, he gave up an opportunity to seriously consider the concerns of Boyle's
report when he passed it on to his assistant Louis Dunham who merely recommended "further study."[78] La Guardia showed some sympathy for the plight of
African Americans, and was praised by many African American leaders as "one
of the most fearless friends the Negro has ever had in or out of Congress."[79] And,
relatively speaking, he was. However, his biographer Thomas Kessner finds that
he offered no special program to single out black communities and treat their
unique problems.[80] Blacks in New York City, therefore, faced their problems
alone. Except that in Jane Bolin, as assistant corporation counsel assigned to the
Domestic Relations Court, they now had an advocate working on the inside of
the city's judicial system who fully appreciated the seriousness of their plight.

Bolin's appointment as assistant corporation counsel inserted her into the popular consciousness through features in both the black and the white press. The black
press celebrated her pioneering status as an African American woman lawyer with
coverage such as that carried in the *Apex News* with a heading that stated simply,
"A Sepia Portia-Jane Bolin." The *New York Age* framed its story with a heading that
read, "Miss Jane Bolin Appointed Asst. to Corporation Counsel," and the *Richmond Planet* simply read "Miss Jane Bolin."[81] Whatever the caption, nothing was

ordinary about the import of the subject or subject matter. In referring to Bolin's appointment, the *New York Times* reported that she was assigned to a tribunal that "handles many cases involving members of her race."[82] The *New York Times* had not missed the political timing of her appointment—or maybe the article intended to delineate ethnic parameters to her authority in an effort to temper the anxieties of the traditionalists who may have found her appointment unsettling.

In 1939, almost four years after Harlem erupted (and from all reports, still an incendiary period for the city), La Guardia reconsidered Bolin, who was then thirty-one years old and in his estimation, no longer "too young for the position he had in mind." La Guardia was in his second term as the city's mayor, yet he had not grasped fully the magnitude of the plight of African Americans nor the conditions that fanned the embers in 1935. He had accepted neither the recommendations of E. Franklin Frazier's report nor those of Alain Locke's. In 1943, during his third term of office, his administration would witness another racial protest in Harlem, one that bore all of the characteristics of root and rumor exposed in the 1935 riot.[83]

La Guardia may have hoped that his appointment of Bolin to the Domestic Relations Court would alter, if not completely reverse, the image of the court's inefficiency and insensitivity in handling cases involving African American children.[84] Bolin's experience as assistant corporation counsel assigned to that court (and specifically the Children's Court) made her a superior candidate for a judgeship there, an observation that was made by Justice Rosalie Whitney who first recommended her to La Guardia. Moreover, such an appointment would be most timely given that the African American demand for jobs now extended beyond Harlem to white-collar jobs throughout the city, and resulted in the March 1937 creation of the Greater New York Coordinating Committee for the Employment of Negroes.

The coordinating committee was led by A. Philip Randolph, the militant trade union leader and future mass movement organizer. In spring 1938 the organization adopted a black-out boycott and bill-payers parade that aimed to pressure the Consolidated Edison and Gas Company to hire African Americans. The organization had the full support of Harlem's black leaders, and specifically Reverend Adam Clayton Powell Jr., who at a mass meeting in April 25, 1938, told the more than three thousand Harlemites that "Harlem is sick and tired of promises. The hour has struck to march!" By early 1939 Mayor La Guardia had weighed in on the growing influence of the coordinating committee when he characterized the Harlem Chamber of Commerce Agreement, which the coordinating committee finally negotiated, as "a tribute to common sense and justice."[85]

It was no secret that La Guardia played the game of race politics. According to Kessner, despite the mayor's frequent denials that "I have never appointed and never will appoint a man [or woman] to office because of his [or her] color," La Guardia played the game of ethnic appointments with rare flair.[86] Summing up his administration's attitude toward African Americans in a characteristic speech before the NAACP convention in Philadelphia a year after he appointed Bolin, La Guardia declared: "I appoint Negroes to office in New York not because they were Negroes, but because they had the qualifications and abilities which the City of New York needed to get a job done, and every one of them has made a fine civil servant of which any municipality could be proud."[87]

But La Guardia understood the importance of a "carefully selected token," according to Kessner, as did the communities from whence those persons came.[88] The respected black daily *Amsterdam News* lauded La Guardia for appointing "more Negroes to big, responsible jobs in city government . . . than all other mayors of the city combined." They believed that such appointments educated New Yorkers to wider possibilities for integration than they had allowed themselves to expect before. Even Walter White, executive secretary of the NAACP, praised the mayor for his forward-looking policies regarding African Americans.[89] In death, La Guardia was editorialized as a friend to African Americans "not because he gave them special, or occasionally sensational, or preferential treatment, but because in his conception of American democratic government and in his administration of it they were *included* as citizens."[90]

The degree to which African Americans themselves pushed city government into action cannot be overemphasized. Francis Ellis Rivers was very influential in this regard and may have single-handedly empowered the black community to determine who sat on the judiciary in at least one municipal district. Assemblyman Rivers, who graduated from Columbia University Law School in 1922 and broke the color bar of the New York State Bar Association and the ABCNY, helped pass the legislative act (Laws of 1930, Chapter 651) that created the new Tenth Municipal Court District in Harlem. Rivers was proud that the new municipal court district, as redrawn, had awakened Republican power in a city that had on the whole become Democratic. The leadership of Assemblyman Rivers and the political participation of the black community had secured the election of two African American judges and opened the way for the future election and appointment of other African Americans, including Jane Bolin.

Bolin's appointment to the bench occurred without much fanfare, though, in the midst of the excitement that was the 1939 New York World's Fair. Bolin was summoned to a meeting with Mayor La Guardia in mid-July that year. She was instructed to come, with her husband, the following Saturday, July 22, to the New York City Building at the World's Fair (which had opened on April 30 in Flushing Meadows, New York).[91] Bolin recalled being frightened not knowing why La Guardia wanted to meet with her because as mayor "he had instituted the practice of an answer for every complaint his office received and the answer had to be given to him within just a few days."[92] She naturally pondered reasons why the mayor would summon her to a meeting, but could not think of anything that she had done to warrant such a summons. Still, she was certain she was "in for a hard time."[93]

On July 22 she and her husband, Ralph Mizelle, arrived at the New York City Building at the World's Fair in the shadow of the Trylon and Perisphere and waited for the mayor who was out on the grounds. But when La Guardia arrived, Bolin said he just breezed past her saying he wanted to speak with her husband. The two men retired to a private office and left Bolin alone in the reception area to ponder her fate. Shortly thereafter they emerged smiling, and the mayor directed one of his assistants to call in the photographers. Bolin remembered that very matter-of-factly, the mayor told her to stand up, raise her right hand, and swore her in as a judge of the Domestic Relations Court.[94]

Presentist positioning might extract from La Guardia's request to first speak with Bolin's husband a chauvinism that would be unacceptable today. Current feminist sensibilities might even suggest that although the professional equal of her lawyer-husband, Bolin was seen (or not seen) and treated as a wife who needed her husband's permission. That the mayor consulted with the husband of the appointee without affording the appointee an opportunity to accept or decline reveals much about the mayor's arrogance. Yet, his request to first speak with the husband of a judicial appointee could well be reflective of a protocol common to the period. Bolin's characterization of the mayor's actions was more pragmatic and she thought it ridiculous that her husband would have to or want to give his permission. She said that she was so overwhelmed and surprised at the time that she really did not think about why the mayor wanted to first meet with her husband, but that she understood why he did, reasoning that it was because the mayor wanted to know the *character* of the man who was her husband.[95] Given the importance of the appointment, this would certainly be a valid inquiry—although nothing suggests that such protocol was followed with other appointees, male or white.

The New York World's Fair, focused as it was on the World of Tomorrow, turned out to be the perfect backdrop for the appointment and introduction of the nation's first African American woman judge. The following summer when the World's Fair opened the new American Common, Judge Bolin's name was featured among the list of forty-one African Americans whose names were inscribed on the Wall of Honor. She was in very good company among the five African Americans listed for contributions to education. The other four were Booker T. Washington, the most powerful black leader of his time and ardent proponent of industrial education for African Americans; William Edward Burghardt Du Bois, preeminent Harvard-trained scholar and black protest leader who was also a founding member of the

NAACP; Archibald Grimké, a Harvard-trained lawyer and leading intellectual-activist of racial equality who was also a founding member of the NAACP; and Herman E. Moore, U.S. Federal District Court judge.[96]

Within moments of La Guardia administering the oath, Jane Bolin was emblazoned onto the collective consciousness as the nation's first African American woman judge. Again, the black press celebrated the significance of her appointment and the progress that it represented. The *Philadelphia Tribune* featured the article, "Judge Bolin Hopes Choice Will Inspire Other Women." More entangled with New York politics, the *New York Age* measured the distance that African Americans had traveled under the La Guardia administration in the article, "New York's Fourth Negro Judge, Now on Bench."[97] When Jane informed her father of the appointment, he was as irritated as he was years earlier when she told him of her plans to study law. Gaius told her, "Judges have so much tension in their lives, they die early of heart attacks."[98] Over the next four decades of her judicial career, despite the pressures of the job, she proved her father wrong, and he frequently expressed his immense pride that may not have been readily discernible upon her initial appointment.

Portrait of Jane M. Bolin at age 15 (1923). Courtesy Jane M. Bolin
Photograph Collection, Photographs and Prints Division, Schomburg
Center for Research in Black Culture, New York Public Library, Astor,
Lenox and Tilden Foundations.

Jane M. Bolin with father Gaius C. Bolin, distinguished lawyer, Poughkeepsie, New York (1944). Courtesy Jane M. Bolin Photograph Collection, Photographs and Prints Division, Schomburg Center for Research in Black Culture, New York Public Library, Astor, Lenox and Tilden Foundations.

Jane Bolin is sworn in by Mayor Fiorello LaGuardia as judge in Domestic Relations Court as her husband, Ralph Mizelle, watches (July 22, 1939). Courtesy *New York Daily News*, photo by Bill Wallace.

"Miss Jane Bolin, first colored woman to become a judge in New York, gets acquainted before convening Domestic Relations Court at 153 E. 57th Street. She took the bench for the first time today. Opening case was that of a man who left his wife in need." Courtesy *New York Daily News,* photo by Ed Jackson.

4. Politics of Practice

*An African American Woman Judge
on the Domestic Relations Court*

On July 24, 1939, two days after Mayor La Guardia appointed Jane Bolin to the Domestic Relations Court, Justice Jacob Panken inducted her as a justice there, making her the nation's first African American woman judge.[1] Bolin entered a very exclusive fraternity in the legal hierarchy, overwhelmingly male and white. She would remain the only African American woman judge for the next two decades. How she experienced this judicial space of authority was therefore greatly informed by her consciousness as an African American woman. That she was a judicial appointee as opposed to an elected one also impacted her tenure on the bench, which was three times considered for mayoral reappointment. Furthermore, as a wife twice widowed and mother, she faced the burden of double consciousness that had always plagued women lawyers as they tried to balance their gender and professional identity. But, in the case of Judge Bolin, might the tension between her gender and professional identity have been mitigated because her judicial appointment was to the Domestic Relations Court—modeled on the principles of family and children's courts that "perpetuated the Victorian emphasis on woman's inherent domesticity" and supposedly allowed women lawyers to be women and lawyers?[2]

By the 1930s few women lawyers were judges in courts outside of Domestic Relations Court, family courts, children courts, and juvenile courts. What was intended as an ideal and separate judicial sphere for women lawyers, beginning with juvenile courts of the late nineteenth century and women's courts of the first decades of the twentieth century, grew into virtually the only opportunity for judgeships accessible to women lawyers. Many male lawyers supported the idea that women lawyers were better suited than men to interpret the law for and protect the rights of women and children.[3] As a result few men wanted these judgeships that for many represented the lowest rung of the judicial hierarchy.[4] Nevertheless, in twentieth-century American society, judges of either gender at all levels of the judicial hierarchy "were the repository of legal knowledge, as well as a model of temperament and respect among other lawyers and the public at large."[5]

As appointed, Jane Bolin was first assigned to the Family Court in Manhattan as a justice of the Domestic Relations Court. On the occasion of her induction, Justice Panken welcomed her on behalf of the staff and lawyers who were assigned to the court, and further added, "I want to express to you my entire and complete gratification that the Bench will be graced by you." "Justice Bolin, I take it that it feels good to be addressed as 'Justice,' and I take it also that the term 'Justice' is not a vain word. I am sure that it will not be a vain word insofar as you are concerned." Panken knew of Bolin's performance as assistant corporation counsel and thought that she had done outstanding work in the two years she had held that position. "You have a great deal of experience in our Court," he said, and reminded her that it was less than a week ago before she was elevated to the bench that he had complimented her on her outstanding work.[6]

Panken went on to say that Bolin would make an excellent justice in the Domestic Relations Court because of her sterling qualities, her ability, and because of her humaneness. He explained that if the rehabilitative method of modern jurisprudence, particularly jurisprudence that dealt with crime and delinquency, was going to be effective, then "in this Court we need humane people as judges, we need people who have common sense." And, he was sure that "no one can rehabilitate or contribute to salvaging when one places himself [herself] on Mount Olympus and tries to pull the maladjusted and underprivileged, the emotionally disturbed, up to Mount Olympus." Panken believed that a justice of the Domestic Relations Court had to be "part of the people" and "subjective in ones objectivity, in order to be able to contribute towards the effort of readjusting, reeducating, and rebuilding that which has, because of disadvantage, economic, moral, social, or otherwise, been destroyed." In Bolin he recognized such a person. "You are not only humane," he said, "but you have a fund of common sense, which will be tremendously helpful to you"; but more importantly, "it will be helpful to those who look to you for justice, justice in the sense of doing that which is humanly possible to help others."[7]

Whether Mayor La Guardia intended to truly integrate city government or just temporarily appease the city's African American community with his appointment of Jane Bolin is a question that obscures the fact that he ended the era of blanket exclusion of black women lawyers in the judiciary. And whatever comfort may have been derived from viewing Bolin's appointment as tokenism was immediately dashed by the reality that even tokens establish precedent, which engenders change. Bolin believed that "no matter what the past, the future will take care of itself and even the law may capitulate as have many other professions thereby becoming a better profession and a truer expression of democracy—because of its acceptance of women jurists."[8] Justice Panken seemed to appreciate or anticipate the change that was to come, when during Bolin's induction he said, "You are quite young, but this is an age of youth anyhow. If the world is to be made better it will not be made so by us of the last generation, it will be made so by your generation."[9]

In the early 1930s, the Seabury investigations had uncovered a level of corruption in New York City government that reached into the courtrooms of judges beholden to the Tammany Hall politicians who appointed them. The investigations and inauguration of the new Fusion administration under Fiorello La Guardia had stemmed the tide of the machine politics and corruption of Tammany Hall, but did not completely eradicate the virus that infected the courts by the time Jane Bolin came to the bench in 1939. Bolin had replaced a judge who was a Tammany Hall political appointee and who ran a racket of selling the disposition of cases for political clout. This Tammany-appointed judge contacted Bolin several times within her first months on the bench regarding the "contracts" that he had made on certain cases and told her what he wanted her to do about them.[10] Bolin came face to face with the very corrupt but common practice that had political clubs making deals with judges to go lightly or dispense with cases in a particular way. Yet her youth had no bearing on her sense of professionalism and integrity. She immediately told the former judge that she could not possibly go along with his contracts and that she had to try the cases.[11] She was never approached again.

Judge Bolin's induction into the Domestic Relations Court occurred six years after the court's establishment on October, 1, 1933. As established, its name suggested functions that were more inclusive than its jurisdiction stipulated. Under the restrictive enabling provision of the New York State constitution, the Domestic Relations Court Act created a statutory court of limited jurisdiction that did not include many of the functions essential to a domestic relations court of general jurisdiction.[12] Nevertheless, the Domestic Relations Court, with its legal procedure and the safeguards of due process that were supplemented by the techniques of social work, psychiatry, and psychology, represented a marked improvement over the purely legalistic approach of the New York State Supreme Court in its exclusive jurisdiction over matrimonial actions and child custody issues.[13]

This "modern court," which Bolin joined in 1939, assumed the jurisdiction of the Children's Court of the City of New York and of the Family Court that was part of the Magistrates' Court system of the City of New York—although the Children's Court had almost exclusive jurisdiction over children, and was therefore separate from the Family Court, which had jurisdiction over a broader spectrum of family issues involving mainly adults. However, besides the Domestic Relations Court, four other courts—some civil, some criminal—had jurisdiction over some aspect of the child and the family. The Magistrates' Court had jurisdiction over disorderly conduct pertaining to the family, which included nonsupport of wives and children; the Court of Special Session handled filiation procedures; the Supreme Court heard matrimonial actions and child custody controversies; and the Surrogate's Court had jurisdiction over adoptions.[14]

This jurisdictional division among the five courts represented for Bolin an illogical dissection of family issues that placed a heavy and often unreasonable burden on petitioners and respondents who were turning to the courts for help. In a speech made before the Bar Association of the City of New York during her second term on the bench, she advised their recognition of the urgency for reform, saying, "One sympathizes with the many women who must go to one court for a legal separation, divorce or annulment, to be followed when there is no money for legal services by action in another court to obtain support for the children. And for wives without children, after possibly action in the Supreme Court for separation and the Domestic Relations Court for support, they must go to the Magistrates' Court or perhaps the Court of Special Sessions to prosecute an assaultive and abusive husband."[15] She was particularly concerned about the "heartless necessity to repeat, without privacy except in the Domestic Relations Court, intimate marital details."[16] She added her voice to those who challenged the practicality of the division and in 1962 welcomed a new integrated court system under the restructured Family Court of the State of New York. Decades later she would still be remembered as a justice who brought "understanding and perception to a family court in transition from being a social court to a due process tribunal."[17]

Bolin assumed her judicial responsibilities the same day she was inducted "without any guidance," a practice she criticized and worked hard to change. She agreed that a lawyer should already know the law before coming to the bench, but reasoned that some lawyers may have to work a little harder in the beginning to learn specialized law that pertains to the particular court of appointment. Bolin came to the bench with solid specialization in domestic relations law because of her years as assistant corporation counsel assigned to the Family Court. Nevertheless, she strongly believed that "no lawyer should be thrown cold into court" to sit as judge. She felt certain that judicial appointees should be given an opportunity, after appointment or election, to observe for a few weeks with another judge before taking on their actual responsibilities. Not surprisingly, she was extremely generous with her assistance to new judges while she was on the bench.[18]

Bolin intended to execute the responsibilities of her judicial position earnestly without regard to ethnic or racial parameters, and said as much when she stated publicly that "I am a judge, not of Harlem, nor the children of Harlem, but for the whole city and for all children who are in trouble. Harlem's problems are the same as those of other communities. Every child who comes before the court needs attention and his case must be heard and judgment made in view of all the factors of personality and environment entering into the particular child's life."[19] More than anything, she wanted to bring Harlem and the concerns of its black youth within the purview of city responsibility.

Bolin was the youngest of three women judges, and the first African American woman judge, in the Domestic Relations Court in 1939. The number of women judges did not increase much during her tenure on the bench. Judge Rosalie Loew Whitney was one of the other judges and another La Guardia appointee. Bolin had argued cases in Whitney's court while assistant corporation counsel assigned to the Family Court. The two women quickly bonded as judicial peers and friends. Along with a handful of other women lawyers who were appointed to various positions within the La Guardia administration, they formed an association they loosely referred to as the "Women in the La Guardia Administration." As a group they would have dinner together once or twice every month as a way to nurture their community of women. This group sustained Bolin as a pioneer in the male-dominated judiciary.

However, with Judge Whitney, Bolin engaged in more intense conversations about the law; these occurred mostly during their private time together away at Whitney's farm in Beacon, New York, or at her home in Brooklyn Heights. Fondly recalling their friendship, Bolin said, "Judge Whitney and I just seemed to be attracted to each other, and really eventually loved each other."[20] Whitney's friendship and sensitivity as a widow herself proved to be of great comfort to Bolin when Ralph Mizelle died four years after Bolin had been on the bench. As a young judge, Bolin learned much from Whitney, whom she counted among her short list of female mentors.[21]

Required to complete the court calendars before court adjourned, Bolin found herself working very long hours. When she first took the bench in family court, judges heard up to seventy cases a day. The court calendars were so heavy that many nights she, like some of her colleagues, worked as late as 9:00 p.m., and on occasion until 11:00 p.m. She believed that, especially when sitting in the Children's Court, "one took time, no matter how late one sat, one took time to give each case all the necessary time."[22] There was later a fixed schedule from 9:30 a.m. to 5:00 p.m., but she shouldered the previous schedule for the greater part of her forty years on the bench. A July 1948 performance evaluation lists Bolin's adjournment record as the best in the Domestic Relations Court. With a volume of 725 hearings for a one-month court term, Bolin had a total of thirteen adjournments, or a 1.8 percent adjournment rate, the lowest in the court.[23] "A courageous, no-nonsense hard worker who never shirked an assignment," is how one of her colleagues, Judge Joseph B. Williams, described her.[24] In some ways she maintained this level of professional excellence at the expense of her family life.

Marriage was always problematic for professional women of the late nineteenth and early twentieth centuries, primarily because of the difficulty of balancing family responsibilities with their careers.[25] However, from all accounts, Bolin and her husband Ralph Mizelle were equal partners in a modern marriage. Their marriage was characterized by the ideals of the "companionate marriage" of the new woman that emphasized friendship and mutuality between husband and wife, rather than the dependency, obligation, and obedience that typified the traditional wife.[26]

Furthermore, the empowerment that such marriages afforded women in the home found expression in Bolin's public life.[27] Fifteen years her senior, Mizelle seemed to have been very supportive of Bolin's career, adding her name to his practice as a partner, and not simply including her as supportive staff, as was commonly the case for many women lawyers who joined their husbands' practice. Mizelle respected and supported Bolin's decision to forego the social practice of name change upon marriage. She was admitted to the bar under her family name and thought it quite natural to continue to use it as a professional woman even after she was married. Her pragmatism notwithstanding, Bolin did ask her husband whether he wanted her to use his name. However, he thought it made good sense for her to keep her family name since she was using it professionally. His agreement with her decision therefore leaves little room to speculate about the philosophy that might have informed her choice. Their private decision, however, did not stop outsiders who adhered to conventional practice from referring to her as Mrs. Mizelle, a name she did not readily recognize. Once at a meeting when someone asked if Mrs. Mizelle would comment, she remembered just sitting there unresponsive to the invitation until "I finally came to and realized by . . . the chairman looking at me that I was the one."[28]

She remembered that when she was assistant corporation counsel and Mizelle was working in Washington, D.C. as assistant solicitor in the Solicitor's Office of the United States Postal Service that he would jokingly ask her if she wanted him to use his paycheck to cash hers since her salary was so much less than his. Two years later when she became a judge she posed the same question to him when she received her first paycheck that was greater than his, a fact that did not bother him. (Even though Mayor La Guardia had reduced the salaries of all city employees, Bolin still made more money than her husband. In 1939 she earned $10,500 per year instead of the $12,000 that she would have earned had the reduction not occurred.)[29]

Mizelle also showed his support of Bolin's decision to join the New York City Law Department as assistant corporation counsel in 1937 by not expecting that she would relocate to Washington, D. C. where he was a member of President Franklin Roosevelt's Federal Council of Negro Advisors, or "Black Cabinet." After the law firm of Mizelle and Bolin dissolved, each partner accepted a governmental appointment, one municipal, the other federal, but in different regions. As a result, the couple had one of the early commuter marriages, with Mizelle coming home for weekends. Having a commuter marriage, however, meant that Bolin assumed the day-to-day responsibilities for their son, Yorke Bolin Mizelle, born on July 22, 1941. Her parental responsibilities increased with Mizelle's death in 1943, when she became a widowed working mother of a two-year-old child with no other reliable means of income. In 1950 she married Walter P. Offutt Jr., a Baptist minister and church secretary of the NAACP, who was very involved in civil rights activism.[30] His employment with New York's Division of Human Rights and his ecumenical responsibilities kept him sufficiently busy such that Bolin's career demands did not really affect him. Offutt was a good stepfather, contributing added parental support until his death of lymphoma in 1976, three years before Bolin's retirement.

Bolin was a modern wife but saw herself as a very traditional mother who believed that "the ideal is for a child to be raised certainly until eight or nine years old by both parents, but with the mother at home." However, evidence suggests that she was more like a traditional *working* mother who felt guilty about having to leave her child with others but who had to work nevertheless. To be sure, Bolin *chose* to keep working after her son was born, two years into her judicial career, but two years after that she felt she *had* to work when her first husband died. She was essentially a working parent before and after the deaths of her husbands. She relished the opportunity to help children and families and would have chosen no other career, but she experienced overpowering guilt for having to spend so much time away from her young son who was under ten years old during her first term as judge. Like every working mother, she said, "I had and still [at age eighty-two] have a sense of guilt."[31]

Bolin was more fortunate than most black women because she could afford to employ a live-in housekeeper to help balance the demands of her private and public lives. Her housekeeper, whom she considered one of the joys of her life, was a young German woman who had immigrated to the United States after living through the First World War in Germany. The woman came to work for Bolin before Yorke was born and continued in her employ (long after Yorke was married) for the remainder of her life. This woman served Bolin in the same way that many African American domestics served many white households in the first half of the twentieth century. They lived in their employers' homes, appearing not to have lives of their own. Bolin's relationship with her housekeeper represents an interesting twist to early twentieth-century race and labor relations even for the North. It is also interesting that Bolin, as the employer, recognized her house-keeper as someone's wife, and allowed the housekeeper's husband to come by in the evenings—a practice that was absolutely forbidden to black housekeepers by their white employers.[32]

It was comforting to Bolin to have someone who was, as she recalled, very devoted to her son, but it did not ease the guilt she felt having to leave him every day and "just have the weekends and evenings" with him.[33] She recalled an instance that made her feel even worse as a working mother: Yorke was quite young and was sick with the measles, and although her housekeeper was devoted to him and Bolin knew he would be taken care of, to her great surprise, her son asked if she was still going to go to work even though he was sick.[34] Had she had the benefit of a two-income household, Bolin was sure that she would have stayed off the bench to raise her son until he was about eight or nine years old. She reasoned that as a trained lawyer, she could have reentered the profession as a sole practitioner or maybe even secured an appointment as a judge again.[35] Bolin concluded, in hindsight, that her first husband's death and the resulting financial difficulty had foiled her ability to be a traditional mother. However, her choice to continue working as a judge after her son was born and years before her husband died tells a less traditional story.

The ordinary life of this very extraordinary woman sensitized her to the prob-lems of those before her in court, especially the issues of working mothers. She approached each case with "her natural compassion rather than a judge's severity."[36] In describing what she considered the qualities of a good judge, Bolin said, "Ac-quaintance with the law—that's basic of course, studying all the cases pertaining to the Court's jurisdiction—even any place in the United States, the United States Supreme Court. Patience, understanding the different cultures that comprise the city, that are reflected in the composition of the litigants in the court. A dignity, of course, and a quiet authority."[37] The Domestic Relations Court, as she saw it, was not simply a court but a social agency—where conflicted men and women could expect more than a court order telling them to go out and live happily ever after. She was a strong proponent of individualized justice, and thought that "in Children's Court you have to take an individual view, dig into the background of the child, his physical and mental endowments, all his emotional patterns" because "he isn't there for punishment. He is there for help."[38]

Bolin's judicial philosophy was simple and in accord with the founding prin-ciples of the Domestic Relations Court. She was therefore thoroughly opposed to the U.S. Supreme Court's underwriting of the juvenile offender law that was being adopted by several states in the 1960s and 1970s. She thought "in its narrow and tortured, retrogressive and even mean-spirited interpretation of the United States Constitution" that the Court had changed the law to hold children to the same standard of conduct as adults, even children as young as thirteen years old. Bolin was discouraged by the juvenile offender law, which she was sure would be the death knell of the original philosophy of the Children's Court.[39] She believed that almost any child who has become delinquent can be rehabilitated if given proper care and attention at the right time, and placed a great responsibility on the community for a child's delinquency. She acknowledged that some youth were very violent, but also acknowledged that "the violence in our society is reflected in them."[40]

Bolin's compassion on the bench was influenced by her personal experiences of marriage and motherhood, of being twice widowed, a working parent and almost unemployed, and hindered by the combination of gender and race. Yet she did not think that "a woman is necessarily better than a man as a Domestic Relations judge." She believed it was more a matter of aptitude and temperament.[41]

Bolin's judicial temperament was tested in an emotionally charged homicide case. The *New York Daily News* reported that just before Christmas 1978, a juvenile male killed his friend during an argument over a bicycle. As the juvenile, who had never been in trouble before, stood before Judge Bolin awaiting disposition, the father of the dead boy pleaded to be heard. Judge Bolin obliged, and the father told the court that he had prayed to find it in his heart to forgive the boy who had deprived him of his son, and that his prayer had been answered. Anticipating the conventional ruling for a homicide not committed in self-defense, the father reportedly reminded Judge Bolin that his only son could not be brought back no matter how she ruled, and begged her not to deprive the parents of the defendant of their only child. (The newspaper reported that there was not a dry eye in the courtroom, including the judge's.) Judge Bolin's "quiet wisdom" in this particular case recalled the biblical story of Solomon. In this instance Solomon was a black woman judge who decided to send the offending boy home on probation. Years later when asked to comment on the case, she proudly remarked that after that appearance the boy was never in trouble again.[42]

Other women judges have captured the attention of the press with their sympathetic and sensitive (albeit sensible) dispositions regarding young people. Being strong proponents of child welfare laws, these judges, like Bolin, believe in equal rights "but not equal wrongs."[43] In deference however to the admonition that "the decider must cerebrate rather than emote about what he [or she] is deciding," many criticized such rulings as too emotional and not based on the merits of the case. The following statement typifies the way some people viewed the performance of women lawyers and judges: "Women are too emotional to make good lawyers. I know, I have had them on my staff. I have had them as opponents and I have even tried cases before women judges. They are all the same. Inevitably, they let emotion supplant cold logic and hard facts on which law is based."[44] The sweeping declarations of this statement recall social scientist Beverly Blair Cook's observation that to speak of a different attitude of women on the bench is to speak of women's different status in society.[45] To the extent that women judges behave differently, they are responding from the gendered experience of women as a group in much the same way that male judges respond from their gendered experience as men in the society.

Yet to equate difference with emotionality is to truly miss an opportunity to discuss the particularity of justice from one tribunal to another. In the case of the Family Court, the philosophy of *parens patriae* would have privileged the preventive approach over the purely punitive approach of the criminal courts.[46] As originally conceived, the juvenile court, apart from the physical separation of the child from the adult offender, inaugurated the concept of the court as a social rather than a penal or police agency.[47] Accordingly, it repudiated as a contradiction in terms the idea of a "juvenile criminal." In line with this philosophy, in 1924, twenty-five years after the inauguration of the juvenile court movement in Chicago and Denver, the State of New York initiated a separate Children's Court. It was to reach beyond the police system into the community for cooperative efforts with child care and other social agencies. And disposition was to be made on the basis of the particular child's personality regardless of the character of the offense.[48] In determining disposition, therefore, the court places great reliance on the social and clinical report of the probation officer. Such a "social study" would determine the root of the child's errant behavior, in an effort to better empower the judge to dismiss the case, warn the juvenile, fine him, place him on probation, arrange for restitution, refer him to an agency or treatment facility, or commit him to an institution.[49]

On the bench Bolin always tried to find Solomon's wisdom for those human tangles that even good laws failed to address. "Every child who comes before the court needs attention," she said, "and his case must be heard and judgment made in view of all the factors of personality and environment entering into that particular child's life."[50] Bolin's ruling in the aforementioned case was therefore compatible with her understanding of the court's philosophy regarding children. She believed that "almost any child who has become delinquent can be rehabilitated if given proper care and attention at the right time"—although she agreed that much depended upon the cooperation that is given by parents and teachers.[51]

Bolin was no less demanding of police cooperation. In *In re John Rutane,* a case that considered "whether the confession of a juvenile was voluntary since an involuntary confession is, by its nature, evidence of nothing," she found that the juvenile's confession, made after seven hours of continuous police interrogation in the absence of parents or counsel, while in a police station, was indeed not voluntary and therefore not reliable. In her decision, which was reported in the

New York Supplement and cited by the U.S. Supreme Court in a landmark decision regarding confessions, Bolin applied the U.S. Supreme Court's repeated emphasis on the responsibility of the police to protect the fundamental rights of adult citizens in custody or under detention, and reasoned that "the Family Court, having exclusive jurisdiction over children the age of this respondent [age thirteen], must be ever vigilant to accentuate this grave, or even graver, responsibility where citizens of extreme youth are concerned."[52]

In the more routine cases involving petitions for child support, custody, and visitation, Bolin demonstrated the same commitment to "the best interests of the child." In *Langerman v. Langerman,* which involved the nature and extent of the exclusive jurisdiction of the Family Court to order support of children after a divorce of their parents procured outside of the State of New York, the father of two minor children opposed the request made by his ex-wife, who was the custodial parent, for an order of support over and above the provisions made at the time of their divorce in Nevada.[53] Judge Bolin affirmed the exclusive jurisdiction of the Family Court in *Langerman,* reasoning that "only a narrow, technical and unrealistic interpretation, contrary to general principles of statutory construction, could lead to the conclusion that the Legislature intended that children, residing in New York City or the subject of proceedings in the Domestic Relations Court of the City of New York because of the father's residence in New York City, should be limited to an award of $50 a week, no matter how numerous the number of children of a particular father nor the extent of his means, while each child elsewhere in the State might be awarded an unlimited sum." She ruled that the original decree of $50 per week plus medical expenses for the two children and the $2,300 voluntary contribution made the year before by the father did not constitute fair and reasonable support according to the means of the father who had a net annual income after taxes of $46,784.[54]

Beatrice Hoffman, in her study of changes in the Domestic Relations Court, found that quite often the attitude of male judges, attorneys, and spouses who leave the children with the woman did not assure them enough financial support.[55] This was not the case in Bolin's courtroom. Ever mindful of the economic realities women faced, she was sensitive to the precarious position in which a divorced mother with children could find herself. But relying first and foremost on what was best for the children, she made a ruling in *Langerman* that was satisfactory to neither parent. With an acute sensitivity to the children's accustomed lifestyle that their father had maintained, but that their mother could not afford, she amended the original support decree to better meet the needs of the children and to reflect the means of the father. As such, the original award of $50 per week support for two children was increased to $150 per week. The fairness of Bolin's ruling is evident in the substance of her amended award that was half of the $300 per week sought by the petitioner/mother. The judge reasoned, "Today's order is made substantially less in the hope it will encourage the respondent [father] to continue voluntarily to provide for the children with occasional toys or whatever gifts will satisfy him most," since "he feels justifiably that he would like the children to receive some contributions directly from him."[56] On the father's appeal to question the nature and extent of the exclusive jurisdiction of the Family Court to order support of children after a divorce had been procured outside the State of New York, her ruling was upheld.

However, in *Martin v. Sparks* she felt "reluctantly constrained" to dismiss a mother's request for increased child support because she determined that the "Family Court Division of Domestic Relations Court of City of New York lacks power to enter support order for minor children of divorced parents in sum exceeding amount awarded by judgment of divorce of New York Supreme Court."[57] Nevertheless, in rendering her decision, Bolin was careful not to leave the mother without remedy, noting that she could apply for increased child support to the Supreme Court of Bronx County, where her decree of divorce was granted. But, Bolin simultaneously criticized the remedy as illusory since she believed that often "the father's resources are so slender as to make unpropitious the prospect of sufficient compensation to induce an attorney to undertake a Supreme Court application." Bolin therefore challenged the wisdom of statutory jurisdiction that would restrict her ability to act in the best interest of the child when she stated, "It is hoped that today's decision may stimulate the Legislature to amend section 137 of the Domestic Relations Court Act so as to open the door of the Family Court, where the staff prepares all necessary papers without fee, to all children of divorced and judicially separated parents without any restriction as to the amount of the order. . . . For the preponderance of cases in this court involves persons of a financial level which renders impracticable recourse to the Supreme Court."[58]

Her rulings in both cases were consistent with the law; yet in her courtroom justice was not a woman blindfolded, but a jurist fully aware of the nuances of each case, and a jurist not reluctant to challenge the reasonableness of the law, legal procedure, or the limits of Family Court jurisdiction. These cases also demonstrate the diversity of the cases Bolin handled. True, many cases that came before her involved persons from Harlem, as the *New York Times* reported at the time of her appointment, but by no means was her court calendar restricted to Harlem's African American community or to any particular ethnic, racial, or economic group. "I am a judge, not for Harlem, nor the children of Harlem" she once said, "but for the whole city and for all children who are in trouble."[59] Her assignment took her into the five boroughs of New York City (Bronx, Brooklyn, Manhattan, Queens, and Staten Island), and into the children's court and family court of each. She was therefore acutely familiar with the city's diverse population, a characteristic she found wanting in many of the city's judges.

As testimony to her brand of justice and her commitment to saving children instead of drowning them in the system of adult criminality, Judge Bolin publicly denounced the 1978 New York Juvenile Offender Act, which permitted thirteen-, fourteen-, and fifteen-year-old offenders to be tried publicly for felonies in the Criminal and Supreme courts, where they could receive longer sentences than could be given a child in the Family Court.[60] Within three months of the law's enactment Bolin would retire, but that did not diminish her displeasure and disappointment with the statute. She warned, "It's a retrogression. I think it is symptomatic of a society that doesn't give priority to its children. It would rather have this kind of law instead of putting money where it should be put, correcting the social and economic conditions where children live."[61]

Bolin understood that violence by juveniles was increasing, and acknowledged that she had never seen anything like the increased violence that was so rampant in the city during the decades of the seventies. But she was unyielding in her belief that the state's stricter juvenile justice law was not the answer. She believed that the course that was chosen by its enactment was more convenient than the more difficult alternative of "a many-faceted, highly financed attack on the social, economic, and family problems responsible for their delinquency with concerted efforts to rehabilitate and reclaim our children."[62] Inherent in her criticism of the Juvenile Offender Act was a criticism of what she perceived to be a glib diagnosis of child crime. Bolin believed that one would be remiss to state offhand either the causes of or cure for juvenile delinquency because there were so many causes and no one cure. The implication that economic factors—such as a mother's need to work—alone accounted for juvenile delinquency was not sound, she said. The forces that drag a child into trouble, she emphasized, were far more complicated than that.[63]

Judge Bolin's years of attention to these cases had taught her that emotional factors in the home, stresses in the child's own personality, and influences outside the home also contributed to the tragic upheaval.[64] "I get very distressed and dismayed," she declared, "when I hear psychiatrists and social workers handing out easy answers, saying it's because of the wars children have seen, or the violent programs on television, or because violence is as American as apple pie." She dismissed such answers as too simple, but believed that society as a whole had a responsibility to its children, and stated such in a newspaper interview: "The failure is ours. You and I and all of us haven't worked out a program to meet it. Only a small start has been made. There's no blackout on human weakness. We can't stop thinking about it."[65] Bolin's commitment to justice and equality, along with her unshakable concern and love for children, were four significant columns that structured her philosophy, which was evidenced in the citywide support for her reappointments.

Each judicial appointment to the Domestic Relations Court was for a period of ten years with no guarantee of reappointment. If it was not forthcoming by the end of his or her term, the judge was expected to seek reappointment from the incumbent mayor. The mayor had the discretion to reappoint or not reappoint regardless of a judge's outstanding record of performance. Mayor Fiorello La Guardia first appointed Jane Bolin to the judiciary, but his successor, William O'Dwyer, was under no obligation to reappoint her. Had La Guardia not bowed out of the mayoral race in 1945 after his third term, he would have, in all likelihood, reappointed Judge Bolin to a second ten-year term on the city's Domestic Relations Court. Her record of performance had not only justified her initial appointment, it had been a source of pride for the La Guardia administration and the African American community at large. Her reappointment, however, was not as certain under the new mayor. O'Dwyer was a Tammany Democrat, whom La Guardia defeated in the 1941 mayoral election, and he let it be known that he had no intention of wasting a judicial appointment on a judge who was not part of his political club.[66] That Judge Bolin had tried over three thousand cases during her first term, never once being overturned on appeal, did not matter much to O'Dwyer.

Armed with the information about O'Dwyer's plans, Bolin enlisted the help of Eleanor Roosevelt. The two women had developed a close friendship years earlier when they founded the Wiltwyck School for Boys, which provided a safe place for African Americans boys who were segregated out of private agencies and neglected because of a lack of public agencies. Bolin, widowed at the time with a young child and terrified at the prospect of having to leave the bench, sought Mrs. Roosevelt's assistance. On February 7, 1949, Bolin wrote to Roosevelt requesting a meeting to discuss a matter that "concerns a personal problem."[67] Within a week Mrs. Roosevelt responded to Bolin inviting her to meet February 23.[68]

Weeks later, O'Dwyer wrote to Mrs. Roosevelt and indicated his willingness to meet with her "any time or place, at your convenience. Just drop me a line or call me and let me know when and where."[69] There must have been a successful meeting between Mrs. Roosevelt and O'Dwyer on Bolin's behalf because shortly thereafter, Mrs. Roosevelt wrote to the mayor and thanked him for his two messages telling her that he would reappoint Bolin. However, in her gratitude Mrs. Roosevelt was also shrewd and let the mayor know that Bolin's "supporters have been anxious about her reappointment."[70] Yet, months passed and O'Dwyer neither contacted nor made a public announcement about his reappointment of Bolin.

As late as early July, weeks before Bolin's judicial term was scheduled to expire, Bolin again wrote Mrs. Roosevelt because she had not heard from the mayor.

Moreover, she was deeply concerned about news that he was scheduled to leave on July 14 for a ten-day trip to Mexico—one week before her judicial term would expire. In desperation Bolin asked Mrs. Roosevelt to suggest anything more that she might do, but she was really asking Mrs. Roosevelt to do all that she could. In the absence of her father (who had died three years earlier), Judge Bolin also sought counsel from her brother in Poughkeepsie who had become a prominent lawyer in his own right. Gaius Charles Jr., unbeknownst to Judge Bolin, enlisted the influence of their father's friend and colleague, an Irish gentleman who was the only other lawyer in Poughkeepsie during their father's early practice. Her brother hoped that this lawyer, who was very active in Democratic politics in New York, would intercede on Bolin's behalf with his political allies. However, to Judge Bolin's surprise and resentment, the lawyer's letter of endorsement made no mention of her judicial record but said only that she had come from a good *colored* family in Poughkeepsie. It is a letter she wished that she had intercepted, but as it turned out it was no more trivial than O'Dwyer's reasons for reconsidering her reappointment.[71]

O'Dwyer was clearly in a predicament because he had told Mrs. Roosevelt that he would reappoint Bolin, but he still had to explain the appointment to his political club. In the end, O'Dwyer honored his promise to Mrs. Roosevelt and reappointed Bolin to a ten-year judicial term with the Domestic Relations Court. The mayor may have felt compelled to recognize Bolin's judicial record, or as he stated, "felt he couldn't turn her [Mrs. Roosevelt] down."[72]

Some may see this as a classic case of politics trumping merit, and Bolin does credit Eleanor Roosevelt with her first reappointment to the bench. However, Bolin's judicial fitness was the single most important factor in Roosevelt's willingness to intercede on her behalf. Still the role of patronage or simple advocacy has been important to the professional survival of African Americans and other similarly excluded groups. But the discourse of advocacy need not supplant the issue or question of competence or the reality of overqualification in the face of exclusion. The fact that O'Dwyer responded to Roosevelt's advocacy and not necessarily to Bolin's judicial record, by itself, reveals little, if anything, about the importance of Bolin's judicial fitness in his decision to reappoint her. Though it is reasonable to imagine that, even at Mrs. Roosevelt's urging, O'Dwyer would not have reappointed someone whose performance would have been a political liability for him.[73]

Citywide support for Judge Bolin's reappointment from those who looked to her "characteristic skill, finely balanced judicial temperament, and profound understanding of the complex problems involved in human relations" was evidence of her record as a judge.[74] In 1959, when her second term was about to end, the president of the Jewish Child Care Association, Irving Mitchell Felt, wrote to Mayor Robert Wagner, saying, "Your reappointment of Judge Bolin to the

Domestic Relations Court will be heartening to the profession and lawyers alike who seek understanding and help for our troubled children."[75] Felt's comments were typical of the endorsements Wagner received, and reflected the support that Bolin engendered from lawyer and layman alike throughout her judicial career. In the same vein, an endorsement from the New York Women's Bar Association reminded Wagner that "Judge Bolin has discharged the duties and responsibilities entrusted to her in a manner which demonstrates that she is fair-minded and en-dowed with mature judgment and judicial temperament." The resolution further testified to the high regard in which Judge Bolin was held and recognized the fine record which she made as a justice of the Domestic Relations Court during her twenty years of distinguished service on that bench.[76] One attorney, aware of Bolin's rare quality for evenhanded justice, wanted to know what she could do to ensure the judge's reappointment. "It's not a court that will help me anymore without you there," she wrote, "you are the first and last judge on the bench for me—I got justice when I came before you."[77]

In a letter of appreciation from the State of New York Youth Commission, Bolin was praised for her commitment to the rights of the city's children. The letter thanked her for being one of the dedicated reasons why the children's courts are a greater hope.[78] The Bronx Women's Bar Association voted unanimously to pass a resolution respectfully urging Wagner to reappoint Bolin for another term as justice of the Domestic Relations Court. The resolution endorsing Judge Bolin's reappointment stated in part,

> WHEREAS, members of the Bronx Women's Bar Association have, on numerous occasions, appeared before Justice Bolin in the Domestic Relations Court, Family Division and Children's Court Division, and
>
> WHEREAS, they have always been deeply impressed by Justice Bolin's outstand-ing ability as a jurist, her sympathetic understanding of the problems facing the adults and children who come into that court for assistance, and the courtesy and humaneness shown to all those who appear before her,
>
> BE IT RESOLVED, that the Bronx Women's Bar Association respectfully recommends to the Hon. Robert F. Wagner, Mayor of the City of New York, that he re-appoint Hon. Jane M. Bolin for another term as Justice of the Domestic Relations Court.[79]

On May 26, 1959, before Judge Bolin's second term ended, Mayor Wagner reap-pointed her to a third ten-year term in the Domestic Relations Court, which would with reorganization become the Family Court of the State of New York in 1962.

Mayor John Lindsay followed suit in 1969, reappointing Judge Bolin to her fourth and final judicial term. The mandatory retirement age then set at seventy years for judges meant that Bolin would retire, though reluctantly, on January 1, 1979, after having spent her professional life serving the children and families of New York City for over forty years.[80] On the occasion of her retirement she received many accolades from women for whom she had been a role model. One such letter of tribute came from Justice Constance Baker Motley of the U.S. District Court. Motley's letter read in part:

> First, I congratulate you on having successfully completed so many years of out-standing judicial service and for having achieved an unblemished record while in public life.
>
> There is a great deal to be said for role model influence. I thought you would like to know that you provided a role model for me at a time when there were very few, if any, black women in the law. I also recall hearing nothing but praise with respect to your legal ability when I first came to New York in 1941. When I thereafter met you, I then knew how a lady judge should deport herself. I want to thank you for that.[81]

Though Fiorello La Guardia was pivotal in Jane Bolin's climb up the profes-sional hierarchy, it was a tribute to her "sagacity and judicial fitness" that she remained on the bench through three more political administrations and may-ors.[82] Aside from her formal qualifications and professional record, La Guardia saw in Bolin someone with immense compassion, which was exactly what she thought a Domestic Relations Court judge should possess. She agreed that any judge should possess an acute acquaintance with the law, but believed that it was equally important for a judge of the Domestic Relations Court to have common sense, patience, courtesy, and "a broad sympathy for human suffering, because she will see enough of it."[83]

Bolin saw enough of it during her more than forty years advocating for the city's children. And she felt certain that to truly serve the city, a judge needed an understanding of the different cultures that comprised the city and reflected the composition of those who come before the court. She found her service to be a most grueling experience, so fascinating and rewarding that she could not imagine herself doing anything else. "Strenuous as it was, stressful as it was," she said, "I don't know any position or practice that I could have had that I would have liked more than that."[84] This in part explains her choice to remain on the Family Court bench although eminently qualified to serve on any court. She believed that she would make her best contribution in a court designed to protect children and families.

To be sure, Bolin was committed to the professional integration of women lawyers, and therefore did not subscribe to the idea of a separate women's legal sphere that touted women's "uniquely feminine qualities of nurturing, sensitiv-ity, and understanding to cases dealing specifically with women and children."[85] Moreover, nothing suggests that she gauged success or value as a judge by jurisdiction in the traditional mainstream courts that were dominated by men. She simply believed that she would make her best contribution in a court designed to protect children and families.

Not surprisingly, Judge Bolin declined any attempts at nominations to "elevate" her to "more prestigious" courts. In a letter to Philadelphia Municipal Court judge Theodore O. Spaulding, who later became the first black appellate court judge in Pennsylvania, Bolin thanked him for his nomination of her to a federal judgeship, but assured him that she was not interested, feeling that she could render the greatest service in the Family Court guarding the rights of women and children, two of society's most unprotected groups.[86]

Bolin was part of the educational elite, but she shared the disappointments of other professionals who were not as privileged. She was influenced by the professional legacy of her father, but she traversed a maze of prejudice and discrimination that he escaped as a man. The threads of gender, class, race, credentialism, and politics wove the fabric of her success and struggle, even as they influenced the structure of her judicial philosophy and her philosophy of activism.

5. Speaking Truth to Power

A View from the Bench of Judge Jane Bolin

In the Family Court of the State of New York and its predecessor courts Judge Bolin presided over the complex and delicate family court matters such as juvenile homicides, nonsupport of wives and children, battered spouses, neglected and abandoned children, adoptions, and paternity suits from every racial and ethnic group of every socioeconomic strata. She imparted and fought for justice with equal vigor, and in so doing, made an indelible impact on the law and on the lives of many New Yorkers.[1] Committed to making the law an instrument of fairness, her reformist zeal excited her judicial colleagues who joined in her crusade for change. Never settling into the "timid inertia" of the bench, Judge Bolin used the authority of her position to challenge injustice in the courts and in the broader community the courts represented.

When Bolin first came to the Domestic Relations Court, racial and religious segregation was widespread among the probation staff, in the children's institutions, and in the social agencies. In addition, "One could count on one's fingers," she recalled, "the number of minorities on our staff—with me the lone one on our bench."[2] When law assistants were first being assigned to family court judges, Judge Bolin began asking "Where are the black law assistants?" Black judges made up a tiny minority in the Domestic Relations Court—or any court for that matter—and accordingly so were black law assistants went the explanation. But Bolin rejected that explanation as an acceptable standard, and before long there were black law assistants. She could not single-handedly remedy the meager representation of black judges, but she could and did effect positive change in the representation of black law assistants.[3] With the aid of judicial colleagues Hubert T. Delany and Justine Wise Polier, she also campaigned to secure racial equity in the court and in its supporting institutions.[4]

Among Bolin's many victories were two that radically changed the fabric and function of the Family Court of the State of New York and its predecessor courts. One involved the assignment of probation officers to cases without regard to race or religion; the other involved private child care agencies accepting children without regard to ethnic background. Probation officers were often seen as a juvenile court judge's "right-hand man." As one of the several nineteenth-century developments incorporated into the juvenile court movement, probation embodied the ideal of individualized, rehabilitative diagnosis and treatment. Probation officers assigned to the juvenile courts served not only as investigators to the juvenile's social history, they also served as liaisons between the judges and the social scientists who guided them.[5] The Department of Probation was therefore central to adjudication in the Family Court.

Bolin had been on the bench only a short time when she discovered that administrative judge John Warren Hill routinely assigned cases of African American children to African American probation officers, and the cases of white children to white probation officers. (She learned further that there were no more than two African American probation officers.)[6] This practice was facilitated by the disclosure on court petitions of the children's race and religion. Shocked by the court's complicity in segregation, Bolin approached Judge Hill. "Well, I was so upset by it that, when I went on the bench," she said, "I went to the presiding justice, as he was called then, and complained, and said that this was not right." She reminded Hill that as public servants, probation officers should not be assigned cases by race. As she remembered, Hill was very annoyed with her, and said there was nothing that he could—or as she put it—"would do about it." As a last resort, she enlisted the assistance of a friend, another lawyer, who threatened the administrative judge with a lawsuit should the practice continue. The threat of court action was sufficient to nudge Hill to discontinue requiring racial and religious disclosures on court petitions.[7]

Similar segregation existed in the larger court system. Local white judges never assigned black lawyers to represent indigent white defendants. In 1936 Horace Gordon, an African American lawyer who practiced in Harlem, complained that local white judges assigned white attorneys to defend blacks as well as whites who were without aid of counsel even when "there are five or more experienced, able and capable Negro attorneys present. . . . [yet] not one of them is asked."[8] It was not until 1940 in a murder case that a black lawyer in New York City was assigned to help defend a white defendant.

Biased hiring and assignment remained "customary practice" in New York City for decades to come. Entire industries were kept lily-white even for menial employment. The subway and surface carriers sprinkled a few African Americans among their janitorial staffs but closed them out from any middle-level jobs and kept them all in Harlem. The dismal record of city government was only surpassed by the private sector. A company such as the Metropolitan Insurance Company, with over 100,000 policyholders in Harlem, hired no African Americans.[9]

That the Office of Probation and the court itself were fraught with segregation adversely affected the quality of the help given to children. The court, after all, depended greatly on the investigations of probation officers to better prepare it for effective case disposition. That only two probation officers were assigned to handle the cases of black children meant that those cases would not have been given the thorough examination usually reserved for the cases of white children. Although new to the bench, Judge Bolin was not afraid to take the probation department and the administrative judge to task for practicing segregation in case assignment.

In the decades before the 1960s many of the private child placement facilities in New York City were also segregated along religious and racial lines.[10] Separate facilities catered to Jewish children, Catholic children, and Protestant children. The African American children who were mostly Protestant were sent to what Bolin saw as the very inadequate and segregated facilities provided by the Protestants. The Colored Orphan Asylum catered to African American children since, for the most part, none of the agencies would accept them. All of these private placement facilities received public monies for their operation, a fact that Bolin would later use to challenge and eradicate segregation in child placement facilities. In some instances there were no public child placement facilities to accommodate children of certain age groups. As a result many young African American children, some as young as eight years of age, were forced to remain in abusive and neglectful homes simply because there were no facilities open to them.

Bolin was so moved by the sad state of child placement agencies in New York City that she cofounded, with Judge Polier, Eleanor Roosevelt, and some other "forward thinking people," the new Wiltwyck School for Boys in upstate New York in 1942.[11] The school was located in Esopus, on the opposite side of the Hudson River from the Roosevelts' family home. Originally established in 1936 under the leadership of the Episcopal City Mission Society, the Wiltwyck School catered to African American boys who were adjudged to be delinquents, but by 1942 Wiltwyck was in danger of closing because of a severe lack of funds.[12] Judges Bolin and Polier and Mrs. Roosevelt seized the opportunity to establish a new facility that would fill the void left by a lack of public agencies and segregated private agencies to assist the young African American children who had been brought before the Domestic Relations Court for help.

As a Domestic Relations Court judge, Bolin brought a unique perspective to the directorship of Wiltwyck on whose board of directors she served as vice president for several years. The authority of her office and her reputation as a staunch advocate for children combined with Mrs. Roosevelt's stature to ease the flow of private funding for the school's operation. Though Wiltwyck as reorganized in 1942 was in direct response to the discrimination suffered by African American children, its founding principles were anything but discriminatory. The Wiltwyck School for Boys met the needs of African American boys in need of placement, but it was open to boys of any race or religion.

Impatient with the persistence of discrimination in many of the child placement agencies, Bolin appeared before the City Council and the New York City Board of Estimate as a chief spokesperson against the segregation of children and especially against public funds being used to sustain any institution or agency that discriminated on the basis of race. She was instrumental in helping enact the Brown-Isaacs amendment to the city charter in 1942 that prohibited segregation by race in the private child care agencies receiving public funds.[13]

However, segregation in child placement and support facilities still continued, often with the complicity of local government agencies. In 1950 Madelyn E. Turner, an African American woman, shared with Bolin her letter of resignation from the Protestant Big Sisters of New York. In the letter, Turner accused the organization of condoning segregation because a white child had never been assigned to her in compliance with the governing board's ruling "that I could not work with white children, because white people did not want colored people going into their homes."[14]

As late as 1955, Bolin was once again reminding New York City officials of the pronouncement of the Brown-Isaacs amendment and of their responsibility to all of the city's children without regard to race or religion. In a letter to Henry Mc-Carthy, the commissioner of welfare, Bolin assailed his department's complicity in the continued segregation of children in placement facilities. She had referred an African American child to the Department of Welfare for temporary placement, but was informed by the probation officer in the Manhattan Children's Court that although the Department of Welfare had located space for the child at one of the facilities, a white Catholic child was preferred.[15] As a result, the African American child was denied immediate placement and therefore denied the immediate help intended by the court.

As was her style, Judge Bolin used the information to conduct her own investigation of the rules and regulations governing the Allocation Division of the Children's Placement Service. She discovered that the Department of Welfare's policy had been to acquiesce to the racial and religious preferences of placement facilities. She reminded the commissioner that "these temporary detention facilities are theoretically non-sectarian and since they are in receipt of public funds are required by the law not to discriminate because of race or religion." Bolin stated that she found it even more disturbing that the department would permit the facilities to express a preference and then do its best to accommodate such preferences. Although she had confirmed the department's complicity, she still wanted the commissioner to inform her of his policy regarding such preferences and instructions to the Allocation Division on how to handle such requests from child placement facilities.[16] In a very diplomatic way her letters summoned accountability and compliance, grounded as they were in her commitment to every child who appeared before her and her adherence to the law.

Two decades after the city prohibited segregation in child placement facilities that received city funds, Bolin discovered specification of a child's race (if African American or Puerto Rican) in the reports of some probation officers, and specifically on the face sheet for Juvenile Term (Form #50-23 Rev1//62) where a space labeled "RACE" was to be filled in with "N" (Negro) or "PR" (Puerto Rican). In a letter to John A. Wallace, director of New York City Office of Probation, she inquired into the reasons for the racial specification on the forms, knowing full well it was to simplify the matching of children with placement facilities. She underscored what the probation officers had already known—that most placement agencies appeared more concerned with a child's race than with his or her needs. Judge Bolin objected to the probation department's gratuitously providing information about a child's race to an agency, knowing there were other means by which the agency could obtain such information. She figured that if these agencies were put to the task of asking for the information, then a better case could be built against them to show a pattern of discrimination—thereby justifying the withholding of public funds. Bolin did not disguise her displeasure in her letter to Wallace, who readily complied with her instructions to issue a directive that racial designation be excluded from all probation records including face sheets and probation reports.[17] The probation department was, after all, a public agency, and ought to be held, she thought, to a higher standard of compliance with the law.

The Colored Orphan Asylum, on whose Special Gifts Committee Bolin served, became a most unlikely target in an era of persistent racial segregation. The asylum was established before the Civil War to meet the needs of African American children who were excluded from placement facilities. It was destroyed by fire in 1863 as antiwar riots that became known as the New York Draft Riot erupted, and later rebuilt and maintained for generations as segregation in placement facilities still existed. However, with the passage of the antidiscrimination amendment in 1942, Bolin questioned the existing name and purpose of the Colored Orphan Asylum. In a 1943 letter to the Maceo Thomas, chairman of the Special Gifts Committee, she wanted to know about the organization's plans, suggesting that compliance with the law would involve not only changing the asylum's name but also changing its intake policies regarding the race of children accepted.[18]

Although "unalterably opposed to segregation by race, in child caring institutions as well as other places," Bolin understood the dilemma of the Colored Orphan Asylum and other similarly situated institutions whose existence was justified because of de facto segregation against African Americans. Nevertheless, they were in violation of antisegregation laws. As she explained to Thomas, "Before the passage of the Board of Estimate amendment, there may have been temporary excuse for such a setup even though it was undemocratic." But, she insisted, the responsibility was now to abolish segregated schools receiving money from the City of New York.[19] The dilemma of the Colored Orphan Asylum was indeed her dilemma because her intention was not to deprive African American children of one of the few facilities completely available to them. Rather, she intended to effect total integration of all placement facilities to increase the availability of placement facilities to all children. She understood that to allow segregation, however well-intentioned, was to perpetuate segregation, however ill-intentioned.

Bolin's position opposing segregation was further demonstrated in her rejection of the proposed reorganization of Sydenham Hospital into a voluntary interracial hospital in Harlem. From its founding in 1892 up to 1943 (the time of the proposal for reorganization), most of Sydenham's ward patients were black while its white patients occupied the private and semiprivate rooms. The utility staff was mixed and there were a few black nurses, but all the doctors were white.[20] Harlem Hospital was the only public hospital in that area in 1943—most hospitals elsewhere in the city refused to admit African Americans and the few that did practiced segregation. Harlem Hospital was routinely overcrowded and severely understaffed because it too discriminated against African American doctors and nurses.[21]

The temptation of a new facility to serve the African American population versus the compromise of segregated institutions elsewhere was therefore understandable, as was the objective to "set a pattern for initiating interracial principle in other hospitals" while providing Harlem with "more effecting and appropriate hospital and medical care."[22] Nevertheless, Jane Bolin was not convinced that Harlem needed such a hospital, nor did she agree that it would improve the welfare of the Harlem community. On the contrary, she thought the community's welfare would be "prejudiced, viciously harmed and indeed set back many years by such a hospital at this time." Writing to Reverend James Robinson, one of the African Americans newly appointed to Sydenham's reorganized board of trustees, she said, "If the hospital you have in mind for purchase is so generous as to want to sell itself for the purpose of an inter-racial hospital, it might accomplish the same result, and in more democratic fashion, by continuing operation and simply opening its medical and nursing staff, as well as its Board of Trustees to Negroes."[23]

She saw beneath the veneer of the idea and was adamant that such a hospital as was proposed would not solve the problems of African American physicians in respect to hospital affiliation (where they could send private patients and continue to treat them). As she saw it, "The number of staff positions open would be so small that it would benefit only an extremely small percentage of the Negro physicians in New York." In addition, she was certain that if an interracial hospital was established, then the other voluntary hospitals that admitted African American patients would be eager to destroy those gains by suggesting that future African American patients "go to their own hospital in Harlem." "If segregation is forced on us in the matter of living quarters," she said, "let us not take steps to provide it ourselves in the matter of hospital service."[24]

In Bolin's opinion, the time, energies, and money to be expended for the so-called interracial hospital could be better used in a campaign to open all public and voluntary hospitals in the city to African American physicians, nurses, and technicians. She informed Robinson that "when this is done, the need for your proposed hospital will have vanished. Unless it is done, the establishing of an 'inter-racial' hospital in Harlem, in my belief, will be a setback to the progress of our race." An ardent integrationist, Bolin resisted any enterprise that undermined citywide desegregation. She did not help the committee's cause when she gave permission for her comments to be published should the proposal be submitted to the public for consideration, reasoning that the public should have the views of those disapproving as well.[25]

But on the very day that she responded to Reverend Robinson, the reorganized Board of Trustees of Sydenham Hospital held its first meeting and accepted the assignment to "establish for the people of New York City an interracial voluntary hospital in the Harlem area" and "to work for the fuller integration of Negro civic leaders, physicians, nurses and other technical and administrative staff into the organizations of other voluntary and public hospitals in New York City." The first annual report of the reorganized board, which counted six African Americans among its ranks, stated that significant progress had been made toward the objectives. "Three other voluntary hospitals in Greater New York have added Negro physicians to their Medical Staffs, six hospitals have added colored nurses, and several other hospitals are known to be seriously considering the acceptance of Negroes for internships and other staff positions." Additionally, Dr. Peter Marshall Murray, an African American physician, had been the attending physician in obstetrics and gynecology at Sydenham for the preceding twelve months.[26] Still, Bolin's opposition to Sydenham was not totally unjustified, as *Time Magazine* reported one year later that "the hospital's Negro backers hope the proportion of Negroes does not get too high—Sydenham might become known as a Negro hospital, and the whole experiment of interracial hospitalization would be defeated."[27]

Bolin was relentless in her crusade for children's right to equal treatment before the law, which literally put her at odds with many department heads within and outside city government. For example, in a 1947 letter, Salvation Army territorial commander Ernest Pugmire invited Judge Bolin to join their proposed Harlem advisory board, saying that her name had been suggested by their officers and friends in Harlem "as a person mindful of her responsibilities to the borough and to its citizens."[28] The Salvation Army, he said, wanted to share this responsibility with Bolin, and with her advice help those in need.

Unimpressed with the gratuitous proposal, Bolin declined the invitation. In her response of February 4, 1947, she wrote, "In the first place, I am out of sympathy with your feeling that a special Advisory Board is necessary for Harlem while your other Advisory Boards throughout the city are set up on a borough basis." Since Harlem was not a separate borough, but a neighborhood within the Borough of Manhattan, she saw no need for a separate advisory board when one already existed for the Borough of Manhattan. She continued, "I should be much more impressed to find the names of some civic-minded Negroes on your borough Advisory Boards than to be invited to a Jim Crow Advisory Board for an agency that is city-wide."[29]

In particular, she was disinclined to join any advisory board of the Salvation Army because she had become aware of, and was investigating, the Jim Crow policy that the organization maintained at its Booth Memorial Hospital, which was a referral facility for pregnant girls. Booth Memorial had reportedly been segregating the black girls from the white girls. Bolin investigated further only to be alarmed "by the reports these [black] girls bring back of the heavy work they are required to do—lifting heavy wash from the machines, lifting heavy trays of dishes and even mopping and waxing floors on their knees during the advanced stages of their pregnancy."[30]

Bolin was so incensed by what the girls had told her that she paid a surprise visit to Booth Memorial to observe conditions for herself. And, although authorized by law to visit any institutions to which she, as a judge, sent children, she was unsuccessful in getting past the front door, having been curtly told that it was inconvenient for her to make an inspection of the facility since some guests were expected for tea that day.[31] This presumption was to Bolin quite telling of what the facility had to hide irrespective of the public principles of the Salvation Army. Invoking the motto of the Salvation Army to frame his letter of invitation to Bolin, Pugmire had written that since 1880 when the first Salvation Army officers landed in New York, the organization had engaged in numerous activities designed to serve community needs with a spiritual purpose and with material service in accordance with its motto, "Service to God Through Service to Man."[32] Judging the organization by its deeds rather than by its words, Bolin responded, "When the Salvation Army begins to practice its motto 'Service to God Through Service to Man' without reservations and without distinction as to the color of 'Man,' I shall be happy to contribute even more of my service than you requested in your letter."[33]

The Red Cross endured a similar scrutiny and criticism for its practice of segregating human blood by race during World War II. This was another way that white America demonstrated its determination that the war would not alter race relations.[34] The process of storing blood plasma was developed by an African American scientist, Dr. Charles Drew, but the Red Cross refused to mix donations of African Americans and whites in their blood banks. Bolin was as outraged as the rest of black America, and boldly withheld her service and contributions from the Red Cross in protest.[35] One could argue that Bolin's protest was part of the larger Double V campaign—for victory abroad against fascism and victory at home against racism—that was waged by African Americans who supported the war effort and responded as patriotic Americans in the face of the rampant segregation of the Department of War, the war industry, and the civilian society. In a 1943 letter of reproach to the general chairman of the Red Cross War Fund of Greater New York, she emphasized the seriousness of her position by stating that only "when blood segregation by these Chapters is discontinued I shall be glad to contribute my service and my money and urge others to do likewise."[36]

The Red Cross attempted to diminish its culpability by deferring to the mandate of the war department, which maintained a policy of segregation. Specifically, the Army maintained segregated troops, the Navy recruited African Americans only as messmates, and the Marines and Army Air Corps generally excluded African Americans.[37] Nevertheless, Judge Bolin felt strongly despite the war department's request that blood be segregated, an organization of supposed international high repute such as the Red Cross could—and ought to—refuse to participate in what she saw as "undemocratic and scientifically unsound action." In her opinion, the Red Cross had "control over any action under its name which divides people instead of uniting them, which saps morale rather than bolsters it during the time of war." The Brooklyn Chapter of the Red Cross had apparently refused to segregate blood according to race, so she saw no real merit in the chairman's position that the Red Cross was somehow bound by directives from the war department. The Red Cross was, after all, an organization, though quasi-governmental, that received its financial and moral support from private citizens, to whom it owed some accountability. In Bolin's estimation, the Red Cross lacked sufficient courage and determination to stand up and say it will not advance the war effort by offending part of the population whose support the war department and the Red Cross needed and wanted.[38]

Bolin consistently pointed out such contradiction in a most incisive manner. Her sentiments were echoed in a commencement speech she delivered to the 1946 Cheyney State Teachers College graduating class titled, "A Standard to Which the Wise and Honest Can Repair." Bolin spoke of the hypocrisy of a war intended to crush fascism abroad while maintaining it at home. She challenged

the graduates not to apply a high level of intellectual and moral integrity in international relations without applying a correspondingly high level at home. Her
words were anchored in the Double V discourse that reverberated from the pages
of the *Pittsburgh Courier,* the black daily newspaper that mounted the campaign for
the double victories against racism at home and fascism abroad. Bolin highlighted
for the graduating class the racial hatred, discrimination and segregation, as well
as the denial of equal educational and occupational opportunities so rampant in
a country that extolled the virtues of democracy abroad. She told the graduates that "it is as incomprehensible as it is degrading to see how any standard of
intellectual and moral integrity can be maintained while accepting a proscribed
citizenship status for any minority group."[39]

She challenged this class of postwar leaders to be socially responsible, by which
Bolin meant moving "in the direction of making a complete, full, inclusive, political
and economic democracy, both on an immediate and on a long-term basis, a living
reality." To effect the ideals for which the society had sacrificed so many and so
much, it was imperative that the "domestic expressions of fascism be eradicated,
completely, effectively, rapidly and ruthlessly." This elimination, she believed,
could "be accomplished only by constant day to day effort to achieve it," which is
exactly what she did.[40] Bolin did not believe in sideline citizenship. Her own life
was a testimony to constructive citizenship. She therefore hoped to impress upon
Cheyney's graduating class their own social responsibility that was born of their
newly acquired knowledge and empowerment.

Described by a judicial colleague as a militant and a fighter, Bolin never faltered
in her responsibility to the city's children, advocating for them on every front.
Along with colleague Justine Wise Polier of the Domestic Relations Court, she
succeeded in persuading the New York newspapers to withhold names of children
under age sixteen who were accused of delinquency, and to discontinue racial
designation of those so accused since it was applied solely to African Americans.[41]
In one instance, however, several years after the committee's success, an attorney's
insensitivity and lack of professionalism almost reversed much of what they had
fought for.

Following up as she did routinely with the children who appeared before her,
Judge Bolin noted that the offending attorney had represented a child before
her in Brooklyn Juvenile Term on September 1, 1962, and later had given an
interview and posed for a photograph with the child and his father for a local
newspaper, *El Diario.* Shocked that the attorney would permit any publicity regarding the very child he was assigned to represent and protect, she wrote him
a scathing letter saying, "It took some of us judges in this court several years,
much correspondence and many conferences to obtain the consent of our New
York newspapers to withhold from their news items the names of children al-

legedly or actually involved in acts leading to their appearance in the Children's Court." She reminded the attorney that "this court extends itself to protect the identity of children appearing here in the belief that when they reach maturity they should not be socially or economically handicapped or emotionally damaged by newspaper stories concerning incidents occurring in their less responsible and less mature years. Nor do we wish either that some children get a mistaken idea that they are 'big shots' because their names have been in the newspapers."[42]

That a sitting judge would make the time to communicate her disappointment about incidents involving children who had long since left her court room only supports the position of a probation supervisor who described Bolin "as one of very few judges—if not the only judge—who really cared a lot about all the individual families, not just the person to whom something was charged."[43]

Bolin's insurgency as a young judge is demonstrated in her crusade against discrimination and segregation. Within the first five years of her appointment to the bench, she challenged the presiding justice over discriminatory practices she had uncovered. With the full import of her office, she simply used the letter of the law, a device accessible to all judges, to create change. Or, more accurately, she used the full import of her office to bring private and public agencies into compliance with the letter of the law. What is certain is that, by her common judicial activism, she may have risked reappointment to the bench (see chapter 4). What set her apart then was her courage to disturb "the timid inertia" so common to the bench, even at the risk of professional ruin.[44] Each challenge she directed toward the Office of Probation or the Department of Welfare was indeed a challenge to the incumbent mayoral administration. The criticisms she hurled at the various city agencies during her first term on the bench were in essence aimed at the La Guardia administration, to which she owed her appointment. This may have soured Mayor O'Dwyer on her reappointment. He may have dreaded the prospect of having his own appointee criticize his administration.

In 1943 Bolin joined judicial colleagues Delany and Polier of the Domestic Relations Court on a citywide committee of community leaders who confronted the metropolitan press about the manner in which it reported crime committed by African Americans.[45] The memorandum, which criticized the press for failing to live up to its responsibility to improve the social conditions and racial relations in the city, stated in part:

> It is noted with alarm that the Metropolitan Press has recently played up crime happenings in Harlem to the extent that the impression is now city-wide that crime among Negroes in Harlem is on the increase. . . . It is to be noted that almost invariably when a crime is committed by a Negro the fact that it was a Negro who committed the crime is so reported that the Negro and the crime are tied together to the extent that whenever people think of one they think of the other. . . . con-

sider the howl that would go up over the land if the press were to report "MIKE
O'CONNOR, IRISH CATHOLIC KILLER" or "JAKE ENSTINE, JEW KILLER"
or "JOE THOMAS, ESPISCOPALIAN KILLER." . . . As it is now, only the Negro
is singled out in this manner.[46]

The memorandum demonstrated just how dangerous this reporting, which racialized crime, was to race relations and, by extension, just how dangerous it
was to the well-being of the city. The memo described the treatment of crime in
Harlem and the unfair policing that caused African American youth to be arrested
without a warrant while white youth who engaged in similar behavior escaped
arrest. The committee deemed the press complicit in exacerbating friction between black youth and white youth, who formed clubs (gangs) to oppose each
other and to protect the interests of each racial group as a result of the press's
negligent reporting of crimes committed in Harlem.

The committee did not restrict its concerns to the immediate impact on New
York City race relations. It utilized this forum of criticism to call attention to the
disproportionate representation of African Americans in the U.S. armed forces,
on whom the coverage of crime in Harlem had "a demoralizing effect."[47] Connect-
ing the local to the national and the civilian to the military, the memo sought to
remind the press that their image of the African American actually distorted the
actions of African Americans as citizen-soldiers. This was not the first time that
these community leaders had taken the metropolitan press to task. Years earlier
community leaders had fought and forced the metropolitan press to begin "capitalizing the word Negro" in its reporting.[48] The activism of this civil rights group of
Domestic Relations Court justices, National Association for the Advancement of
Colored People and National Urban League officers, Department of Correction
and Office of Probation commissioners, and church officials was clearly part of
a broader citywide African American agenda for criminal justice reform in 1940s
New York City.[49] The recklessness of the metropolitan press therefore provided
yet another lens through which to highlight the assault not just on African American youth, but on the African American community in general.

Harlem had erupted eight years earlier in 1935, and although the riot was
sparked by the pilferage of a ten-cent penknife and rumors of abuse and death,
it was made explosive by years of institutional neglect. As if anticipating the future, community leaders warned the press and public alike of a similar outburst
should the voice of the community continue to be ignored. "The riot and its
results," said the committee, referring to 1935, "is a page in history which no
citizen of New York City can view with pride." The group called for a conference
with representatives of the metropolitan press to "correct the present manner
of reporting crime committed by Negroes by ceasing to indicate or emphasize

the fact that the crime was committed by a Negro, and ceasing to play up crime news all out of proportion to the prevalence of crime and the significance of the crime committed."[50] Four months after this call to action, the second Harlem riot erupted on August 1, 1943, when police mistreatment of an African American woman led to rumors that an African American serviceman had been shot by a white policeman.

Although conditions in the African American community had improved a little since the 1935 riot, heavy-handed policing and a housing shortage still remained a problem for the black community into the 1940s. The influx of African Americans who made it northward as part of the Great Migration that peaked during World War I had created a strain on housing in Harlem. For his part, Fiorello La Guardia had done more than any other mayor to address the problems of this growing community.[51] Nevertheless, the announcement that the city and the Metropolitan Life Insurance Company had agreed to build a new housing complex called Stuyvesant Town, which by all indications would exclude African Americans, quickly destroyed any confidence the African American community had placed in La Guardia. The two-day riot in August 1943 left six people dead and 185 injured, and proved to be a lingering disappointment in the city's commitment to the civil rights of African Americans. La Guardia—who had chosen segregated housing over no housing—then belatedly created the Mayor's Committee on Unity to research and prevent discrimination and racial intolerance.[52] He managed to secure an agreement in 1944 with Metropolitan Life to build the Riverton housing project in Harlem. But the Stuyvesant controversy festered nevertheless.

In his study of La Guardia and modern New York, Thomas Kessner writes of two Americas. One was powerful, prosperous, and confident; the other was the slum where everything flourished that prosperous America denied: poverty, illiteracy, unemployment, decrepit housing, and an outspoken angry representative with his arm raised in perpetual objection.[53] Harlem was without a doubt that other America, and Judge Bolin was, from all accounts, an embodiment of that representative with an arm raised in perpetual objection.

Bolin joined this very public discourse over housing discrimination because she knew firsthand of its effects on the children and families who appeared before her in court. She began a letter-writing campaign against segregated housing that spanned a decade and targeted all members of the City Council as well as the mayor and even the president of the United States. In 1950, speaking in her capacity as Domestic Relations Court judge, she implored council president Joseph Sharkey to vote affirmatively on the Brown-Isaacs amendment prohibiting racial and religious discrimination in city-aided housing developments. She described the impact poor housing had on the lives and possibilities of the young people who appeared before her. "I feel obliged to tell you," her letter said, "that as a judge in the Domestic Relations Court I see daily the effects not only of inadequate housing but of segregated housing on families and children."[54]

Her letter depicted little bodies dwarfed by overcrowded, substandard homes and little minds warped by the knowledge that "we are considered somehow different and inferior. We cannot even live any place we want." With that obvious injustice as a starting point and festering over a period of time, Bolin felt that it was perhaps inevitable there should finally be rebellion against the law and authority. She reminded the council president of his duty to each resident of the city whom she believed ought "to feel that all public monies are used for the benefit of all people" and not be "humiliated by the knowledge that his taxes are being used by his City to perpetuate the evils, both material and psychological, of discrimination."[55] Bolin had added her voice to a civil rights chorus that had grown louder since the 1943 riot. In March 1951 the City Council approved the Brown-Isaacs amendment barring discrimination in all publicly assisted private housing. By 1954 Councilman Sharkey had sponsored a bill that would become the Sharkey-Brown-Isaacs Law, barring discrimination in all future private multiple dwellings built with government guaranteed mortgages.[56]

But new private housing still was not made available to African Americans. Bolin therefore joined forces with other community leaders and many civil rights organizations, such as the NAACP, the Urban League, and the New York State Committee against Discrimination in Housing, to fight for a comprehensive fair-housing law. In letters to Mayor Wagner and City Councilman Robert E. Barnes, she urged strong support of the Sharkey-Brown-Isaacs bill. Bolin stated quite bluntly that justice was simply the most compelling reason for supporting the bill. Hinting at the rhetoric of politicians and also at the American ideals that had eluded African Americans for so long, Bolin said, "We talk incessantly of the equality of all Americans and the dignity of man. Here is a small opportunity to put in practice some of our professions."[57]

The real estate boards had reportedly promoted vicious and distorted propaganda about the financial and social horrors of integrated housing. Bolin pointed out that the general experience of everyone who rents or has ever rented an apartment in New York City has never included being consulted by a landlord about prospective neighbors, yet the propaganda had the effect of deepening a fear of no longer being able to choose one's neighbor. Nevertheless, she was confident that New Yorkers would not be so insecure as to fear the enriching experience of living among people of different racial and religious backgrounds. Reiterating her concerns about the impact of segregated housing on the welfare of children and families, she said, "In addition to the justice and democracy of the bill, it would eliminate the sad and destructive effects of discrimination in housing—antisocial children rebelling against patent discrimination as well as unwholesome living conditions, the criminal adult similarly reacting, segregated schools, human beings diseased by slum living, the blatant exploitation by unscrupulous real estate interests of people they consider trapped because of their race, religion or national origin."[58] As a Domestic Relations Court judge, and one who was intimately involved in dispensing justice and help to those who appeared before her, she was in a position to draw those conclusions.

Though many of the men, women, and children who came into her courtroom returned to see her, more often than not she followed up with them. Judge Bolin believed that "you can't deal with human beings and forget them as soon as you leave a court room."[59] Her sense of social responsibility was not restricted to the bench however. It permeated her entire life. Her letters of protest were selective, targeting those citizens who held public office. Writing from the bench, she in essence put the entire weight of her office behind her while putting public office holders on notice. By the end of 1957, the municipal Sharkey-Brown-Isaacs bill became law. Although the law was restricted to developments of ten or more homes, the mayor was pleased that New York was leading the way in such sweeping legislation against discrimination in the sale or rental of privately owned housing.[60]

Uncommonly outspoken, this petite jurist (she stood only five feet two inches tall) was equally caustic with the spoken word as with the written word. One of her more militant and memorable stands against discrimination was occasioned by a 1944 invitation to be guest of honor and principal speaker at a dinner given by the City of Poughkeepsie in observance of American Brotherhood (United Americans) Week. This dinner, to which the public was also invited, was arranged by the United Americans Committee of Poughkeepsie and by such prominent Poughkeepsie residents as municipal judge Charles Corbally and Mrs. Ruby Kennedy of the Vassar College faculty. Cochaired by Mrs. W. W. Smith and Dean H. Temple of Vassar, it was held at the Nelson House, which stood as a reminder of Jim Crow in Poughkeepsie. Like so many boarding houses and hotels, the Nelson House discriminated against African Americans. Even the most well-known artists and performers, such as Marian Anderson and Langston Hughes, were refused accommodations at the Nelson House during their visits to Poughkeepsie.[61]

Perhaps memories of how Poughkeepsie had treated its native daughter and other African Americans had long since faded from the city's collective consciousness. Or maybe local custom had so changed that Bolin's experience of twelve years earlier was eclipsed by Poughkeepsie's progressive politics that integrated its African American citizens.[62] What was certain was that Poughkeepsie intended to honor its native daughter. Its celebration of American Brotherhood Week seemed like the perfect venue for this honor. Bolin accepted the invitation and the honor, but with a shrewdness characteristic of her style turned the attention away from herself and her accomplishments and placed the gaze fully on her host, the City of Poughkeepsie.

Mindful of the discriminatory practices of government agencies and colleges in Poughkeepsie, Bolin told the audience that "an annual brotherhood dinner is of absolutely no significance or of no assistance unless it stimulates all of us to work unceasingly and tirelessly throughout the year toward a brotherhood in action and in deed." She then reminded them that she left Poughkeepsie to start practicing law in New York City because despite the success of her father and brother, she did not see an opportunity in Poughkeepsie to pursue her aspirations and ambitions. She also said that when asked why she left such a beautiful town as Poughkeepsie, her response was, "Yes, it is physically beautiful, but I hate fascism whether it is practiced by Germans, Japanese, or by Americans and Poughkeepsie is fascist to the extent of deluding itself that there is a superiority among human beings by reason solely of color or race or religion."[63]

What might have been for many an opportunity to extol the virtues of hard work and determination in the face of discrimination became for Jane Bolin yet another platform for exposing injustice. As the guest of honor in her hometown and where her father and brother were distinguished lawyers, a few gracious remarks about her own success and that of her father and brother were probably expected and would have sufficed. However, Jane Bolin was mindful not to have her exceptional life be mistaken for the common experience of the majority of African Americans in Poughkeepsie. She therefore exposed the degree to which her life was indeed the exception by focusing on just how poorly Poughkeepsie had treated most of its African American citizens.

Querying the degree of progress that Poughkeepsie had made and simultaneously calling the city to action, she said that when asked about the status of minorities in Poughkeepsie, "I truly should like to reply with pride that there is at least one Negro on the bench, that there are Negroes on the staff of the District Attorney, in the Police and Fire Departments, in the City Council and every City Department. I should like to say that Negro physicians are welcomed on the staffs of the Poughkeepsie hospitals, that Negro nurses are employed there, that there are Negroes teaching in the schools, that in industrial plants Negroes are employed in skilled positions according to their ability." To ponder the status of progress in Poughkeepsie was to essentially expose the lack of progress in Poughkeepsie. The city was no more inclined to share its opportunities with its African American citizens in 1944 than it had twelve years earlier. Bolin told the audience that she still could not say that the YMCA and the YWCA of Poughkeepsie "are no longer hypocrites and no longer degrade the word 'Christian,' that they practice true brotherhood which knows no limitations because of color or race or religion."[64] Speaking in the affirmative, Bolin then spoke of the possibility of integration.

In their oral history project documenting African Americans in Poughkeepsie, scholars Lawrence H. Mamiya and Patricia A. Kaurouma found that with
the arrival of the International Business Machines (IBM) Corporation during
the 1940s and its practice of open employment and affirmative action, employment conditions improved somewhat for African Americans. The requirements
of education and technical skills, however, considerably narrowed access for the
majority of local African Americans.[65] Sadly, accusations that were leveled against
the YMCA and the YWCA twenty-five years earlier still had currency in 1944.
As an editorial in *The Advocate* declared, "Much as we would like to disguise the
fact that the Y.M.C.A. and the Y.W.C.A. movement among Colored people is a
form of segregation, we are forced to admit that the funds contributed by white
philanthropists to aid in maintaining Colored branches are contributed to pre-
clude the possibility of Colored men and women desiring to gain admission and
membership in the white branches."[66] Realizing that nothing had changed, Bolin
urged the men and women of Poughkeepsie to "break down the traditions of this
city and to begin the practice of democratic principles," because "brotherhood"
as she saw it was pointless unless Poughkeepsie ended its intolerance.[67]

It is debatable whether Judge Bolin succeeded in shaming the city into the
"practice of democratic principles." What is interesting, and much more than a
coincidence, is that exactly one year after Bolin's keynote address at the American Brotherhood dinner, her father, Gaius Charles Bolin Sr., who had practiced
law in Poughkeepsie and throughout Dutchess County since 1891, at age eighty
was elected president of the Dutchess County Bar Association, becoming the
first African American to fill that position. Though justifiably proud and happy
about his election, he pondered the distance that Poughkeepsie had traveled, and
concluded that it had much farther to go. Gaius believed that although African
Americans had come a long way, they still had the hardest fight on their hands of
any since the Civil War.[68]

What his daughter saw was that Poughkeepsie had a fight on its hands because
the winds of change were blowing strongly from the lungs of its youth. She believed in the dreams of all children, whether African American, Puerto Rican,
Jewish, or Catholic. She believed that their hopes were a direct challenge to the
City of Poughkeepsie and likeminded cities across the United States, because, as
she said, "they too study the Constitution and the history of America," and "unlike
the United States Supreme Court during much of our history, they take it literally
[and] they mean to have liberty and a full, rich life, free of want, oppression and
inequality of opportunity, whether economics, social, or political."[69] Though a
veiled criticism of the intransigence of the Supreme Court in propping up segregation sanctioned by its 1896 "separate but equal" ruling in *Plessy v. Ferguson,*[70]
Bolin's remarks also signaled the gestation of the modern civil rights movement

that would be won on the backs of young people who held the nation to the guarantees of its Constitution.

Judge Bolin was committed to making the law an instrument of fairness but did not confine her activism to the physical halls of justice. A staunch integrationist, she confronted discrimination throughout municipal government and the private sector without regard for the security of her reappointment. Her activism over the course of four decades is therefore nothing short of a crusade that fits within the broader civil rights struggle in New York City. What follows is yet another chapter in this crusade. She was a leader in the NAACP who never lost her respect for, and responsibility to, the masses of African Americans who were the foundation of the organization. Her commitment to "participatory democracy," however, put her at odds with the national leadership of the NAACP. Still she remained true to her philosophy even at the risk of public ridicule and organizational alienation.

6. Persona Non Grata

Jane Bolin and the NAACP, 1931–50

African American women have always boasted a strong presence in the National Association for the Advancement of Colored People (NAACP). From its inception women have played key roles. They numbered among those who signed the Call for the National Negro Conference in 1909 that led to the formation of the NAACP, which was organized in response to two days of racial violence in Springfield, Illinois, in August 1908. Of the founding members, women comprised a full third, representing leadership in suffrage, settlement-house work, child-labor activism, and racial reform.[1] Two were African American women—Mary Church Terrell of Washington, D.C., and Ida B. Wells-Barnett of Chicago—who both actively participated in the National Association of Colored Women (NACW) as leaders, speakers, and liaisons with local reform organizations.[2] Terrell and Wells-Barnett served on the twenty-one-member executive committee with five white women, while the sixty-six-member general committee included Maria Baldwin of Boston; Maritcha Lyons and Mary Talbert of New York; and Elizabeth Carter, leader of the New Bedford Club.[3]

Nevertheless, from all accounts, black women predominated in traditional female roles as fundraisers and proselytizers, which did not generally lead to greater influence in the national headquarters. They were, however, effective in tying the NAACP to the communities, which in turn created a black-led NAACP.[4] Terrell served on the board of directors in the decade after the organization's founding. Yet, as historian Thomas Holt notes, the singular irony is that a race woman like Wells-Barnett, "the most prominent voice opposing lynching over the preceding decade and the most persistent advocate of a national organization to combat racial oppression, was not among the leaders of the NAACP."[5]

It is therefore significant that a generation later, Jane Bolin, an African American woman of singular judicial prominence and equally outspoken, would be among the national leadership of the NAACP. An active member of the New York Branch of the NAACP and a recent judicial appointee, her nomination for election to the board of directors came as no surprise. The stipulation that she was being nominated as "the woman member of the Board of Directors" portended the gender and organizational dynamics of a board that would find itself at odds with Judge Bolin. From this "positioning" within the NAACP leadership Bolin found herself at the center of an intraorganizational conflict that would render her persona non grata to the organizational leadership. It was a controversy the likes of which the NAACP had not experienced since W. E. B. Du Bois resigned in 1935 after he publicly criticized the organization's lack of a program to address the economic misery of African Americans and advocated for all-black economic initiatives that many believed undermined the NAACP's commitment to complete integration.

This chapter will examine Bolin's philosophy of leadership and its authority over her abrupt resignation from the NAACP in 1950. In so doing, it will also examine her membership and leadership in the New York Branch and analyze the branch's relationship to the national office. An examination of the place reserved for Bolin and how she positions herself within the national leadership is long overdue. Moreover, such an examination would enrich any analysis of an NAACP leadership model and even complicate the tendency to essentialize early black leadership. The question that frames this chapter is not how this independently vocal female African American jurist rose to prominence in the NAACP, but, more important, how and why she plummeted to the depths of its disregard.

To be sure, the NAACP counted African American women among its leadership, though principally as branch directors, youth secretaries, and in other non–policy-effecting positions such as vice presidents. Such notable educators and clubwomen as Mary McLeod Bethune and Nannie Helen Burroughs were among the few African American women who served as vice presidents in the NAACP. The organization's true leadership, as in its policy-effecting and policy-directing offices, however, seemed reserved for men. Because of gender inequality, women did not have full access to decision making in the national office. Executive custom revealed just how reticent the national office had been in fashioning its decision-making body. A 1943 memorandum from NAACP Executive Secretary Walter White, Assistant Executive Secretary Roy Wilkins, and Special Counsel Thurgood Marshall to the Nominating Committee illustrates the gendered construction of this decision-making body. To elicit support for its recommendation of Judge Bolin for membership on the organization's board of directors, the executive officers asked the Nominating Committee, which was manned by Messrs. Arthur Spingarn, Charles Toney, A. A. Lucas, James Robinson, Clayborne George, John

Hall, and Theodore Spaulding, to accept Bolin as their nominee for "the woman member of the Board of Directors for whom the Committee on Nominations left a vacancy."[6]

Bolin's standing in the legal community no doubt influenced her nomination and subsequent election to the NAACP board. She brought with her a sense of commitment that was clearly manifested in her leadership, in the length of her volunteer service to the association, and most importantly in her civil rights crusade as a professional. Conscious of her achievements, the executive officers stated in their recommendation that "Judge Jane M. Bolin of New York City, who both herself and through her family, has had a long record of hard work for the N.A.A.C.P." and who "is particularly skilled in the problems of domestic relations, being the first colored woman to be appointed to the Domestic Relations Court in New York City," was qualified to serve as a member of its national board of directors.[7]

Not surprisingly, her first appointment as a board member was to the Committee on Delinquency, where she worked closely with Hubert Delany, her judicial colleague and friend who would become an important advocate against the machinery of the national office. This appointment, on its face, was not unlike Bolin's appointment to the Legal Advisory Committee of the National Council of Negro Women (NCNW), where she served with other African American women lawyers such as Sadie Alexander and Eunice Carter. It was within a few months of Bolin's appointment to the Domestic Relations Court when Mary McLeod Bethune designated her as a legal advisor, who would be able "to study bills relating to women and to interpret them for benefit of the Council."[8] The NCNW clearly intended to make use of Bolin's legal expertise, and although her standing in the legal profession would not have been totally irrelevant to the council, it was not intended to be a substitute for her actual contribution as a legal advisor.

To the contrary, Bolin's nomination to the NAACP board may have been intended for reasons other than those associated with her leadership in the NCNW. Perhaps her nomination to the NAACP board was also intended to curtail her outspokenness on behalf of the branches by bringing her into the fold of the national office. To one less committed, membership in the national leadership may have signaled an end to branch advocacy. But Bolin remained unflinching in her support for the branches, and saw no contradiction in taking that advocacy to the national office. Her backing of the branches, as she saw it, was not at variance with her membership in the national leadership. She was therefore eager to take up her responsibilities as a national board member.

Jane Bolin's involvement with the NAACP dated back to her childhood in Poughkeepsie. Her family's intimate involvement with the association preceded her personal commitment to the organization, and no doubt inspired her active participation. In 1931 she and several family members joined with a representative number of Poughkeepsie's prominent black families to found the Dutchess County Branch of the NAACP.[9] The leaders of Poughkeepsie's elite group formed the nucleus of this chapter. The newly established branch named her brother, Gaius Charles Bolin Jr., president; Dr. Robert Wesley Morgan, vice president; Eleanor Vaughn, secretary; and Marie Anderson, treasurer.[10]

Shortly after the founding of the Dutchess County Branch, Jane Bolin's sister Ivy headed the committee in charge of the branch's Junior Division, which, by 1935, appeared to be the only vibrant organizational representation the NAACP had in Dutchess County for a while.[11] Under Ivy's guidance, the Junior Division had inaugurated the Phyllis Wheatley Scholarship Fund for promising black youth wishing to go to college, and had earned the respect of the national office, which saw the group as the only hope for resuscitating the regular branch.

The vitality of the Dutchess County Branch had not grown much since its founding. The Dutchess County area was decidedly conservative, winning small battles for integration, but committed to "a quiet and efficient sort of pressure."[12] When the national office suggested a meeting with the branch shortly after its founding, the response was lukewarm. Branch members explained to the national office that "conditions here in this County are not perfect, but as it is a small community the newspapers would take up any such meetings as you desire and any definite propaganda might create an atmosphere that would be harder to overcome than if we went to work quietly and tried to overcome the smaller things that stand in the way of our people getting certain kinds of employment in this County."[13]

Gaius Bolin Sr. seemed far less concerned about the sensibilities of the white residents when, a few months after the branch was established, he requested information about the Scottsboro case from the national office in an effort to acquaint local members with the NAACP's attempts to protect the rights of the Scottsboro defendants and to urge branch participants to subscribe to *The Crisis,* the official organ of the NAACP. Although the Communist Party's International Labor Defense (ILD) had taken the lead in defending the nine young African American men accused of raping two young white women, the NAACP involved itself with fundraising as it fought to wrest control from the ILD. Consequently, even new branches like that in Poughkeepsie raised money for the NAACP's Scottsboro defense fund, while at the same time increasing subscriptions to *The Crisis.*[14]

Gaius Sr. had made *The Crisis* accessible to his own family for years, and had used it and open debates at home to expose his children to the works of the NAACP, to nurture in them a commitment to its ideological and programmatic goals of bringing about a racially egalitarian society. Jane Bolin's early socialization, reading *The Crisis* regularly, and knowing that "there were people like Dr. Du Bois on a larger scale and my father on a smaller scale who were uncompromising and tireless in fighting for the democratic ideal" certainly shaped her subsequent twenty years of commitment to the NAACP.[15] She became active in the New York Branch of the NAACP when she relocated to New York City in 1932 upon passing the bar examination. Bolin moved up the organizational ranks of the NAACP almost as quickly as she did the professional ranks of her career. To be sure, her rise in the NAACP seemed to have occurred concurrently with her rise in the legal profession. In 1937 (the same year that she was appointed assistant corporation counsel), she joined the New York Branch's leadership when she was elected first vice president and a member of the executive committee.

By 1945 when Jane Bolin was elected to the NAACP's national board of directors, she was already serving as second vice president of the New York Branch. Elected to a three-year term as a national board member, Bolin was suddenly positioned among the national leadership with whom she had dissented on behalf of the branches, particularly the New York Branch, for more than a decade. Working closely with the likes of Judge Hubert Delany and Lindsay White of the New York Branch, she had developed a reputation for being an outspoken advocate of the branches.

Bolin knew firsthand just how important and indispensable the branches were to the success of the NAACP. Through countless volunteers the branches had sustained the organization. From fundraising to membership drives, the branches made it possible for the national organization to sustain its commitment to the struggle for full citizenship. All funds raised by branches were to be shared equally with the national office.[16] But Bolin believed that the national office did not always respect the branches' commitment to the program of the NAACP. For years she had observed and criticized the prevailing attitude that "the branches should raise money for the national organization and do whatever work they are asked to do by the national organization but are arrogantly overstepping their bounds if they make suggestions or protests to the national office."[17] Much like Ella Baker, former field secretary and director of branches, Bolin adhered to the principles of participatory democracy, and as such resented what she saw as the "contemptuous and scornful attitude on the part of the paid staff and a majority of the Board toward the NAACP Branches and people who work in the branches."[18]

The national office and the New York Branch of the NAACP were both located in New York City, which presented its own peculiar dynamics. Moreover, having national board members who also assumed great saliency in the New York Branch leadership magnified problems that were inherent in an organization constructed with clear internal hierarchies. Disagreement over and dissatisfaction with the exercise of authority were inevitable, as with any decision-making institution. But being housed in the same city seemed to have compounded whatever disagreements existed between the New York Branch and the national office—so much so that the chairman of the Committee on Branches once proposed that an arbitration committee be set up to discuss the differences (labeled by the press an ongoing feud) that continued to arise between the national office and the Harlem Branch.[19] Problems ranged from the commingling of national and branch funds to the branch's unauthorized protest actions that included the picketing of the Faye Loevin Women's Apparel Shop in Harlem, which resulted in a $100,000 legal suit against the New York Branch and the National Office. The New York Branch even asked the board of directors in 1949 for the ouster of NAACP Executive Secretary Walter White because of "the bad publicity centered around him and the crippling effect it had on their membership and fund-raising campaigns."[20] In a memorandum to the National Board of Directors, the branch stated, "Be assured the New York Branch does not intend to be presumptuous. However, its position is unique in that it functions within the shadow of the National Office and quickly receives any repercussions, favorable or unfavorable, that come as a result of any action of the N.A.A.C.P. or paid member of the personnel." In an internal national office memorandum addressed to Roy Wilkins, Director of Branches Gloster Current dismissed the branch's charge as an excuse for its unsuccessful membership campaign that he blamed on a failure to organize properly.[21]

Like Judge Bolin, Judge Hubert Delany and A. Philip Randolph numbered among the New York Branch leaders who also held positions on the national level. And like Bolin, they saw no contradiction in their concurrent service. But to many they wore hats of competing authority that intensified existing tensions between the branch and national office. The national office, through Acting Secretary Roy Wilkins, regularly questioned the loyalty of its board members who were too vocal on branch issues, and had even been accused once of verbally spanking Lindsay White, president of the New York Branch, "as though he were a school boy" because he requested strict protocol in the matter of an independent petition to renominate Jane Bolin to the national board.[22]

Judge Delany, a longtime member and committee chair in the New York Branch, was upbraided on several occasions for his close involvement with branches, although at the time he was chairman of the board's Committee on Branches. Delany worked closely with the New York Branch to cultivate a better working relationship between it and the national office. But he detected only deep resentment on Wilkins's part for "attempting to revitalize the effectiveness of the Association and to bring the branches and the National Office into closer harmony."[23] In a three-page reprimand Wilkins flatly accused Delany of being "an outright spokesman and protagonist for the New York Branch" while serving as a national board member.[24] Referring to the concerns Delany raised at a board meeting, Wilkins said, "At no time and on no question did you give the impression that you were a part of the national policy-making and administrative machinery of the *National Association*."[25] Without apology and in a four-page response, Delany informed Wilkins as Bolin had done before that "the problem the Association faces now, in my view, is for the staff of the National Office to recognize that the branches are an integral part of the Association without which we cannot function effectively, and that the complaints of the officers and members of the branches are entitled to careful consideration and not arbitrary actions."[26]

While a New York Branch officer, Bolin had offered similar advice to the national office about innumerable branch complaints that their correspondence went unanswered—or was answered in a sarcastic, insulting manner.[27] In one such instance, the national office had ignored for over a year the New York Branch's request for a conference to meet with board representatives and staff to iron out conflicting and overlapping problems of the two offices.[28]

Being elected a board member did not suddenly nor over time stifle Bolin's critique of the national office. If anything, being a board member sharpened her critique. Many might have expected that she would be co-opted by the board to stand against the branches. But a simple board membership, however significant, could not sway Bolin's commitment to the democratic principles that defined the NAACP's very existence. Never able to turn a blind eye to board malfeasance, Bolin dissented continuously while a board member. "I could not sanction the paid staff overwhelming the Board to the extent of usurping the Board's function of making policy," she wrote to Arthur Spingarn. "Nor could I condone the practice of the Executive Secretary, as revealed by a member of the Board, calling together in advance of a Board meeting a secret gathering of a selected few Board members to inform them what would be on the agenda at the Board meeting and what action he wanted the Board to take." Bolin did not appreciate the "contemptuous and scornful attitude on the part of the paid staff and a majority of the Board toward the NAACP Branches and people who work in the branches." She was unequivocal in her conviction that the NAACP uphold democratic procedures within its own organizational setup, because as she saw it, "an authoritative set-up, whether Fascist, Communist, or NAACP is abhorrent."[29]

It had become clear to Bolin and others, like Delany, that the "Hague attitude of 'I Am the Law'" that Wilkins and some board members exhibited had begun to adversely affect membership and thus the buoyancy of the organization as the branches were not going to stand for such treatment for much longer.[30] One of the complaints of both board members and the branches was that the national officers seemed to feel that they controlled the association and were within their rights to liquidate those who disagreed with the board. Delany believed that if the board's relationship with the branches was more cordial and respectful, "our membership would not be dropping at such [an] alarmingly rapid rate."[31] What

Bolin and Delany witnessed was the damaging effect that such an attitude had on branch operations. They both rejected the association's published membership of 500,000 in 1949, identifying 150,000 as a more accurate number.[32]

Wilkins refused to consider that the decrease in membership could be remotely related to any "high and mighty" attitude of the national office. Instead he pointed to the inordinate latitude permitted in the operations of local branches in many areas such as San Francisco, Los Angeles, Houston, Chicago, Detroit, Cleveland, Washington, D.C., and Philadelphia. In a letter to Delany he insisted that many factors had entered into the decline in membership, not the least of which was maladministration in Chicago, high salaries and an ineffective local program in Detroit, a strike against a fifteen-year branch president in Los Angeles, and what he (Wilkins) saw as failed membership drives in the New York Branch, whose "concentration on a raffle which raised $10,000 for the Harlem Branch treasury . . . did not secure any members."[33] Despite his effort to dispel any suggestion that the attitude of the national office contributed to the decrease in association membership, Wilkins had conceded that indeed there was a grave decline in numbers. Nevertheless, as he told William Gibson, editor of the *Baltimore Afro-American,* in 1950: "I should like to point out that if the NAACP national office had a consistent policy of 'contemptuous and arrogant' treatment of branches of the Association, we would—by this time—have no branches, no support, no members, no money. Instead, we have more than 1,200 functioning units, 28 state organizations as going concerns, and are in the process of holding five regional conferences."[34]

Bolin's analysis of the decrease in membership was more programmatically informed. She truly believed that the NAACP program had become "sterile and barren," and considered this a major reason for the drop in numbers from nearly half a million to about 125,000. "The only part of the NAACP which is not programmatically bankrupt today," she said in a letter to Arthur Spingarn, "is its legal department which is doing an important and superb job. This, however is limited in scope and the NAACP in my opinion can no longer justify its failures in larger areas by the success of its legal arm in its limited area."[35]

Like Hubert Delany, Bolin was completely opposed to the elitist leadership that assumed that "all the brains in the NAACP lie only in the national Board and staff." In an open letter, she reminded President Arthur Spingarn that as "a member of nearly twenty years standing in the Poughkeepsie and New York Branches I have seen too many earnest people working on a volunteer basis with sincere devotion to the program of the NAACP to subscribe to these attitudes of the national organization."[36] She believed strongly that branch positions and requests should be thoughtfully and respectfully considered, if for no other reason than the fact of their service to the organization.

If the NAACP national office was the sum of its separate parts, then it remained a very divided whole for the duration of Jane Bolin's tenure. While thoroughly committed to the association ideologically, in administrative matters Bolin constantly challenged the "principle of centrality" that left the branches in a perpetually subordinate position to the national office.[37] Bolin believed in "participatory democracy," a philosophy of leadership that Carol Mueller attributes to Ella Baker, former NAACP field secretary and director of branches.[38] Baker may have given formal statement to what Bolin practiced and fought for as an NAACP member and officer. What is certain is that in the pre–civil rights era, a cadre of progressive African American women challenged the leadership structure of the nation's premier civil rights organization.

As a board member, Bolin was a policy maker, and theoretically better positioned as a peer to effectively dissent and protest in behalf of the branches, especially the New York Branch.[39] But precisely because of this dissidence, grounded in her philosophy of leadership, she was positioned as an "outsider within" the inner circle of NAACP national leadership. Furthermore, dissenting from the seat left for "the woman member" proved to be a source of profound irritation and embarrassment for the national office, which was therefore committed to ending her tenure as board member even if it meant compromising democratic principles.

What occurred during Bolin's second term of office, despite efforts to secure her renomination, was the uncharacteristic removal of an incumbent board member despite having the highest attendance record of any renominated board member. Bolin was first considered for board membership in 1943 when the executive officers recommended her to the Nominating Committee for nomination in February 1944. Duly elected at the NAACP Annual Meeting on January 2, 1945, she assumed office for a three-year term to end December 31, 1947.[40] She was actually still serving her second term when the decision was made to remove her from the board. However, in removing Bolin's name from the ballot for renomination, the Nominating Committee had not anticipated just how belligerent her supporters would become. More importantly, the committee could not have predicted that their decision would have met a challenge of public proportion. At most, the committee probably imagined some minor opposition from a few board members, such as Delany, whom they hoped to placate with Bolin's subsequent appointment as an NAACP vice president. They could not have been more wrong on all counts.

The headline in the *Afro-American* on October 8, 1949, read "REMOVAL OF JUDGE BOLIN FROM NAACP BOARD BARED." According to the accompanying article, an unidentified source revealed that the NAACP seven-man Nominating Committee had moved to drop Judge Jane Bolin as a member of the board of directors.[41] (In actuality, by a 4 to 3 vote the committee had agreed not to recommend Judge Bolin for another term. The failure to renominate her was in fact a tie vote, with the tie broken by a vote of Dr. J. L. Leach, the committee chairman.)[42] But even the legitimacy of this vote was called into question. What was supposed to be strictly internal association business, not yet authorized for release, had suddenly become available for public consumption and criticism. To make matters worse, neither the standing board collectively, nor Judge Bolin individually, had been notified of the committee's action. As a result, Bolin found out about her ouster through the morning paper and not by internal memorandum.

According to the source, Bolin had been dropped as a board member after a staff meeting was called at the national office where it was stated that "Bolin has to go." It was further reported that two top staff members at that meeting opposed Judge Bolin's continuance as a board member on the ground that "we can't get along with her."[43] The reference to a staff meeting, and not necessarily a Nominating Committee meeting, suggested that members of the paid staff (as in the executive or acting secretary) might have discussed their position on Bolin's renomination with select members of the committee in an effort to influence the committee's decision. Judge Delany, staunch Bolin supporter and member of the Nominating Committee, had no knowledge of the meeting in question. Tantamount to abdication by the board to the staff, such a meeting would not have been uncommon, but characteristic of the lack of propriety Bolin so often challenged throughout her tenure with the NAACP.[44]

Bolin welcomed cooperation between the board and the staff. She only objected to situations like the one reported in the *Afro-American,* and similar incidents, such as the executive secretary calling secret meetings in advance of board meetings to inform board members of what action he wanted them to take.[45] Like Judge Delany, her partner in protest, Judge Bolin respected the board of directors as the association's policy-making body and therefore expected the staff to carry out policy without attempting to undermine or in anyway interfere with the board's responsibilities.[46]

As soon as the story broke, rumors and whispers about the clandestine operations of the Nominating Committee circulated freely. As a result, the national office found itself under the microscope. The board of directors called a meeting on October 10, 1949, where Judge Bolin asked to speak on a point of personal privilege. She began by saying that she was not addressing her remarks to the action of the Nominating Committee in failing to renominate her. She had accepted their decision, or so it seemed. Her remarks were, instead, "to the article on page 1 of this week's *Afro-American,* which I am sure all of you have seen." She reminded the board that she was obviously not present when the Nominating Committee made its recommendation, yet "to date I have not been officially notified of the failure of the Committee on Nominations to redesignate me—although the press was notified at once."[47] Bolin made full use of the platform she had; without wavering, she announced that the information must have been given to the press by some member of the staff who was present at both meetings. (This type of behavior was not uncommon, and maybe that made it more revolting to her. As she recalled, not quite a month previously, a press release circulated days before a board meeting stating that the board had selected Roy Wilkins as acting executive secretary.) Although Bolin was not asking for action to be taken against whomever was responsible for such a leak, she felt obliged to share with the board that "one of the most outstanding members of our race and a founder of the NAACP, Dr. Du Bois, was summarily dismissed by this Board for letting something get to the press before it had gone through the proper channels."[48]

Bolin was not so much concerned about the lack of respect shown her as she was about the staff interference in the Nominating Committee's business. It was ironic that the very practice she challenged throughout her tenure with the NAACP should be the reason for her demise organizationally. "Since I have been on this Board," Bolin said, "I have been called on by people who are nationally known in the field of social action to justify the domination of the organization by the staff." She could not justify the action, and was not about to apologize for the action because for her it represented a complete reversal of the traditional functions of a policy-making board and a policy-executing staff—a clear situation of "the tail wagging the dog rather than the dog wagging the tail."[49]

"We do have a reputation," she informed the board, "for being a supine board of puppets which does everything expected of us by the executive secretary and his staff."[50] At this moment, Bolin had a captive audience, one that she would no longer have at the close of her term on the board. More importantly, she stood before a board made vulnerable because of its own deeds. It could not, in good faith, dismiss her remarks because, quite simply, the verdict was in and the evidence was in black and white on the pages of the black press. The October meeting was the opportune time for Bolin to set the entire board straight, one last time, on her integrity as a board member and to distinguish her service from theirs. Thus, in closing at the meeting, she declared:

> I must say I feel we are not meeting the obligation we have to the masses of the people. Yet I have not gone out and tried to operate behind the scenes. I have said what I had to say right in this room. I have not tried to engage any member of the board or staff in any politics. I have not gone to the press with my differences of opinion. In fact, at least two members of the Board can affirm that when they wanted to go to the press with their differences of opinion, I discouraged it when my advice was sought. I have been very outspoken in what I have to say. I have been so not because of any personal hostility towards any member of the staff or

Board. I was expressing myself the only way I know how in the interest of the masses of the people who are clamoring for the attention of this association, but are not receiving it.[51]

No sooner had this board meeting adjourned than there appeared in the *New York Amsterdam News* an account of matters discussed there, with specific reference to the remarks made by Judge Bolin. This prompted the acting secretary to state openly at the November board meeting (at which Bolin was conspicuously absent without regret), that "someone is giving out information that is detrimental to the Association . . . the Board should realize that it is creating publicity which is hurting the Association, and which is making it very difficult to carry on a program."[52]

Once leaked, Bolin's criticism of the NAACP seemed to galvanize the branches even as it alienated the national office. The *Atlanta Daily World* likened Judge Bolin to Dr. Du Bois, noting that they were both generally regarded as "persona non grata" at the national headquarters of the NAACP. The newspaper reported that "battle lines between the national office of the NAACP and its local branches were more tightly drawn . . . as nineteen of the state's forty-two branches approved a resolution recommending the placing of Dr. W. E. B. Du Bois on the national board of directors of the organization and a move was started to have Judge Bolin placed back on the national board."[53]

Since the Nominating Committee failed to recommend Bolin for reelection to the board, the only way for her to get on the ballot (should she desire reelection) was by a petition containing the signatures of at least thirty members who wanted to retain her on the board. The election ballot would go to the branches in December.[54] Her supporters wasted no time in securing as many signatures as possible. It is difficult to tell whether Bolin was truly determined to retain her seat on the board or whether she simply acquiesced to the enthusiasm of her constituency. Either way she was on the road to becoming persona non grata to the national office.

By October 28, the New York Branch had submitted a nominating petition with close to one hundred signatures, including those of Hubert Delany, Nominating Committee member; Lindsay White, New York Branch president; Channing Tobias, national assistant treasurer; and Ella Baker, a dedicated member of the New York Branch, who from all accounts shared Bolin's disdain for the particular style of leadership in the national office.[55] Though closer examination revealed duplicate signatures, the petition represented well in excess of the thirty signatures required. The petition, whose preamble read "We, the undersigned members in good standing of the National Association for the Advancement of Colored People, hereby nominate as a member of its Board of Directors JUDGE

JANE M. BOLIN," also included a paragraph detailing the accomplishments of the nominee, a courtesy that was not extended to all other nominees.[56] The petition submitted by the Jamaica Branch of the NAACP did not include a paragraph like that in the New York Branch's petition, but it did have more than the thirty required signatures.[57]

The national office tried to not arouse further the ire of the New York Branch. Moreover, it wanted to avoid any further appearance of impropriety regarding the election. Following the branch's submission of the nominating petition, Roy Wilkins supposedly sang the praises of a favored nominee publicly from his desk in the national office. His public support of one nominee over others was a conflict of interest that was not lost on Hubert Delany. "I also consider that it was improper in a recent release going out from the National Office about two weeks ago [early November] to pick out one nominee from along all the rest, and tell of his great work for the Association," he told Wilkins. "If that is democracy, then I think we need a new definition of democracy for the Association."[58]

The New York Branch was equally vigilant in holding the national office to strict administrative propriety. Along with the petitions were forms to be signed by the acting secretary upon his receipt of said petitions. Though Wilkins obliged, he could not contain his outrage at such a request. In a letter to Lindsay White, New York Branch president, Wilkins said he had never before been asked by a branch to provide a signed receipt for a petition of nomination. "The implications contained in this request from you are not pleasant," he told White, "nor do they reflect favorably upon you or the New York Branch or any other agents for whom you may have been acting."[59] With obvious reference to Bolin, Wilkins went on to say, "The National Office has never been accused of 'losing' a petition, or suppressing one, or in any fashion interfering with the constitutional right of 30 or more persons to make independent nominations. To have you or the New York Branch or any other persons involved in this transaction so crudely imply that dishonesty and mishandling could be expected is indicative . . . of the origin of the alleged difficulties between the New York Branch and the National Office."[60] It should not have been difficult for Wilkins to conceive of the national office mishandling information since its current practices had thrust private association business onto the press. Less than a month earlier those practices had prompted Bolin to demand a correction of the minutes to indicate her presence at the board's November meeting.[61]

White simply chalked up such invective to Wilkins's being "hypersensitive." Though sincerely concerned about the implications of dishonesty imputed to his office, Wilkins was even more concerned that his signature, acknowledging the receipt of the petitions, could be construed as something more. But, as White told him, "To think that your signature meant anything else is difficult to reconcile with reason."[62]

Some members of the Nominating Committee were not willing to defer totally to the prescribed election process. In an effort to seal the outcome of the election, the national office, through the agency of committee chairman Dr. J. L. Leach and committee secretary Daisy Lampkin, sent out a craftily worded letter to all branches, asking them to vote for the nominees presented by the Nominating Committee and to ignore the New York Branch petition, saying it was trying to undermine the committee's process. The letter stated, "Your Committee was not aware of any New York feud that may or may not have been going on. Our business, as the elected representatives of the convention and of the Board, was to try to select good nominations to the Board."[63]

Though sent out in an official capacity, this letter did not necessarily represent the opinions of all seven members of the Nominating Committee nor the national office as a whole. Yet the impression was that it did. As a result, the national office became further embroiled in this cauldron of controversy. After all, if the national office supported this letter, then implicitly, it also condoned interference with the election process. As will be seen from the New York Branch's response, at least five national officers were willing to publicly accuse the national office of doing just that.[64] The letter further polarized the Nominating Committee, which was already sharply divided on the issue of Judge Bolin's renomination to the board. The letter also elicited a similarly crafted and more direct letter from the New York Branch.

The New York Branch's letter was similarly addressed to branch presidents who were asked to "bring this matter to the attention of your Executive Committee and read this letter to the membership at the annual meeting just before the ballots are distributed and before the votes are cast for the members of the National Board of Directors."[65] The architects of this letter were Judge Hubert Delany, James E. Allen, William Lloyd Imes, Earl B. Dickerson, and Lindsay H. White, four of whom were currently affiliated with the national office. The exception was Lindsay White, president of the New York Branch.

The authors framed the content of their protest with the following opening sentence: "This letter trumpets the call to action of every Branch as we face a great democratic crisis in the N.A.A.C.P. today."[66] In their estimation, members of the Nominating Committee had gone to great lengths to deny the NAACP an outstanding leader in Judge Bolin. Therefore, acting with due authority, and with endorsements from prominent national officers, the New York Branch assumed the responsibility for exposing the politics surrounding the Nominating Committee's failure to renominate Judge Bolin to the board of directors. The branch had surreptitiously secured a list from the national office of the officers of all NAACP branches across the country and proceeded to counteract the impact of Dr. Leach and Daisy Lampkin's letter. The New York Branch wanted all other branches to know that Leach and Lampkin's letter was unauthorized and that an unauthorized letter was sent on the official stationery of the NAACP only substantiated what they had suspected all along, "that Judge Jane M. Bolin after serving twelve years on the Executive Committee of the New York Branch and five years on the National Board was not renominated because of the opposition of some of the top national office paid staff. . . . Even if the letter purporting to come from the Nominating Committee was authorized—and it was not—it would in effect be attempting to prevent the election of any candidates nominated by the Branch by independent petition as provided for in the N.A.A.C.P. Constitution."[67]

The New York Branch saw the Nominating Committee's vote against Bolin as a direct result of the political engineering of top paid staff in the national office. And, before ballots would be cast, they wanted all association members to know that the opposition to Bolin "was based on Judge Bolin's fighting in the National Board for greater *democratic participation* by the Branches in the policies and work of the N.A.A.C.P." (emphasis mine). They underscored the fact that "Judge Bolin has always insisted that the people in the branches be regarded as more than just fund raisers for the national staff but rather as interested citizens working toward the professed goals of the N.A.A.C.P."[68]

The association's membership, "the principal stockholders" of the organization, would determine who would represent them on the board of directors. Yet, as late as early December, though all branches had received letters from the New York Branch as well as Leach and Lampkin, several branches had not received an official ballot. In a letter to the national office, dated November 25, the president of the Williamsport Branch, Reverend Madison Bowe, informed National Youth Secretary Ruby Hurley that while he had not received the list of candidates, "we have had two letters, one from the New York Branch and one from the Nominating Committee, I believe from your office, recommending certain persons for the Executive Board for the next term and to me they are conflicting."[69]

This "New York" feud between the branch and the national office had touched and even disturbed the confidence of the association's membership. Which letter were branches supposed to believe? Could they accept the veracity of the New York Branch and still remain loyal to the association? Could they obtain unbiased clarification on issues that both letters raised? Would questioning the national office automatically make their branch suspect in the eyes of the national office? Was there sufficient time to investigate all relevant issues before the December 31 deadline for ballot submission? These were only a few of the questions confronting the branches. And if they hoped to have a truly informed ballot, those and many more questions would have to be answered.

With an impending deadline, many branches probably just chalked up the conflicting letters to a New York City problem involving a New York Branch nominee and bowed out of further inquiry. But at least one branch chose an informed ballot over a merely on-time ballot. A very telling letter was sent to the national office from Everett R. Lawrence, president of the Merrimack Valley Branch in Andover, Massachusetts, on November 21. Though the Merrimack Valley Branch had received the official ballot and had started to vote on it, the branch decided to table the vote until its December meeting or until such time as all issues raised in both letters were addressed. Lawrence said, "As it stands now, no one knows whether to believe that the Committee actually *did* act in the best interests of the Association,—*did* consider each nominee fairly. Whom do we believe? Do you feel that this is the sort of action that builds confidence in our National Staff? Do you realize that this questionable business offers just the argument needed for those who are reluctant to join?—that it is just this sort of childish bickering that has many of your supporting branches on their heels?"[70]

Roy Wilkins was unable to assuage the concerns of the Merrimack Valley Branch with perfunctory statements about the recalcitrance of a "problem child" branch because Lawrence clearly stated: "I expect an explanatory reply to present to my Branch at our December meeting, and I will not consider a form letter as a satisfactory means of supplying the answers to my direct questions."[71] Wilkins promised to pass on Lawrence's letter directly to the chairman of the Nominating Committee, whom he supposed was better situated than he to answer the branch's inquiries without it being "branded immediately as an unwarranted attempt, on the part of an employed staff member who is already accused of bias, to influence a situation."[72] But, interestingly, Chairman Leach might not have been the most objective person at that particular time to answer the concerns of the branches. He was, after all, a party to the controversy that had ensued. As it turned out, Judge Delany's earlier proposal of an arbitration committee may have been the fairest, though not the most efficient, way to handle the root of the problem that had surely tainted the election.

Delany, who served on the Nominating Committee with Leach, Lampkin, Joshua Thompson, Rosa Johnson, W. K. Saxon, and Alfred Baker Lewis, sought to distance himself from the committee's decision denying renomination to Bolin. He had announced bluntly in the Nomination Committee's infamous meeting that he would "help Judge Bolin fight" for reelection.[73] Delany was clearly one of the committee members who voted to retain Judge Bolin as a member of the board. He had even lent his name to the New York Branch's letter of response, along with James E. Allen, William Lloyd Imes, Earl B. Dickerson, and Lindsay H. White. Later, he questioned whether the proceedings that resulted in the committee's 4 to 3 vote against Bolin's renomination were valid. As he recalled, at no time before or during deliberations was there a committee secretary, a title he says Lampkin later assumed for the single purpose of lending legitimacy to the letter she and Leach wrote. In addition, he noted that the committee chairman was unilaterally selected by Roy Wilkins who was present during deliberations.[74]

In a letter to Wilkins that threatened to expose his interference, Delany said, "I think it will be you who will need to do some explaining as to why a duly authorized committee of the Board and the convention proceeds to conduct its business pursuant to your selection of the Chairman, and after the business is completed proceeds then to select a Secretary." To support his charge, Delany recounted the following to Wilkins: "At 1 o o'clock there were three persons seated on each side of the table where the Committee sat, which table was adjoining your desk. At about 5 minutes passed [*sic*] 10, as Dr. Leach came in, you arose and said substantially, 'Dr. Leach, we have a seat ready for you. You may act as Chairman.' And Dr. Leach proceeded to act as Chairman, pursuant to your designation."[75] Such an indictment might have had more currency had Delany not participated in the proceedings he later discredited. Yet, he hoped that by putting the information before the branches that somehow the masses of association members would "storm the bastille" that was the national office, demanding answers or heads. Instead, either because of too much information, not enough information, not the right information, or simply because of confusion with all of the information, the members voted for the committee's nominees. As a result, at the January 3, 1950, annual association meeting, Judge Bolin was not reelected to the national board of directors.[76]

However, at the next board meeting on January 3, 1950, Judge Bolin was elected as one of the association's vice presidents for the regular one-year term ending December 31, 1950. In his letter of congratulations, Wilkins told Bolin: "Because of your interest and activity in the past, we are confident that in the capacity of a vice-president you will continue to give us your advice and support in the many matters that will come before the Association."[77] Bolin wrote Wilkins the following day inquiring about the duties of vice presidents. Referring to Article IV, Section 2 of the NAACP constitution, which stated, "The Vice Presidents shall perform such functions and exercise such duties as may be voted by the Board of Directors," Bolin requested that Wilkins send her a copy of the minutes of the meeting at which the board had determined the functions and duties of vice presidents. It is entirely possible that Bolin knew that no such record existed. She may have made the request as a formality in an effort to create a record for herself.[78]

This simple request sparked a new flame of contention, not wholly unrelated to the issue of Bolin's removal from the board. Many in the national office saw her inquiry as an affront to the board's graciousness in electing her a vice president. Not coincidentally, the New York Branch had specified in its letter to all branch presidents months before, "Do not be fooled by the offer of the

Nominating Committee to make Judge Bolin a Vice-President of the N.A.A.C.P. This is part of their plan to continue to use Judge Bolin's name and prestige for the benefit of the N.A.A.C.P. while depriving her of participating in making Board policy."[79] Maybe it was hoped that Bolin would have accepted her "consolation prize" of a vice presidency and quietly retired to the letterhead of the association hierarchy. Had she been a person easily swayed and silenced by titles, she might have. But she was not, having always operated with the full force of her office behind her. Therefore, she needed to know exactly what the force, and not merely the title, of her office was. Bolin was also too aware of the internal politics of the association's national office to simply accept a title without understanding its import and responsibility. What followed was a full-blown intraorganizational conflict that exploded onto the pages of the black press from New York to Kansas City, Missouri.

Within a week of Bolin's request for the minutes, Wilkins had his secretary call Bolin, not because he had the information she requested, but simply "because she asked for a reply in a week." This was the kind of paranoia that gripped the national office. A few days later, Wilkins himself wrote to Bolin: "Within my recollection, over the past eighteen years, the Board has not formally determined the functions and duties of Vice Presidents of the Association, or assigned to them any specific tasks." Wilkins had evidently spoken to President Arthur Spingarn on the matter, and though he also did not recall any board action on this matter, he suggested that maybe the language of Article IV, Section 2 meant only "that the Board might assign such duties from time to time as occasions might arise."[80] The question then still remained: For what duties and functions were vice presidents responsible?

It is entirely possible that Bolin knew the answer to the question. She had clearly worked with many of the association's vice presidents during her six years as a board member and could easily have tapped her memory on the extent of their involvement in policy making. She may well have been unsure about the actual duties and responsibilities of vice presidents because quite possibly she could not reconcile what she had witnessed as a board member with what others, inside and outside of the New York Branch, were saying. During her time on the board she had observed the mostly male vice presidents who attended board meetings voting without the imposition of any disqualification by the chairman. Yet the New York Branch's letter to the vice presidents (about which Bolin must have known) stated in relevant part, "This is part of their plan to continue to use Judge Bolin's name and prestige for the benefit of the N.A.A.C.P. while depriving her of participating in making Board policy—for under the N.A.A.C.P. national constitution Vice-Presidents may not vote!"[81]

With such conflicting information, it was wise for Bolin to request clarification before assuming the office. The national office took the position that vice presidents had no constitutionally assigned duties—but duties could be assigned at the discretion of the board as the occasion arose. Bolin found this position ridiculous. In a letter dated February 8, 1950, to the board chairman Dr. Louis T. Wright, she said, "It is inconceivable and inconsistent that there should be an office in an organization without duties. It must be concluded that since the Board has failed to state specifically the functions of a Vice-President, the generally conceived and publicly accepted meaning of the Office is accepted by the NAACP." Bolin reasoned that in the absence of explicit duties, vice presidents were bound by the customary practices of the office. She was convinced that this interpretation was also accepted by other vice presidents in the association because, as she recalled, "During my six years as a member of the Board I have observed Vice Presidents attending Board meetings, expressing their valuable opinions and participating in the voting." Any other interpretation, she believed, would grossly mislead the public because, as she told Dr. Wright, the public believed, and had a right to believe that "any person who accepts election as an officer in the NAACP, as in every other organization, shares in the grave responsibility of making the Association's policy and in the general administration of its affairs." With her position clearly stated, Bolin concluded her letter (which was copied to all vice presidents) by accepting the vice presidency "with its concomitant responsibilities, including those of attending Board meetings and discussing and voting on the business of the Association."[82]

Having accepted the position of vice president, she attended the national board meeting on February 14, 1950, intent on participating fully in the business of the association. However, when Bolin raised her hand to vote against a motion made by Lampkin, Chairman Wright ruled that as a vice president she was ineligible to vote on the affairs of the association.[83] This was a ruling that, by the facts, could not be supported by either association practice or constitutional provision. Wright directed the acting secretary to read Bolin's letter of February 8 to the entire board. He then asked Special Counsel Thurgood Marshall to read the memorandum that he had been asked to prepare on the issue of vice presidents.[84] After hearing both the letter and the memorandum, the board decided as a body that vice presidents could not vote. At that moment, "Judge Bolin asked to be excused from the meeting, stating that she had neither the time nor the desire to sit and listen to the discussions unless she was able to participate by voting."[85]

When Bolin left the meeting she had already made the decision to resign. But however quick, her resignation would not be quiet. Hers was a very public resignation, exposing deep fissures in the organization and confirming earlier reports that like Du Bois she too had become an irritant and liability to the national office with every public criticism. A few days after the board meeting, William Imes tried to convince Bolin that although she had good and sufficient cause to resign, if she did so she would be doing "just what the reactionary crowd at our NAACP wants you to do." Imes, who had been a close friend and associate of Bolin's second husband, Walter Offutt, and a dear friend to Bolin, strongly believed that to save face, the board had made a gesture of their respect for her in the nomination and election to a vice presidency. He was, however, convinced that if Bolin resigned, "even though they have tried to render a vice-presidency *innocuous,* they will feel they have entirely triumphed over you." He pleaded with her not to resign, saying, "[The NAACP] needs you and hundreds more like you."[86]

Many on the board supported Bolin, but she found staunch supporters in Judge Delany and William Lloyd Imes. Many responses from the other NAACP vice presidents backed Bolin's position on the duties and responsibilities of the office. Bishop W. J. Walls of Chicago wrote: "Being one of the same status, that is vice-president of the Association, I am naturally interested. I fully agree with the position taken in your letter and will support it unreservedly. I am simply acknowledging same in order to say, more power to you."[87] A. Philip Randolph, one of the elders of the civil rights movement and a national vice president, acknowledged that he too did not know that vice presidents could not vote in the affairs of the association. He echoed Bolin's admonition that the board be more specific about the duties and responsibilities of the office. Even sitting board member Earl B. Dickerson admitted that he was unsure of the voting rights of vice presidents, and that he had simply referred Judge Bolin to the constitution when she inquired about his opinion on the issue.[88]

Of course there were those vice presidents who believed that Judge Bolin had read too much into the function of the office. Buell Gallagher, of Washington, D.C., wrote directly to the board chairman saying, "For whatever it is worth, may I enter in the record the fact that, as a Vice-President of the NAACP I have never suffered from the delusion that I had voting power." He went on to say that if it were physically possible, he would gladly attend meetings regularly for the sole purpose of sharing in the discussion. Gallagher said that he had enough confidence in the democratic process to feel that the intelligent and persuasive statement of a position was the only effectively democratic procedure, and that voting was merely a means of recording the results of sound deliberations. (Gallagher was obviously not familiar with the power of a vote.)

Maybe Gallagher and others like him were willing to sacrifice meaningful input for the sake of powerful titles. Bolin had been both an active branch official and an active national board member and did not have half as much confidence as Gallagher did in the democratic process of the national office. Gallagher believed that the power of a vice president was no more than that of any member not directly elected by the membership, because as he saw it, "Only those who are subject to the direct votes of the membership ought to have the power to vote in Board meetings."[89] He seemed unwilling to apply the same logic to the board. Could it be that, like many in the national office, he saw the real power as sitting on the board and not necessarily in the "persuasive" voice of the membership? Gallager's attitude about surrendering to the "democratic" procedures of the association only reaffirmed what Bolin had been fighting against all along—the notion that all the brains of the association reside only in the national board and staff.

On March 9, 1950, two months after her election as vice president, Judge Bolin formally submitted her resignation in the form of a three-page letter to President Arthur Spingarn.[90] She also released the letter to the press in mimeographed copies that were in the hands of newspapers before it was delivered to Spingarn on March 13. By noon that day, the national office had been bombarded with telegrams from newspapers asking for comment on Bolin's resignation. The *Norfolk Journal and Guide* wrote: "PLEASE IMMEDIATELY WIRE COMMENT ON RESIGNATION STATEMENT RELEASED BY JUSTICE BOLIN STATEMENT ATTACKS POLICY OF NAACP TOP COMMAND ETC." The *Carolina Times* (Durham, North Carolina) made a similar request, as did *The Call* (Kansas City, Missouri).

The national office wired responses that were mechanical at best. To the *Norfolk Journal and Guide,* Roy Wilkins wrote: "BOLIN LETTER RELEASED TO PRESS BEFORE IT REACHED BOARD YESTERDAY. REGRET I CANNOT COMMENT. HOWEVER STATEMENT FROM DR. LOUIS T. WRIGHT, CHAIRMAN OF BOARD, WILL BE RELEASED IN TWENTYFOUR HOURS." To the *Carolina Times,* he wrote: "REGRET THAT COMMENT ON JUDGE BOLIN LETTER BY CHAIRMAN OF OUR BOARD HELD UP AND CANNOT REACH YOU BY YOUR DEADLINE TONIGHT." He told reporters for the *Baltimore Afro-American* and the *New York Amsterdam News* that he personally could not comment, but that the board had authorized the chairman to issue a statement that would be released in a few days.

Surprised, embarrassed, and exposed, the national office needed time to regroup, but until then Judge Bolin's letter stood "as a true statement of conditions," in the absence of any other to refute it.[91] Her letter read in part:

> As you know I accepted the Vice Presidency with the interpretation of its responsibilities as including that of participating in the business of the association. At the Board meeting on February 14th, the Chairman of the Board ruled that as Vice President I am ineligible to vote on the affairs of the association. In view of Mr. Wilkins' letter to me of January 23rd stating that the Board had never provided for any duties or functions for Vice Presidents as it is required to do by the NAACP constitution and in view of the Board Chairman's ruling that Vice Presidents cannot participate in determining policy or program for the organization, I find that twenty Vice Presidents (a ridiculous number) are merely names on NAACP letterheads, used to lend prestige to the association and to mislead the public that these persons

have responsibility in formulating policy. I refuse to share in this deception and I refuse to let the public hold me in part responsible for the actions of the NAACP without having the power to vote on these actions.

There are several areas in which I have dissented while a Board member. I could not sanction the paid staff overwhelming the Board to the extent of usurping the Board's function of making policy. As I stated in a Board meeting last year, we have in the NAACP the spectacle of the tail (the staff) wagging the dog (the Board).

Nor could I appreciate the contemptuous and scornful attitude on the part of the paid staff and a majority of the Board toward the NAACP Branches and people who work in the Branches. In other words, all the brains in the NAACP lie only in the national Board and staff.

I am further of the belief that the NAACP program has become sterile and barren and that is a major reason for its membership dropping from nearly a half million to about one-eighth of a million in the last few years. The only part of the NAACP which is not programmatically bankrupt today is its legal department which is doing an important and superb job.

I have become persona non grata to the NAACP hierarchy because of the positions I have taken and I have been duly purged on the Board. . . . It appears to me that for some time now the NAACP high command has been more interested in personal and political intrigue than it has been in discharging that trust efficiently and to the fullest.[92]

Bolin did not simply resign as vice president. She used her resignation as a public platform for challenging the structure, program, policies, and leadership of the NAACP. She was not the first African American woman to oppose the style of leadership of the NAACP on the national level, but she was one of the first to do so immediately and publicly. Her tenure of protest on the board had resulted in her removal without personal appeal. But she was determined that her withdrawal from the vice presidency would never be relegated to the margins of internal correspondence. Information about her resignation was therefore not leaked, but well-timed and shared fully with the press. This woman who had always lent her voice to the struggles of others made a decision to speak for herself in a loud, resounding voice. She summarily preempted any misinformation about her resignation by baring all that she had said to the NAACP president. How empowering that must have been for a woman who had only months earlier endured the insult of learning about her impending removal from the national board in the morning paper.

It was now the national office's turn to play "catch up" with Bolin's statement that had already saturated the collective consciousness of the association's membership. The national office had authorized the chairman of the board to issue a statement to get the board's viewpoint into the newspapers. However, in accordance with resolutions passed at the March 13 board meeting, the statement was withheld pending a committee conference with Bolin. At that meeting, Arthur Spingarn made a motion (seconded by Judge William Hastie, an early black cabinet member) that the chairman be authorized to send a letter to Judge Bolin that essentially accepted her resignation. Upon substitute motion made by Judge Delany, it was decided by a 10 to 5 vote that the chairman should appoint a committee, including himself, to confer with Judge Bolin to see whether she would reconsider her resignation.[93]

In commenting on the board's actions, Bolin stated, "I shall always be pleased to meet with this committee or any N.A.A.C.P. Board committee, to discuss not only my resignation, but any matter or interest to the Association.[94] Arthur Spingarn was one of five board members who opposed Delany's motion to confer with Bolin regarding reconsideration of her resignation. His opposition stemmed from what he perceived to be the lack of "good faith" on Bolin's part.[95] However, Bolin felt that the vote to confer with her "indicates that a two-thirds majority of the Board, aware of my twenty years' service to the N.A.A.C.P., does not consider my resignation motivated by 'bad faith' or personal reasons as publicly charged by one or two Board members." However, Charles Toney, a municipal court judge since 1931, supported Spingarn's argument as well as Thurgood Marshall's earlier memorandum. He stated that since the association was a membership corporation and the laws of New York State applied, then the control of the organization was placed only in the board of directors.[96]

However relevant and truthful these summations were, they could not negate the fact that during Judge Bolin's years on the board vice presidents frequently voted on the affairs of the association. Thus Bolin, and not necessarily the office of vice president, may have been the intended target of the board's timely interpretation of the vice presidency.

A month after Bolin released her letter of resignation to the press the committee still had not conferred with her. Wilkins managed, however, to convince the board to release Wright's comment on Judge Bolin's letter. He was convinced that the longer the board waited to publicly address Bolin's letter, the more they would have to prove. Wilkins referenced the leading editorial in the *Afro-American* for March 18 as an indication of the type of impact Judge Bolin's letter had. Headlined "Rumblings At the NAACP," the column said that Judge Bolin's charges called for a searching inquiry with the public being fully informed of the findings. It called for "direct and positive replies," saying that until this was done, "the future of the NAACP seems to be definitely in jeopardy." The editorial also stated that "unfortunately, the charges made by Justice Bolin have been heard rather frequently within the past year and following the theory that where there is smoke there usually is fire, the public has become increasingly confused by the charges and counter-charges."[97]

Similar concerns were raised in other newspapers, whose headlines ranged from the dramatic "NAACP Branded Sterile, Barren Judge Bolin Rips Officers And Quits Job" (*New York Amsterdam News*) and "Justice Jane Bolin Quits NAACP: Blasts 'Contemptuous Attitude'" (*New York Age*) to "Judge Jane Bolin Quits NAACP: Protests Lack Of Power Of Vice President" (*The Call*). Every story, however, contained the sense that Bolin's resignation was expected. For example, the March 18 *New York Amsterdam News* story stated that Judge Bolin's resignation had been expected in New York circles since early in January when she was not returned to the board of directors.[98] On the same day, a *New York Age* article spoke of a "long simmering feud between Domestic Relations Justice Jane Bolin and national officers of the NAACP.[99] The notion that disunity continued within the association hierarchy certainly justified Wilkins's suspicion that the organization's ability to stand together in the long fight for African Americans was being questioned.

Wilkins was equally concerned that any further delay of comment from the board would place the association in a more embarrassing position should the conference with Bolin result in her return as vice president. Wilkins told Wright, "Suppose, in your conference with Judge Bolin, she should accept the invitation of the committee and agree to withdraw her resignation. Could the Association then issue any statement condemning her letter? Would we not be in the position of having begged a person to return to her office and thereby tied our hands to criticize her views publicly?"[100] In consideration of Wilkins's statements, and that scheduling further delayed the committee conference with Judge Bolin, the following comment by the chairman of the board was set for immediate press release:

> This action suggests strongly that Judge Bolin's principal purpose was not to discuss a point of difference with the Association and its Board, but to attack the organization itself.
>
> The ostensible reason for the writing of the letter and the tendering of her resignation as a vice president is the alleged fresh discovery by Judge Bolin that vice presidents of the NAACP do not have the power of directors of the NAACP, that is, they do not have the power to vote on issues. Judge Bolin's letter tries to give the impression that she was unaware of this, and that as soon as she discovered it she offered her resignation. In the light of several known facts and incidents, as well as in light of reasonable intelligence, it is doubtful that this contention is in good faith.[101]

The national office was not pleased with the type of coverage given to the board's response to Bolin's letter of resignation. Wilkins, however, was quite pleased with the manner in which the *Norfolk Journal and Guide* handled the whole matter. In a letter to Bernard Young of the *Journal and Guide,* Wilkins commended the paper for treating the board's response "as important news and in a manner calculated to give your readers a rounded picture of the situation." He lamented that "Eastern papers . . . gave Judge Bolin's letter front-page prominence," and carried the board's comment "on the next to the last page and the other tacked a few paragraphs on to another story over on an inside page."[102] The "Eastern papers" to which Wilkins referred were clearly the *New York Amsterdam News* and the *New York Age*. (The black press, as a tool of the African American community, was as involved in the matter of this controversy as well as in its dissemination. For obvious reasons, the *New York Amsterdam News* and other New York–based African American newspapers would have been sensitive to the position of the New York Branch of the NAACP.)[103]

For whatever reason other newspapers outside of New York seemed to favor Bolin's and the New York Branch's position. William Walker's "Down the Big Road" column in *The* [Cleveland] *Call and Post* of March 25, 1950, truly angered Wilkins. In a very bitter letter to Walker, he complained that although Walker had grasped Judge Bolin's "specious reasons for resigning as vice-president" and had published the board's reply, he chose nevertheless to continue to "heap praise upon Judge Bolin's calculated attack upon the Association."[104] Wilkins was truly incensed by Walker's article, feeling that it showed very little, if any understanding of the national office's position. Walker's article began as follows:

> Judge Jane Bolin of the New York City Domestic Relations Court, has done a real service to the NAACP by resigning. Her letter of resignation from the national board as one of its twenty vice-presidents, brings out into the open, most of the complaints hundreds of other members have been making but have not been able to get into public print as did Judge Bolin. . . . I congratulate Judge Bolin for having courage enough to resent being made a figurehead or stooge. The obvious reason for denying Judge Bolin the right to vote was because previously she had shown independence and voted her conscience rather than being a yes-member for an already agreed upon program.[105]

Bolin had pierced the veil of this corporate body from the inside out. In the process she had exposed the weaknesses of an organization that needed to be strong for all African Americans. Many, like Walker, praised her for her courage and commitment, but others harshly criticized her. Denton J. Brooks Jr. of New York City wrote to board chairman Louis Wright bemoaning just how grieved he was to read of "Judge Jane M. Bolin's attack on the NAACP." Brooks further complained that while he could not pretend to comment on any of the issues involved, he felt that "this method of airing differences can be more harmful than helpful."[106]

A memorandum from Charles H. White, NAACP member and self-proclaimed expert witness for the U.S. Justice Department on policies, program, activities, teachings, and philosophy of the Communist Party and front organizations since 1937, represented the tone of several pieces of communication sent to the national office and the newspapers regarding Bolin's letter of resignation. Addressed to the editor of the *Pittsburg Courier,* NAACP Acting Secretary Roy Wilkins, and New York Branch Secretary Charles A. Levy, the memorandum stated: "Justice Jane Bolin has resigned from the NAACP—I say GOOD RIDANCE. [*sic*] I hope she has the decency to resign as Justice of Family Court as well. It occurs to me that it is worth mentioning that Bolin, Delany, and Justine Wise Polier, all of Family Court NY City, are all bed fellows of such be kind to Commy causes as Justice Frankfurter of the Supreme Court showed for the traitor Alger Hiss. Not being able to use the NAACP for a Soviet Trojan Horse, they now hope to destroy it."[107]

Bolin's consistent activism on and off of the bench, at times with the help of her judicial colleagues Delany and Polier, had obviously ruffled the feathers of the more conservative board as well as branch membership of the NAACP and even of ordinary citizens. She considered this a small price to pay for "informing the membership of some internal conditions which appeared to me to need correction, if our Association is to be the effective and powerful instrument we want and need."[108]

Bolin's resignation stood firmly as did her criticism of the association's national leadership. Yet the board again nominated and elected Bolin as vice president at a subsequent meeting on January 2, 1951. Whether in response to membership pressure, internal pressure, or past service, the board seemed eager to make amends—or at least committed to having Judge Bolin, the nation's first and, at the time, only African American woman judge, counted among the names on their letterhead. In a letter to the chairman of the board, she thanked board members for their gracious action, and stated that her resignation in 1950 was a "considered decision reached after long thought and great deliberation." She resigned immediately from the 1951 vice presidency and reiterated, "My feeling has not changed that I do not care as a national officer to assume responsibility to the public for the Association's decisions when I am powerless to affect those decisions through voting."[109]

Judge Bolin risked more than a board membership and an NAACP vice presidency in her crusade to expose and hopefully correct inconsistencies in association proceedings and management. In her fight for participatory democracy she may have risked her livelihood and her career. She may even have risked reappointment to the bench by Mayor O'Dwyer. As discussed in chapter 4, her 1949 reappointment to the bench proved to be the most difficult, though evidence suggests that political reasons could have been the problem. Just as much evidence suggests that the entire NAACP controversy, complete with daily headlines, might have hardened O'Dwyer's reluctance to reappoint her. The O'Dwyer's era, according to Thomas Kessner, was the era of the Cold War mentality when fears led to House Un-American Activities Committee (HUAC) excesses, of the new conservatism, and of the passing of insurgency politics.[110]

Judge Bolin's dissident vocality was, therefore, as out of place in O'Dwyer's administration as it was within the NAACP. Duly purged from the NAACP board, and essentially silenced as a vice president, she had become persona non grata to the national office. Nevertheless, she spoke the loudest and risked the most as a national officer. Hubert Delany's years of activism placed him on the same philosophical plane as Bolin, yet interestingly, he eluded the "machinery" of the national office. Though many spirited exchanges occurred between him and the executive and acting secretary, none ever resulted in his banishment from the policy-making body. Maybe as a woman—an "unruly" woman—Bolin's insider status within the inner circle of NAACP national leadership was not as secure as Delany's.

Bolin's legacy with the NAACP has only just begun to unfold. Undoubtedly, it will be debated through her positioning as charter member, branch official, member of the board of directors, vice president, and persona non grata to the NAACP. Though the expansive contouring of her organizational life is susceptible to portrayal as conventional and insurgent, it was nonetheless characterized by her palpable commitment to the democratic ideals of the NAACP and the philosophy of participatory democracy, a brand of leadership frequently quoted but rarely realized. This chapter utilized the portrayal of insurgency to best answer the question raised in the beginning: How and why did Judge Bolin plummet to the depths of the association's disregard?

As the historical record is reassessed to reflect the contributions and significance of this little-known civil rights trailblazer, the question still remains: How did such a visible political subject become invisible to the historical eye?

Epilogue

Judge Jane Bolin retired from the Family Court of the State of New York on December 31, 1978, at age seventy, then the mandatory age for retirement. Her departure after four decades on the bench elicited as much media coverage as did her appointment as the nation's first African American woman judge in 1939. On the occasion of her retirement, however, there was some fanfare—unlike the occasion of her appointment. But characteristic of her humility and her relentless concern for civil rights, Judge Bolin asked that the tribute not focus on her but instead on the rights of children and minorities. Therefore, the event held December 7, 1978, to honor Bolin was a symposium that featured two civil rights scholar-activists, the Honorable A. Leon Higginbotham Jr. (U.S. Court of Appeals, Third Circuit), and Thomas I. Emerson, Lines Professor of Law of Yale Law School and former classmate of Bolin's at Yale. Higginbotham gave the keynote address on the continuing efforts to secure and enforce through judicial systems when necessary, the rights of children and minorities in twentieth-century America; then Emerson responded.[1]

The symposium was held at New York University School of Law in the Vanderbilt Auditorium, where approximately 150 of Bolin's colleagues gathered to honor her and discuss recent legislation, court decisions, and trends in the rights of children and minorities. This was a fitting tribute for a judge who spent her entire career fighting for the rights of the disempowered. It was a promise she made to herself as a young girl growing up in Poughkeepsie when her innocence was shattered by reports of lynching in the South. And it was a promise that she kept throughout her career even when the stakes were high. It came as a surprise to no one that she was not ready to leave the bench because she still had at least a generation of fight left in her. The Juvenile Offender Law enacted two years earlier that allowed children as young as thirteen to be charged as adults for felonies had shaken her confidence in the new philosophy of children's courts. Although enacted, she did not stop publicly denouncing its fundamental logic. One can only imagine the intensity of her opposition to its implementation in her courtroom had she remained on the bench.

Described as a "militant and a fighter" by judicial colleagues, Bolin's letters of protest that insisted on accountability for segregation present a good text of her progressivism. How she wielded the pen and the power of her office is therefore telling of her brand of activism. An integrationist of irreducible dedication, Jane Bolin mounted a veritable campaign against segregation yet managed to keep herself off the roster of civil rights trailblazers. The foregoing chapters in this book attest to her place on that roster and how she was etched onto it.

Jane Bolin's lived visibility as private practitioner, assistant corporation counsel, and Domestic Relations Court judge situates her in the professional and political milieu of New York City. A member of the professional elite, Judge Bolin was also in the mainstream of political activity, exercising legitimate authority to dispense justice and directly or indirectly "allocate the tangible benefits in our society" to one or more persons among several competing for them.[2] Moreover, as the first African American woman judge she became what one political scientist calls a "highly visible political minority" who stayed under the proverbial political microscope.[3] As a civil rights advocate, however, she used the authority of that political space to effect change beyond the corridors of the court, thereby placing herself in the midst of the city's early civil rights struggle.

The judiciary's usual conservatism may have disguised Bolin's activism and obscured its examination in the historical record. Historical invisibility, according to historian Ann Firor Scott, is the process by which "a significant phenomenon for which all the data have existed, much of it readily available," still remains almost totally hidden to historians.[4] In the case of Jane Bolin, the data that extols her activism have always existed in the very public instruments of press, profession, and organization. But if we see, as Scott contends, things we are prepared to see and overlook those we do not expect to encounter, then we can be oblivious to the unconventional—however visibly outspoken Bolin may have been.

Bolin's dissidence within the NAACP was not uncommon, but singular in its importance to an understanding of the place of African American women in the evolution of black organizational leadership. The scale of the 1949–50 controversy understood within the context of community solidarity has much to teach about the gender and class dynamics of dissidence and about her as a progressive member of the board. Who Jane Bolin was professionally clearly aroused the media interest in her criticism of and exit from the nation's premier civil rights organization. To be sure, the black press had earlier inscribed her onto the popular consciousness of the nation when she became the nation's first African American woman judge. Nevertheless, the black press had always worked in concert with the NAACP and other civil rights organizations "toward breaking down segregation and injustice for the Negro, court case by court case, boycott by boycott, and headline by headline," according to Amistead S. Pride and Clint C. Wilson II in their groundbreaking *A History of the Black Press*. And with each succeeding victory, they remind us, a price was paid, and sometimes "it was the pain of a race member going 'outside' to air criticisms that most preferred to keep within the ranks."[5]

Bolin had indeed transgressed convention and had been chided by many, though applauded by most. Nevertheless, standing firm against the solid male leadership of the NAACP national office was not easy; neither was being scapegoated for the near unraveling of the organization at a time when it was most desperately needed. Might this fallout have engendered a deliberate forgetting on her part and an overlooking on ours? In her interview with Jean Rudd (the only interview given), Bolin says very little about her involvement with the NAACP and never mentions the public controversy that ensued.[6] Might her reluctance to relive her contentious relationship with the NAACP national office or her willingness to marginalize it, in part have been what Deborah Gray White identifies as a manifestation of the black woman's perennial concern with image born of centuries of vilification?[7] Or might her avoidance be better understood through the lens of dissemblance or that "self-imposed invisibility" that black women so often employ to protect their inner lives?[8]

Bolin traveled extensively later in her life, visiting all the continents except Antarctica. She regretted not having done more traveling when she was younger, but attributed that restriction to having a young child. She was in her early fifties when she first traveled to Africa. The two-month trip took her from one coast to another, but her stay in Ghana and Kenya proved most memorable. Armed with letters of introduction from colleagues at the United Nations, Bolin met several leaders of the African community including African nationalists President Kwame Nkrumah of Ghana, President Jomo Kenyatta of Kenya, and Mrs. Mary Paitoo of Ghana, whose civic activities left Bolin convinced that "no one need feel uncertain about the future of any new country while there are people like you so devoted to the interests and welfare of other people."[9] Bolin possessed a genuine interest in the status of women and children in other countries and, not surprisingly, was among the few key people in the field of child welfare who were afforded an opportunity to meet with Indira Gandhi, during a brief visit to the United States, "for intensive discussion of problems of mutual interest."[10]

This transnational consciousness evoked in Bolin an early identification with the women of Haiti. In responding to a request from the head of the Haitian Bar for a report on the status of "Negro" women lawyers in the United States, Sadie Alexander was anxious to include Bolin as an African American woman lawyer who was engaged in active practice. The Haitian Bar had scheduled a first-ever discussion about the status of Haitian women at its conference in Port-au-Prince just months before Bolin's judicial appointment, and wanted to include information about the accomplishments of African American women lawyers. Bolin obliged with a thorough accounting of her legal education and practice, but cautioned that it was "in no attempt to arrogate any distinction to myself but only because I think it might prove encouraging to our Haitian women friends to know that new fields are opening to us."[11]

Bolin may or may not have been aware of the broader collaboration that existed between African Americans and Haitians in the 1930s on a range of issues from business to education. Still, her efforts and those of other African American women lawyers were consistent with what historian Millery Polyné describes as "a commitment by Haitians and U.S. blacks to a program of international racial uplift." Bolin's professional standing therefore inserted her into a wider discourse of uplift since, according to Polyné, "demonstrating achievement in the black diasporic world continued to be a significant activity as the Haitian government tried to reshape its image and rejuvenate its economy during the post–U.S.-occupation era."[12]

On the occasion of her retirement, Jane Bolin expressed gratitude to former Mayor Fiorello La Guardia for having the courage to appoint her to the bench forty years earlier in a very different social climate. What her record reveals is her own courage to inhabit that appointment with a progressive and effective brand of activism within that climate. Bolin will always be remembered as the nation's first African American woman judge. Upon her death in 2007, a year and three months shy of her one hundredth birthday, Bolin graced the headlines of the nation's magazines and newspapers as she had in 1939, and was reinscribed as the nation's first African American woman judge for another generation of Americans. An examination of her lived visibility and her place on the roster of early civil rights trailblazers, however, would have to wait.

Notes

Preface

1. Constance Baker Motley to Bolin, 26 January 1979, Bolin Papers, Box 3, Schomburg Center, New York City Public Library.

2. The Althusserian concept of interpellation, as discussed by Judith Butler, whereby a subject is constituted by being hailed, addressed, or named, is useful to my understanding of how Bolin moves from invisibility to visibility in the historical record. See especially, chapter 3 in Judith Butler, *Theories in Subjection: The Psychic Life of Power* (Stanford: Stanford University Press, 1997).

3. Kenneth Mack does an excellent job of theorizing black women's professionalization in the legal profession, and Bolin is squarely positioned in this process as a member of the second generation of black women lawyers. See generally, Kenneth W. Mack, "A Social History of Everyday Practice: Sadie T. M. Alexander and the Incorporation of Black Women into the American Legal Profession, 1925–1960," *Cornell Law Review* 87, no. 6 (September 2002): 1405–74.

4. Judith Butler's analysis of gender is instructive here in terms of general subject construction. Judith Butler, *Gender Trouble: Feminism and the Subversion of Identity* (New York: Routledge, 1990). Also, Sidonie Smith's essay, "Performativity, Autobiographical Practice, Resistance," in Sidonie Smith and Julia Watson, ed., *Women, Autobiography, Theory: A Reader* (Madison: University of Wisconsin Press, 1998): 108–15.

5. Jane Bolin's 1990 interview with Jean Rudd, Bolin Papers, Box 1, Schomburg Center, New York City Public Library.

6. Michelle M. Wright, *Becoming Black: Creating Identity in the African Diaspora* (Durham: Duke University Press, 2004), especially introduction and chapter 1.

7. Lawrence H. Mamiya and Patricia A. Kaurouma, ed., *For Their Courage and For Their Struggles: The Black Oral History Project of Poughkeepsie, New York* (Poughkeepsie, NY: Urban Center for Africana Studies, Vassar College, 1978); Denise Love Johnson, "Black Migration," *Poughkeepsie Bicentennial Forum* (New York: Poughkeepsie High School, June-July, 1976): 6.

8. Hilary Sommerlad, "The Gendering of the Professional Subject: Commitment, Choice and Social Closure in the Legal Profession," in Clare McGlynn, ed., *Legal Feminisms:Theory and Practice* (Burlington,VT: Ashgate Publishing Co., 1998), 3–20.

9. Joyce Ann Hughes, "The Black Portia," *The Crisis* (May 1975): 168. Kenneth Mack's work (as referenced in note 3) offers a most analytical examination of this unique positioning. However, earlier scholarship touched on the lives of black women lawyers, but without a full examination of their professionalization as was done in Mack's work. Karen Berger Morello's *The Invisible Bar:TheWoman Lawyer in America 1638 to the Present* (NewYork: Random House, 1986) dedicates a chapter to what she terms the "double impairment" faced by black women lawyers. J. Clay Smith Jr., *Emancipation:The Making of the Black Lawyer, 1844–1944* (Philadelphia: University of Pennsylvania Press, 1993) filled the void in the historical record as it pertained to black lawyers generally, but missed the mark on black women lawyers when it came to the particularity of their experience in the legal profession. But in Smith's *Rebels in Law:Voices in History of BlackWomen Lawyers* (Ann Arbor: University of Michigan Press, 1998), an edited collection of articles that includes the voices of early black women in the law, we hear directly from black women in the legal profession.

10. See Butler, *Psychic Life of Power,* especially the introduction and chapter 3.

11. Ibid, 11. Emphasis in original.

12. Geraldine Joncich Clifford, "Women's Liberation and Women's Professions: Reconsidering the Past, Present, and Future," in John Mack Faragher and Florence Howe, ed., *Women and Higher Education in American History: Essays from the Mount Holyoke College Sesquicentennial Symposia* (NewYork:W.W. Norton, 1988), 165–182.

Chapter 1. Her Standing in Poughkeepsie

1. Interview with Jean Rudd, 1990, Bolin Papers, Box 1, Schomburg Center, New York City Public Library.

2. The elder Bolin's Christian name is at times spelled "Abram" and at other times "Abraham." I have chosen the former spelling because that appears on photographic references although "Abraham" appears on Gaius Bolin's "Vital Statistics" student form at Williams College. Alumni Records, Gaius C. Bolin folder, Alumni Office, Williams College, Williamstown, MA.

3. Donald L. Robinson, *Slavery in the Structure of American Politics, 1765–1820* (New York: Harcourt Brace Jovanovich, Inc., 1971), 36.

4. Lawrence H. Mamiya and Patricia A. Kaurouma, ed., *For Their Courage and For Their Struggles:The Black Oral History Project of Poughkeepsie, NewYork* (Poughkeepsie, NY: Urban Center for Africana Studies,Vassar College, 1978), 2–4. Also, Denise Love Johnson, "Black Migration," *Poughkeepsie Bicentennial Forum* (New York: Poughkeepsie High School, June-July, 1976): 6.

5. Interview with Jean Rudd, 1990, Bolin Papers, Box 1; Alumni Records, Gaius C. Bolin folder; Dorothy W. Thomson, "51 Years a Lawyer," *Poughkeepsie Sunday NewYorker,* 22 November 1943.

6. Thomson, "51 Years a Lawyer"; *Poughkeepsie Daily Eagle,* 21 April 1910.

7. Ibid.

8. Ibid. By 1872, the College Hill Reservoir was built when the Hudson River became the supply for the city water system as opposed to Poughkeepsie's earlier reliance on cisterns and wells as sources of water for domestic use. See Joyce C. Ghee and Joan Spence, *Images of America, Poughkeepsie: Halfway up the Hudson* (Charleston, SC: Arcadia Publishing, 1997), 65.

9. His son remembers him with great pride in an interview done for a newspaper article. See Thomson, "51 Years a Lawyer."

10. Carleton Mabee, "Toussaint College: A Proposed Black College For New York State in the 1870's," *Afro-Americans in New York Life and History* (January 1977): 25–35.

11. Ibid.

12. Ibid., 27.

13. Ibid., 26.

14. Mamiya and Kaurouma, *For Their Courage,* 88.

15. Mabee, "Toussaint College," 26.

16. Ibid. Since the admission of African Americans was the result of a Republican administration directive rather than the result of institutional reform, Smith's ostracism was to be expected.

17. Ibid., 27

18. Ibid., 28

19. Millery Polyné, *From Douglass to Duvalier: U.S. African Americans, Haiti, and Pan Americanism, 1870–1964* (Gainesville: University Press of Florida, 2010), 87–88.

20. Mabee, "Toussaint College," 29–30.

21. Ibid., 29–32.

22. Ibid., 32–33.

23. Ibid., 26.

24. Ibid., 31.

25. *Poughkeepsie Daily Eagle,* 20, 21 April 1910; *New York Age,* 28 April 1910. The *Poughkeepsie Daily Eagle* reported that the funeral services were very impressive and touching, and particularly so "when Mr. Bolin's aged widow, very ill and infirm had to be carried in the arms of her sons to his casket to look at him for the last time in the home where they had lived together for fifty-three of the fifty-six years of their married life."

26. Thomson, "51 Years a Lawyer."

27. Ibid.

28. Dennis Dickerson, "Success Story. . . . With a Difference," *Williams Alumni Review* (Fall 1979): 3.

29. Thomson, "51 Years a Lawyer."

30. Ibid. Up to 1870 few African Americans in New York had attended college; few were adequately prepared academically and fewer still had the necessary funds to attend the handful of colleges that admitted blacks. These conditions no doubt influenced Abram's efforts to found a black college.

31. Dickerson, "Success Story," 3; Thomson, "51 Years a Lawyer." Gaius Bolin was followed one year later by his brother, Livingsworth Wilson, and in 1948 by his grandson Lionel (his son's child).

32. W. E. B. Du Bois, ed., *The College Bred Negro* (Atlanta: Atlanta University Press, 1900), 14, 29–30, 38–39.

33. Dickerson, "Success Story," 3–4; Edwin C. Andrews, comp., *Fifty Years After: A Report of the Class of 1889, Williams College* (Williamsiana), 7.

34. Dickerson, "Success Story," 3–4

35. Ibid.

36. Theodore Roosevelt to Gaius C. Bolin, 16 April 1899; Gaius C. Bolin to Theodore

Roosevelt, 18 April 1899, Theodore Roosevelt Papers, Library of Congress, Manuscript Division, Washington, DC. It is interesting that Bolin was appointed to the position for which he had recommended Charles W. Anderson to the governor. Anderson was a black Republican leader in the state who had joined the chorus of black leaders demanding that the governor appoint more blacks to state offices. It might explain why in responding to the governor, Bolin promised to keep the governor's letter and nomination "entirely confidential." For a discussion of Governor Roosevelt and blacks, see Thomas G. Dyer, *Theodore Roosevelt and the Idea of Race* (Baton Rouge: Louisiana State University Press, 1980), 89–122.

37. William H. Loos, Ami M. Savigny, Robert M. Gurn, and Lillian Serece Williams, *The Forgotten "Negro Exhibit": African American Involvement in Buffalo's Pan-American Exposition, 1901* (Buffalo, NY: Buffalo & Erie County Public Library and the Library Foundation of Buffalo & Erie County, 2001). Theodore Roosevelt to P. Butler Thompkins, 5 July 1899, Theodore Roosevelt Papers; *Journal of the Senate of the State of New York, 132nd Session*, vol. 2 (Albany: Wynkoop, Hallenbeck, & Crawford Company, 1899), 1532. Bolin's fellow board members were Daniel T. Lockwood, Buffalo, who was also designated as president of the board of general managers; Jacob Amos, Syracuse; Nicholas V. V. Franchot, Olean; William H. Gelshenen, New York City; Frederick Greiner, Buffalo; John T. Mott, Oswego; Leopold Stern, New York City; and George E. Vost, Theresa.

38. Dickerson, "Success Story," 4–5; Gaius C. Bolin to Theodore Roosevelt, 11 April 1900; Theodore Roosevelt to Gaius C. Bolin, 12 April 1900, Theodore Roosevelt Papers.

39. Thomson, "51 Years a Lawyer."

40. Dickerson, "Success Story," 4; Mamiya and Kaurouma, *For Their Courage*, 82; interview with Jean Rudd, 1990, Bolin Papers, Box 1.

41. Interview with Jean Rudd, 1990, Bolin Papers, Box 1.

42. Dickerson, "Success Story," 5.

43. Interview with Jean Rudd, 1990, Bolin Papers, Box 1; Dickerson, "Success Story," 5.

44. Letter from Jane Bolin to Dennis Dickerson, 2 February 1979, Bolin Papers, Box 3, Correspondence Folder; Letter from Gaius Bolin Jr. to William Pickens, 30 August 1931, NAACP Branch Files, Poughkeepsie, New York folder, 1932–34, NAACP Papers, Library of Congress, Manuscript Division, Washington, DC.

45. Mamiya and Kaurouma, *For Their Courage*, 6.

46. Ibid. Also, for a general discussion of this type of approach to social change see Richard Pierce, *Polite Protest: The Political Economy of Race in Indianapolis, 1920–1970* (Bloomington: Indiana University Press, 2005.)

47. Letter from William Pickens to Ivy Bolin, 7 October 1935, NAACP Papers, Branch Records, Manuscript Division, Library of Congress.

48. Dickerson, "Success Story," 11.

49. Untitled newspaper article without author. Bolin Papers, Box 3, Clipping File.

50. Bolin Papers, Box 1, Biographical Folder.

51. Jim Haviland, "Local Attorneys Recall First Black to Head County Bar," *Poughkeepsie Journal*, 28 February 1991.

52. Interview with Jean Rudd, 1990, Bolin Papers, Box 1.

53. Ibid.

54. Ibid.

55. Ibid.

56. Ibid.

57. Ibid.

58. Ibid.

59. Ibid.

60. Ibid.

61. Ibid. The *Chicago Defender,* founded by Robert Abbott in 1905, became a daily in 1956—the fifty-second black newspaper to do so. With its published letters, news, and employment advertisements, the *Defender* was largely responsible for the "Great Northern Drive" of southern black people. The *Pittsburgh Courier,* first published in 1910, was headed by Robert Lee Vann who guided the paper to a commanding position in the 1930s. Some of the highlights of its record include the launching of a self-respect program tied in with the protest against the racial caricatures in the "Amos 'n' Andy" radio show, and an all-out campaign to give blacks fuller recognition in the armed forces. The *Baltimore Afro-American* was born in 1892 out of the union of three small church newsletters: the *Ledger,* a church and community newspaper run by Dr. George Bragg, pastor of Baltimore's St. James Episcopal Church; the *Sunday School Helper,* started by John H. Murphy, Sunday school superintendent at the St. John A.M.E. Church, as a vehicle for uniting state Sunday schools; and the *Afro-American,* published by the Reverend William Alexander, pastor of Sharon Baptist Church, to advertise his church and community enterprises. See generally, Armistead Pride and Clint Wilson, *A History of the Black Press* (Washington, DC: Howard University Press, 1997.)

62. Interview with Jean Rudd, 1990, Bolin Papers, Box 1.

63. Letter from Jane M. Bolin to Honorable Justine W. Polier, 24 October 24 1978, Bolin Papers, Box 1.

64. Interview with Jean Rudd, 1990, Bolin Papers, Box 1.

65. Ibid.; speech presented in honor of the pioneer role of Dr. W. E. B. Du Bois by the Schomburg Center, Bolin Papers, Box 3, "Speeches" Folder.

66. Interview with Jean Rudd, 1990, Bolin Papers, Box 1.

67. Ibid.

68. "Wellesley in My Life," in *Wellesley After-Images,* Bolin Papers, Box 1.

Chapter 2. On Her Own

1. Ralph Ellison, *Invisible Man* (Vintage International, 1952), 402.

2. During the 1927–28 academic year, educator and social reformer Charlotte Hawkins Brown was a "special student" at Wellesley. However, at age forty-four and a non-degree-seeking student able to choose any courses she wished including graduating courses, Brown would not have socialized with Bolin nor Ruth Allison Brown or Lillian Lee Washington, the other black women in the undergraduate class of 1928. See *Black Alumnae List: 1887–1970,* compiled by Elizabeth Miranda, April 2002, Wellesley College.

3. Oberlin College, in 1833, was the first institution of higher education to admit all students regardless of race or sex—although, women here took a shortened literary course in accordance with the belief that their minds could not assimilate the same fare as men's and the belief that their education better prepared them for intelligent motherhood. In 1837, with the founding of Mount Holyoke, the concept of improved education for women took hold, and later developments in the nineteenth century saw the opening of Vassar (1861), Smith (1871), and Wellesley (1870), and Radcliffe (1879). See Helen Lefkowitz Horowitz,

Alma Mater: Design and Experience in the Women's Colleges from Their Nineteenth-Century Beginnings to the 1930s (Amherst: University of Massachusetts Press, 1984), especially chap. 3; also D. Kelly Weisberg, "Barred From the Bar: Women and Legal Education in the United States, 1870–1890," in D. Kelly Weisberg, ed., *Women and the Law: A Social Historical Perspective, Volume II* (Cambridge, MA: Schenkman, 1982), 246–48.

4. Horowitz, *Alma Mater,* chap. 3.

5. Interview with Jean Rudd, 1990, Bolin Papers, Box 1, Schomburg Center, New York City Public Library.

6. Carleton Mabee, "Toussaint College: A Proposed Black College For New York State in the 1870's," *Afro-Americans in New York Life and History* (January 1977): 26.

7. Ruth Ann Stewart, *Portia: The Life of Portia Washington Pittman, the Daughter of Booker T. Washington* (Garden City, NY: Doubleday and Company, Inc., 1977), 41–42.

8. Interview with Jean Rudd, 1990, Bolin Papers, Box 1.

9. Ibid.

10. Katherine Freedman, "The History of African-Americans at Wheaton College: 1834–1950," Ethnic Time Lines, 6–8, Madeleine Clark Wallace Library, Wheaton College, Norton, MA.

11. Ibid.

12. Bolin, "Wellesley in My Life," 91, in *Wellesley After-Images,* Bolin Papers, Box 1.

13. Ibid.; interview with Jean Rudd, 1990, Bolin Papers, Box 1.

14. Evelyn Brooks Higginbotham, "African-American Women's History and the Metalanguage of Race," *Signs* 17, no. 2 (Winter 1992): 255.

15. See general discussion in Richard B. Markham, "Blacks at Wellesley Discover Indifference Swallows Its Own Children," *The Harvard Crimson,* 19 December 1968; "Wellesley Class of '73," *Ebony* (August 1973).

16. Bolin, "Wellesley in My Life," 91. Historian Wilma King discusses a similar instance of ostracism involving Shawnee students and African Americans at Hampton Institute in the early decades of the twentieth century when Hampton experimented with the multicultural education of African Americans and American Indians. In one particular case when segregated dining rooms gave way to segregated tables and there was insufficient space at the "Indian table," an Indian student chose not to eat rather than eat at the "colored table." See "Multicultural Education at Hampton Institute—The Shawnees: A Case Study, 1900–1923," *Journal of Negro Education* 57 (1988): 524.

17. Bolin, "Wellesley in My Life," 91; interview with Jean Rudd, 1990, Bolin Papers, Box 1.

18. Letter from Jane M. Bolin to Honorable Justine W. Polier, 24 October 1978, Bolin Papers, Box 1.

19. "Mammy" became a national symbol of perfect domesticity, immortalized by Hollywood, at the very time that millions of black women were leaving the cotton fields of the South in search of employment in northern urban areas. See generally, Kenneth W. Goings, *Mammy and Uncle Mose: Black Collectibles and American Stereotyping* (Bloomington: Indiana University Press, 1994); and Micki McElya, *Clinging to Mammy: The Faithful Slave in Twentieth-Century America* (Cambridge: Harvard University Press, 2007).

20. Deborah Gray White, *Ar'n't I A Woman?: Female Slaves in the Plantation South* (New York: W. W. Norton & Company, 1985), 165; also, bell hooks, *Ain't I A Woman: Black Women and Feminism* (Boston: South End Press, 1992), 83–85. Cheryl Thurber aptly points out that such myths

offered a way of praising the past and dealing with a younger generation of blacks that was viewed as "uppity." See Thurber, "The Development of the Mammy Image and Mythology," in Virginia Bernhard, et al., ed., *Southern Women: Histories and Identities* (Columbia: University of Missouri Press, 1992),

21. McElya, *Clinging to Mammy,* 3, 259.

22. Bolin, "Wellesley in My Life," 91.

23. Ibid.

24. Ibid.

25. Interview with Jean Rudd, 1990, Bolin Papers, Box 1.

26. Ibid.

27. Bolin, "Wellesley in My Life," 92.

28. Interview with Jean Rudd, 1990, Bolin Papers, Box 1.

29. Bolin, "Wellesley in My Life," 92.

30. As quoted in Gerda Lerner, ed., *Black Women in White America: A Documentary History* (New York: Vintage Books, 1973), 332.

31. J. Clay Smith Jr., *Emancipation: The Making of the Black Lawyer, 1844–1944* (Philadelphia: University of Pennsylvania Press, 1993), 613.

32. See Sadie Tanner Mossell Alexander, "Women as Practitioners of Law in the United States," *National Bar Journal* 1 (1941): 56, 61.

33. J. Clay Smith, Jr., ed., *Rebels in Law: Voices in History of Black Women Lawyers* (Ann Arbor: University of Michigan Press, 1998), 284–86.

34. As quoted in Lerner, *Black Women in White America,* 330.

35. Interview with Jean Rudd, 33–34, Bolin Papers, Box 1.

36. Gaius Bolin's less-than-progressive perspective reflected the sentiment of many men and of many of the nation's law schools, and was not unlike that held half a century earlier by Justice Joseph P. Bradley in the infamous *Bradwell* case of 1872, in which he reasoned that "the natural and proper timidity and delicacy which belongs to the female sex" make it unfit for a career in the law. See *Bradwell v. The State,* 83 U.S. 130 (1872); see also Jeanne Noble, "The Higher Education of Black Woman," in John Mack Faragher and Florence Howe, ed., *Women in Higher Education in American History: Essays from the Mount Holyoke College Sesquicentennial Symposia* (New York: W. W. Norton, 1988), 87–106.

37. "Speech in honor of Du Bois," Bolin Papers, Box 3.

38. Ibid.

39. Bolin, "Wellesley in My Life," 92.

40. "Speech in honor of Du Bois," Bolin Papers, Box 3.

41. Some women were not as fortunate as Jane Bolin. Dr. May Edward Chin, born in 1896, and the only woman doctor in Harlem for fifty years, recalled that her father was deeply embarrassed by her educational pursuits and not only discouraged her but provided no financial support because he believed that "a girl that went to college became a queer woman." See Linda M. Perkins, "The Education of Black Women in the Nineteenth Century," in Faragher and Howe, *Women in Higher Education,* 83–84.

42. Willard Gatewood's study of the black elite suggests a demonstrated continuity in the educational achievement among upper-class blacks. He maintains that "a considerable correlation existed between upper-class status and educational achievement in the black community in the forty years following Reconstruction, as it did in previous generations," essentially

because literate blacks reinforced their claims to positions at the top of the class structure by "perpetuating traditions of educational achievement." This is not to suggest that class mobility was the impetus for educational achievements in the black community. The issue of education for African Americans in the decades after Reconstruction had much to do with uplifting, of course, but not so much with individual uplifting as with race or community uplift. The complexity of the pursuit of education within the black community therefore cannot be sidestepped for the facility of a simple class analysis more suited to the white middle-class model. Further, that an overwhelming number of black leaders came from the "learned" class does not in and of itself suggest that education was pursued to secure leadership status within the black community, since leadership within the black community was not limited to the professional class of teachers, lawyers, and ministers, but also included laborers, washerwomen, and farmers, as was the case with Abram Bolin in the nineteenth century. See generally, Willard B. Gatewood, *Aristocrats of Color: The Black Elite, 1880–1920* (Bloomington: Indiana University Press, 1990); Stephanie Shaw, *What A Woman Ought to Be and to Do: Black Professional Women Workers during the Jim Crow Era* (Chicago: University of Chicago Press, 1996); Kevin Gaines, *Uplifting the Race: Black Leadership, Politics, and Culture in the Twentieth Century* (Chapel Hill: University of North Carolina Press, 1996).

43. Interview with Jean Rudd, 72, 1990, Bolin Papers, Box 1.

44. Karen Berger Morello, *The Invisible Bar: The Woman Lawyer in America 1638 to the Present* (New York: Random House, 1986), especially chap. 6 (145).

45. "Race Uplift" took on an additional obligation for black college women as they were to advance the educational goals and moral character of the race, the implication being that teaching was the only acceptable way for black women to enter the public arena and still somehow maintain their virtue. See, Noble, "The Higher Education of Black Women," 91.

46. As quoted in Smith, *Emancipation*, 405.

47. Bolin, "Wellesley in My Life," 92.

48. Ibid.

49. Ibid. Today, Wellesley boasts an impressively large population of black women that engenders a forum for debate about the lingering issue of the sisterhood of women at Wellesley.

50. Interview with Jean Rudd, 1990, Bolin Papers, Box 1.

51. Louise Overacker to Jane Bolin, 10 September 1974, Bolin Papers, Box 1.

52. Darlene Clark Hine, "Rape and the Inner Lives of Southern Black Women: Thoughts on the Culture of Dissemblance," in Virginia Bernhard, Betty Brandon, Elizabeth Fox-Genovese, and Theda Perdue, ed., *Southern Women: Histories and Identities* (Columbia: University of Missouri Press, 1992), 182–83.

53. Ellison, *Invisible Man*, 402. Here I offer a paraphrasing of the Ellison's words, "Outside the Brotherhood we were outside history, but inside of it they didn't see us."

54. Wayne Hobson, *The American Legal Profession and the Organizational Society, 1890–1930* (New York: Garland Publishing, Inc., 1986), 104–6.

55. Cynthia Fuchs Epstein, *Women in Law* (New York: Basic Books, 1981), 49. See also Morello, *Invisible Bar*, 89.

56. Morello, *Invisible Bar*, 89.

57. Epstein, *Women in Law*, 49–51.

58. A reading of sociologist Linden Lewis's theorizing on the status of poor whites in Barbados is instructive here. See generally, Linden Lewis, "The Contestation of Race in Barbadian Society

and the Camouflage of Conservatism," in Brian Meeks and Folke Lindahl, ed., *New Caribbean Thought: A Reader* (Kingston, Jamaica: University of the West Indies Press, 2001), 144–95.

59. Smith, *Emancipation,* 37. Nathan Young was elected to the debating club, the first black student elected to such a position. This phenomenon of individual black students excelling during periods of segregation needs analysis that gets to the psychology of inclusion within communities of men and communities of women and how they differ. Also, evidence of "first" does little to enhance our understanding of the numbers of others who were excluded. For every black student admitted to a northern institution, literally hundreds with equal ability were denied a legal education.

60. Before Yale Law School voted to admit women, a white woman, Alice Jordan, managed to take advantage of a loophole in the school's policy and negotiated her admission in 1885. It appears that the men who had drafted Yale's catalog had not anticipated a woman applicant, and therefore were not specific about those who would be excluded. However, subsequent to the "Jordan incident" as it became known, Yale's policy of exclusion became unambiguous as to sex. See Morello, *Invisible Bar,* 90–92, 106.

61. David Margolick, "In Retrospect, Father Didn't Know Best in the Case of a Daughter With a Habit of Making History," *New York Times,* 14 May 1993.

62. Bolin's frequent reference to "Southern" students both at Wellesley and Yale appear to be more of a reference to the racist behavior of the students than their region of origin.

63. Interview with Jean Rudd, 24–25, Bolin Papers, Box 1.

64. Ibid., 67–68.

65. Morello, *Invisible Bar,* 106–7.

66. Hilary Sommerlad, "The Gendering of the Professional Subject: Commitment, Choice and Social Closure in the Legal Profession," in Clare McGlynn, ed., *Legal Feminisms: Theory and Practice* (Burlington, VT: Ashgate Publishing Co., 1998), 5.

Chapter 3. Politics of Preparation

1. In 1912, the inadvertent admission of three black male lawyers to the ABA led the organization to adopt a resolution that effectively barred African Americans from its membership for the next three decades. It was not until 1943 that the official action that barred African Americans was in effect rescinded. See Geraldine R. Segal, *Blacks in the Law: Philadelphia and the Nation* (Philadelphia: University of Pennsylvania Press, 1983), 17–18.

2. Beverly Blair Cook, "Women as Judges," in Beverly Blair Cook, et al., *Women in the Judicial Process* (Washington, DC: American Political Science Association, 1987), 9.

3. The Fourteenth Amendment brought African Americans into the national polity as citizens in 1868; the Fifteenth Amendment guaranteed male suffrage regardless of race in 1870; and the Nineteenth Amendment guaranteed white female suffrage in 1920. But it took a civil rights movement and several civil rights acts later in the twentieth century to ensure the guarantees of those amendments.

4. This sociological study of professionalism shows that the development of specialized roles and functions within professions is broadly determined by the inseparable and dependent structure of inequality, since a political system is only as egalitarian and representative as the society in which it is based. Magali Sarfatti Larson, *The Rise of Professionalism: A Sociological Analysis* (Berkeley: University of California Press, 1977), 2.

5. Cynthia Fuchs Epstein, *Women in Law* (New York: Basic Books, Inc., 1981), 303.

6. Segal, *Blacks in the Law,* 17–20, 97.

7. Segal, *Blacks in the Law,* 18; Edward J. Littlejohn and Donald L. Hobson, *Black Lawyers, Law Practice, and Bar Associations—1844 to 1970: A Michigan History* (Detroit: Wolverine Bar Association, 1987), 57; see also a discussion of the early black bar and their responsibility to social justice in Darlene Clark Hine, *Black Victory: The Rise and Fall of the White Primary in Texas* (Millwood, NY: KTO Press, 1979).

8. *New York Herald Tribune,* 18 April 1943.

9. Epstein, *Women in Law,* 80.

10. By 1950 there was still only one black woman judge, and of the 6,271 women lawyers, only 83 were African American. And of these 19 were in New York, 13 in Illinois, and 10 in Washington, D.C. The 1950 U.S. Census as cited in J. Clay Smith, Jr., ed., *Rebels in Law: Voices in History of Black Women Lawyers* (Ann Arbor: University of Michigan Press, 1998), 284–86; Alvin E. White, "Women Judges," *Dawn Magazine* (26 October 1974): 4; "Why Aren't There More Women Judges," *The Afro-American* (21 February 1959): 1, 7.

11. See generally, Smith, *Rebels in Law;* Karen Berger Morello, *The Invisible Bar: The Woman Lawyer in America 1638 to the Present* (New York: Random House, 1986); Epstein, *Women in Law;* Segal, *Blacks in the Law.*

12. See Sadie Tanner Mossell Alexander, "Women as Practitioners of Law in the United States," 1 *National Bar Journal* 56 (1941): 61; letter from Jane Bolin to Sadie T. Mosell Alexander, 25 April 1939, Sadie Tanner Mossell Alexander Papers, University of Pennsylvania Archives, Box 13, Folder 17.

13. Segal, *Blacks in the Law,* 31; Kenneth Mack, "A Social History of Everyday Practice: Sadie T. M. Alexander and the Incorporation of Black Women into the American Legal Profession, 1925–1960," *Cornell Law Review* 87, no. 6 (2002): 1406.

14. Morello, *Invisible Bar,* 150–53. Carter is also referred to as "Mrs. Lisle Carter" in Smith, *Rebels in Law.*

15. White, "Women Judges."

16. Smith, *Rebels in Law,* 284–85, as reported in the 1950 census.

17. Darlene Clark Hine, "Black Lawyers and the Twentieth-Century Struggle for Constitutional Change," in *African Americans and the Living Constitution,* ed. John Hope Franklin and Genna Rae McNeil (Washington, DC, and London: Smithsonian Institution Press, 1995), 41; Littlejohn and Hobson, *Black Lawyers,* 2–53; see generally J. Clay Smith, *Emancipation: The Making of the Black Lawyer, 1844–1944* (Philadelphia: University of Pennsylvania Press, 1993); Segal, *Blacks in the Law.*

18. Morello, *Invisible Bar,* 197.

19. Littlejohn and Hobson, *Black Lawyers,* 8.

20. Hine, "Black Lawyers, 41, 47; Segal, *Blacks in the Law,* 17; Charles J. Ogletree, "Blind Justice?: Race, The Constitution, and the Justice System," in *African Americans and the Living Constitution,* ed. John Hope Franklin and Genna Rae McNeil (Washington, DC, and London: Smithsonian Institution Press, 1995), 235–69. Ogletree finds that their citizenship history and their experiences in the justice system have informed their beliefs and fears.

21. Among the black women who secured employment in government agencies are Pauli Murray, who was California assistant attorney general in 1946; Eunice Hunton Carter who, for

ten years, was assistant district attorney in New York City; and Edith Sampson, who became Illinois's first black woman assistant state attorney in 1947. *Ebony Magazine* 2 (August 1947), 19; see also J. Clay Smith, *Emancipation*.

22. Hine, "Black Lawyers," 41; Littlejohn and Hobson, *Black Lawyers,* 7–22.

23. Hine, "Black Lawyers."

24. See generally, Segal, *Blacks in the Law;* Smith, *Rebels in Law;* Morello, *Invisible Bar.*

25. Smith, *Emancipation,* 632.

26. Gaius Charles Jr. attended Howard University and Amherst College before law school, and remained in Poughkeepsie until his retirement, becoming counsel for the Poughkeepsie Housing Authority. Bolin Papers, Schomburg Center, New York City Public Library, Box 1, Biographical File.

27. Morello, *Invisible Bar,* 147.

28. Segal, *Blacks in the Law,* 31.

29. Interview with Jean Rudd, Bolin Papers, Box 1, Schomburg Center, New York City Public Library.

30. Ibid.

31. Without specific evidence about why her brother remained in Poughkeepsie practicing until retirement, one can speculate that as the son, he was naturally positioned to be his father's rightful successor. In *Women Lawyers: Rewriting the Rules* (New York: A.A. Knopf: 1993), Mona Harrington writes about the passing of power and authority from one generation to the next, and highlights the "unnatural" place of the daughter as her father's "rightful successor" (70).

32. Interview with Jean Rudd, 25–27, Bolin Papers, Box 1.

33. Ibid.

34. Ronald H. Bayor, *Fiorello La Guardia: Ethnicity and Reform* (Arlington Heights, IL: Harlan Davidson, 1993), 16–18, 85–90.

35. As quoted in ibid., 95.

36. The term "New Negro" comes from Howard University professor Alain Locke's edited volume of black literature by the same name, but the term came to signify a new more militant generation of African Americans who exalted black culture even as they demanded full citizenship. See Alain Locke, ed., *The New Negro: Voices of the Harlem Renaissance* (New York: Albert and Charles Boni, Inc., 1925).

37. David Margolick, "At the Bar," *New York Times,* 14 May 1993, B8-L.

38. Interview with Jean Rudd, Bolin Papers, Box 1; *New York Times,* 29 January 1944, 7A.

39. "Lady Lawyers," *Ebony* (August 1947): 18–21.

40. *Poughkeepsie New Yorker,* 23 February 1944.

41. *Ebony* (August 1947).

42. Letter from Gaius Charles Bolin Jr. to Dennis Dickerson, 27 December 1978, Bolin Papers, Box 1.

43. See generally Mack, "A Social History," 1405–74.

44. Littlejohn and Hobson, *Black Lawyers.*

45. Interview with Jean Rudd, Bolin Papers, Box 1.

46. Ibid., 8–9. The fact that she identifies prejudice with region speaks to her understanding or expectations of the progressive North versus the Jim Crow South.

47. Ibid.

48. Bayor, *Fiorello La Guardia*, 102.

49. Thomas Kessner, *Fiorello H. La Guardia and the Making of Modern New York* (New York: McGraw-Hill Publishing Company, 1989), 261, 275.

50. Ibid.

51. Ibid., 275.

52. Morello, *Invisible Bar*, 150–52; "Mrs. Carter Seen as Only Negro Appointee," *New York Amsterdam News*, 10 August 1935, 1; "Dewey Gives Post to Harlem Lawyer," *New York Times*, 6 August 1935, 3; "Negro Lawyer Will be Placed on Dewey Staff for Racket Inquiry," *New York Amsterdam News*, 3 August 1935, 1. Carter had discovered in the course of her prosecutions as assistant district attorney that organized crime controlled prostitution in New York City. When she shared this information with Special Prosecutor Dewey, he immediately hired her as a member of his special prosecution team, of which she was the only African American and woman.

53. Morello, *Invisible Bar*, 150–52.

54. Emphasis mine. Sadie Alexander to Eunice H. Carter, 28 April 1939, Sadie Alexander Papers, University of Pennsylvania Archives, 50, A3745, Box 13, Folder 17.

55. Smith, *Rebels in Law*, 18; "Political Graveyard: Black Politicians in New York," n. d., http:// www. Politicalgraveyard.com/geo/NY/black.html.

56. Francis E. Rivers, "Negro Judges for Harlem," *The Crisis* (November 1930): 377.

57. Mason C. Hutchins, ed., *The New York Red Book: 1937* (Albany, NY: J.B. Lyon Company, 1937), 468. The growing strength of the Democratic Party in the cities and the New Deal's responsiveness to social distress combined to make Roosevelt the champion of the urban masses, which included a majority of African Americans.

58. Beverly B. Cook, "Women Judges in the Opportunity Structure," in Laura L. Crites and Winifred L. Hepperle, ed., *Women, the Courts, and Equity* (Newbury Park, CA: Sage Publications, 1987), 143–74. Also see generally, Cook, "Women Judges: The End of Tokenism," in Winifred L. Hepperle and Laura Crites, ed., *Women in the Courts* (Williamsburg, VA: National Center for State Courts, 1978), 84–105.

59. Cook, "Women Judges in the Opportunity Structure," 143–74.

60. Kessner, *La Guardia,* 34.

61. Interview with Jean Rudd, 8, Bolin Papers, Box 1. Gilbert Osofsky explains that although black Republicans composed a majority in the nineteenth and twenty-first assembly districts through most of the 1920s, sometimes the efforts to elect black Republicans in these districts were defeated when blacks joined with the white minority to vote against black insurgents. However, the main problem, according to Osofsky, was political geography that placed those districts in the larger twenty-first congressional district, which included three solidly white and traditionally Democratic assembly districts. See generally, Gilbert Osofsky, *Harlem: The Making of a Ghetto, Negro New York, 1890–1930* (New York: Harper and Row, 1966), 174–77.

62. Dennis Dickerson, "Success Story. . . . With a Difference," *Williams Alumni Review* (Fall 1979): 4–5; Dorothy W. Thomson, "51 Years a Lawyer," *Poughkeepsie Sunday New Yorker,* 22 November 1943. In 1936 almost three-fourths of African American voters voted for Roosevelt, and although 67 percent supported Roosevelt in 1940, only 42 percent identified as Democrats. See Steven F. Lawson, *Running for Freedom: Civil Rights and Black Politics in America Since 1941* (Malden, MA: Wiley-Blackwell, 2009), 18.

63. Kessner argues that when La Guardia failed to win against Michael Farley in 1914 as

a Republican in the Fourteenth Congressional District, his spirited effort, however unsuccessful, attracted the attention of party veterans whose patronage later propelled him into congressional service and the mayoralty. Kessner, *La Guardia,* 34–35.

64. As quoted in Osofsky, *Harlem,* 159, 172; Rivers, "Negro Judges for Harlem," 377, 393.

65. La Guardia's "fusion" administration reflected political diversity, but the same could not be said about the racial diversity of his early administration. Kessner, *La Guardia,* 274–79.

66. Ibid., 368–77; for discussion of the 1943 riot see also Dominic Capeci, *The Harlem Riot of 1943* (Philadelphia: Temple University Press, 1977).

67. "New York's First Black Woman Judge Retires," *American Bar Association Journal* (June 1979).

68. Ibid.; Kessner, *La Guardia,* 275.

69. Osofsky, *Harlem,* 159–78.

70. Ibid.

71. Kessner, *La Guardia,* 372.

72. Ibid.

73. Ibid., 371–73. The impact of the Depression on African Americans has generated volumes of literature not to be addressed in this work.

74. Roi Ottley and William J. Weatherby, ed., *The Negro in New York: An Informal Social History, 1626–1940* (New York: Praeger Publishers, 1969), 275–78.

75. Bayor, *La Guardia,* 130–34.

76. "Police End Harlem Riot: Mayor Starts Inquiry: Dodge Sees a Red Plot; District Still Is Tense," *New York Times,* 21 March 1935.

77. Kessner, *La Guardia,* 374–76.

78. Ibid., 372.

79. As quoted in *The Crisis* (October 1947).

80. See generally, Kessner, *La Guardia,* 374–76.

81. The following are some of the sources that carried stories about Bolin's appointment to the Office of the Corporation Counsel: "A Sepia Portia—Jane Bolin," *Apex News* 9, no. 13 (1937); "Miss Jane Bolin Appointed Asst. to Corporation Counsel," *New York Age,* 27 April 1937; "Miss Jane Bolin," *Richmond Planet,* 17 April 1937.

82. As quoted in David Margolick, "At the Bar," *New York Times,* 14 May 1993, B8-L.

83. Rumors that an African American soldier had been shot and killed by a white police officer outraged an already frustrated population still struggling against racial discrimination in their communities, the military, and the war industry.

84. This image was painted clearly in the conclusion of Justice Boyle's report: "The court has not been able for some years satisfactorily to function in cases involving Negro children." Kessner, *La Guardia,* 371–72.

85. Ottley and. Weatherby, *The Negro in New York,* 288–89.

86. Kessner, *La Guardia,* 376.

87. Ibid.

88. Ibid.

89. *The Crisis* (October 1947).

90. Ibid.

91. Interview with Jean Rudd, 9, Bolin Papers, Box 1; "Fair Honors Mrs. Mizelle," Bolin Papers, Box 3, Clipping File.

92. Interview with Jean Rudd, 9, Bolin Papers, Box 1.

93. Ibid.

94. Ibid.

95. Ibid., 18.

96. "Fair Honors Mrs. Mizelle." This newspaper clipping references "Moor" instead of "Moore," U.S. Federal District Court judge in the U. S. Virgin Islands, and the one who had sworn in William Hastie as governor of the Virgin Islands in 1946.

97. Myles A. Paige was appointed a magistrate soon after La Guardia took office in 1934, and two black judges were elected through the political maneuverings of Assemblyman Francis Rivers who secured the creation of a new Tenth Judicial District that made their election possible. The following are some of the sources that carried stories about Bolin's judicial appointment: *The Crisis* (September 1939); "Judge Bolin Hopes Choice Will Inspire Other Women," *Philadelphia Tribune*, 17 August 1939; "New York's Fourth Negro Judge, Now on Bench," *New York Age*, 29 July 1939.

98. Margolick, "At the Bar."

Chapter 4. Politics of Practice

1. Jacob Panken was an early judicial appointee of La Guardia's. Panken was better known in the black community as the judge who unmasked Father Divine in court when he threatened him with contempt of court should he insist that he was God. Transcript of Justice Jacob Panken's induction of Jane Bolin, 24 July 1939, Bolin Papers, Box 3, Schomburg Center, New York City Public Library.

2. Virginia G. Drachman, *Sisters in Law: Women Lawyers in Modern American History* (Cambridge: Harvard University Press, 1998), 233–34.

3. Ibid., 232.

4. Ibid., 229–34.

5. Ibid., 229.

6. Transcript of Justice Jacob Panken's induction of Jane Bolin, 24 July 1939. Bolin Papers, Box 3.

7. Ibid.

8. See Alvin White, "Why Aren't There More Women Lawyers," *Afro-American* (21 February 1959): 7.

9. Transcript of Panken's induction of Bolin.

10. Interview with Jean Rudd, 21, Bolin Papers, Box 1. See Ronald H. Bayor, *Fiorello La Guardia: Ethnicity and Reform* (Arlington Heights, IL: Harlan Davidson, 1993), especially chap. 4; also generally, Nathan Glazer and Daniel Moynihan, *Beyond the Melting Pot: The Negroes, Puerto Ricans, Jews, Italians, and Irish of New York City* (Cambridge: M.I.T. Press, 1963), 208, 221–29.

11. Interview with Jean Rudd, 21–22, Bolin Papers, Box 1.

12. When created in 1933, the Domestic Relations Court's jurisdiction did not include decreeing divorce, separation, annulment, dissolution, or the nullity of an invalid marriage. Transcript of Jane Bolin's speech to the Association of the Bar of the City of New York (ABCNY), 5 April 1954, Bolin Papers, Box 3.

13. Ibid.

14. In the Domestic Relations Court, each judge had to spend one month in each of its two

sections, the Children's Court and the Family Court, rotating throughout the five boroughs of the city so that in the course of a year every judge would have covered both sections of the court in all five boroughs. In 1962, when the court was restructured, each judge was assigned to their home borough, which was the borough of residence at their initial appointment. At that time Bolin therefore became a Manhattan judge. Interview with Jean Rudd, 49, Bolin Papers, Box 1.

15. Transcript of Bolin's speech to the ABCNY.

16. Ibid.

17. Transcript of speech honoring Jane Bolin with Myles Paige Award, December 1983, Bolin Papers, Box 3, Awards Folder.

18. Ibid.; interview with Jean Rudd, 17–18, Bolin Papers, Box 1.

19. Emma Bugbee, "Justice Jane M. Bolin Shuns Glib Diagnosis of Child Crime," *New York Herald Tribune,* 18 April 1943.

20. Interview with Jean Rudd, 22–23, Bolin Papers, Box 1.

21. Ibid., 33.

22. Ibid., 50. Whereas in the adult section of the court, it would have been the bickering of the lawyers that took up much of the time.

23. Memorandum from Presiding Justice John Warren Hill, 26 July 1948, Bolin Papers, Box 3, Clipping File.

24. Judy Klemesrud, "For a Remarkable Judge, A Reluctant Retirement," *New York Times,* 8 December 1978, Bolin Papers, Box 1, Biographical Folder.

25. Drachman, *Sisters in Law,* 178.

26. Ibid., 241.

27. Ibid., 241–42.

28. Interview with Jean Rudd, 75, Bolin Papers, Box 1.

29. Ibid., 18.

30. Ibid., 8, 54–55. Offutt was born in Indiana and raised in Louisville, Kentucky, where his father was a clergyman.

31. Interview with Jean Rudd, 47, Bolin Papers, Box 1.

32. Ibid., 46–48. The literature on this aspect of women's work is rich. See generally, Elizabeth Clark-Lewis, *Living In, Living Out: African American Domestics and the Great Migration* (New York: Kodansha America, 1996); Tera W. Hunter, *To 'Joy My Freedom: Southern Black Women's Lives and Labors After the Civil War* (Cambridge, MA: Harvard University Press, 1997), especially 58–59, 61, 81, 104–6, 212; Stephanie J. Shaw, *What a Woman Ought To Be and To Do: Black Professional Women Workers During the Jim Crow Era* (Chicago: University of Chicago Press, 1996), especially 112, 113–27, 131–33.

33. Interview with Jean Rudd, 47, Bolin Papers, Box 1.

34. Ibid.

35. Ibid., 46–47.

36. In David Margolick, "At the Bar," *New York Times Law,* 14 May 1993.

37. Interview with Jean Rudd, 20, Bolin Papers, Box 1.

38. In Sidney Fields, "Only Human," *New York Daily Mirror,* 5 March 1943, Bolin Papers, Box 3, Clipping File.

39. Interview with Jean Rudd, 43, Bolin Papers, Box 1.

40. Ibid., 45–46.

41. In Fields, "Only Human."

42. "Legacy of a Family Court Judge," *New York Daily News,* 28 December 1978. Like many other such cases involving children, the records remain sealed to protect the child's identity and delinquency.

43. Karen Berger Morello, *The Invisible Bar: The Woman Lawyer in America 1638 to the Present* (New York: Random House, 1986), 226.

44. In White, "Why Aren't There More Women Lawyers," 1.

45. Beverly Blair Cook, "Women as Judges," in Beverly Blair Cook, et al., *Women in the Judicial Process* (Washington, D.C.: American Political Science Association, 1987), 21.

46. See Sol Rubin, *Juvenile Offenders and the Juvenile Justice System* (New York: Oceana Publications, Inc., 1986), 1–14.

47. As described by Albert Deutsch in "Our Rejected Children," in "The Experience of Domestic Relations Court of the City of New York in Relation to the Proposed Unified Family Court," 5 April 1954, Bolin Papers, Box 3, Speeches Folder.

48. Hearings were to be instituted by petition rather than by formal complaints or indictments as with criminal cases, and were to be informal. See generally, Rubin, *Juvenile Offenders,* 1–14.

49. Ibid., especially chap. 1.

50. In Bugbee, "Bolin Shuns Glib Diagnoses of Child Crime."

51. In Julius Adams, "Meet Justice Jane M. Bolin! The Only Negro Woman Judge in the World's Largest City," *New York Amsterdam News,* 29 January 1944, 7A.

52. See, *In re Rutane,* 37 Misc. 2d 234, 234 N.Y.S. 2d 777 (Fam. Ct. 1962).

53. See *Langerman v. Langerman,* 203 Misc. 230, 116 N.Y.S. 2d 420.

54. Ibid.

55. Beatrice Hoffman, "Changes in Domestic Relations Court," in Winifred L. Hepperle and Laura Crites, *Women in the Courts* (Williamsburg, VA: National Center for State Courts, 1978), 136–59.

56. See, *Langerman,* 203 Misc. 230 . Prior to the separation of the parents the father maintained the children in a Rye, New York, house with gardens, a private swimming pool, three full-time employees, and at least three part-time employees. After the parents' separation, the children were living with their mother in an apartment where the daughter shared a bedroom with the maid and the son slept in a room with the bed next to a pipe and had access to the bathroom only through his mother's bedroom or through the room occupied by the maid and his sister.

57. See *Martin v. Sparks,* 202 Misc. 581, 108 N.Y.S. 2d 259 (Dom. Rel. Ct. 1951).

58. Ibid.

59. In Bugbee, "Bolin Shuns Glib Diagnoses of Child Crime."

60. See Rubin, *Juvenile Offenders,* appendix B, 101–2.

61. Klemesrud, "For a Remarkable Judge."

62. Transcript of Judge Bolin's remarks on occasion of her retirement, 7 December 1978, Bolin Papers, Box 3, Honors and Awards Folder.

63. Bugbee, "Bolin Shuns Glib Diagnosis of Child Crime."

64. Ibid.

65. In Klemesrud, "For A Remarkable Judge."

66. Interview with Jean Rudd, 31–32, Bolin Papers, Box 1.

67. Jane M. Bolin to Eleanor Roosevelt, 7 February 1949, Eleanor Roosevelt Papers, Franklin D. Roosevelt Presidential Library, Hyde Park, New York.

68. Eleanor Roosevelt to Justice Bolin, 12 February 1949, Eleanor Roosevelt Papers.

69. William O'Dwyer to Eleanor Roosevelt, 25 March 1949, Eleanor Roosevelt Papers.

70. Eleanor Roosevelt to William O'Dwyer, 20 April 1949, Eleanor Roosevelt Papers.

71. Interview with Jean Rudd, 19, 12, 31, 34–35, Bolin Papers, Box 1.

72. Ibid., 31–32.

73. The case of Myles Paige is instructive here, because when Mayor La Guardia appointed Paige, who was a Columbia University Law School graduate and Senate nominee, to the New York City Magistrates' Court, he had no doubts about his qualifications, yet the mayor felt compelled to say to Paige, "You just have to make good because the attention of the city will be focused on you." Thomas Kessner, *Fiorello H. La Guardia and the Making of Modern New York* (New York: McGraw-Hill Publishing Company, 1989), 376.

74. "Tuskegee Award," transcript of speech honoring Jane Bolin with Tuskegee Award, Bolin Papers, Box 3, Awards Folder.

75. Irving Mitchell Felt to Robert Wagner, 2 April 1959, Bolin Papers, Box 3.

76. Norma Z. Paige to Robert Wagner, 7 April 1959, Bolin Papers, Box 3.

77. Card from Margie Mae Armstrong to Judge Bolin, Bolin Papers, Box 3, Clipping File.

78. Mark McCloskey to Judge Bolin, 16 March 1955, Bolin Papers, Box 3.

79. "Resolution by Bronx Women's Bar Association," 5 May 1959, Bolin Papers, Box 3.

80. Transcript of remarks by Judge Jane M. Bolin on the occasion of her retirement, 7 December 7, Bolin Papers, Box 3.

81. Justice Constance Baker Motley to Judge Bolin, 26 January 1979, Bolin Papers, Box 3.

82. Fiorello La Guardia, a Republican/Fusion candidate, was mayor of New York City from 1934–45; William O'Dwyer, a Tammany Democrat, from 1946–50; Robert F. Wagner Jr., a Democrat, from 1954–65; John V. Lindsay, Republican/Liberal/Democrat, from 1966–73.

83. In Fields, "Only Human"; interview with Jean Rudd, 20, Bolin Papers, Box 1.

84. Interview with Jean Rudd, 19, Bolin Papers, Box 1.

85. Drachman, *Sisters in Law,* 233.

86. Jane Bolin to Theodore Spaulding, 23 August 1949, Bolin Papers, Box 3; also see Geraldine R. Segal, *Blacks in the Law: Philadelphia and the Nation* (Philadelphia: University of Pennsylvania Press, 1983), 30–31. Having dealt with the angst of reappointment by Mayor O'Dwyer just a month earlier and a protracted public challenge by the NAACP, Bolin may have also anticipated and sidestepped the scrutiny associated with such nominations.

Chapter 5. Speaking Truth to Power

1. Access to Judge Bolin's decisions, except for those that have been published, remains restricted.

2. Transcript of Judge Bolin's comments on the occasion of her retirement, 7 December 1978, Bolin Papers, Box 3, Schomburg Center, New York City Public Library.

3. In Judy Klemesrud, "For a Remarkable Judge a Reluctant Retirement," *New York Times,* 8 December 1978.

4. Hubert Delany was appointed tax commissioner by Mayor La Guardia in 1934, and later appointed a justice of the Domestic Relations Court. Justine Wise Polier joined the Domestic Relations Court a few years after Bolin had been on the bench, but they had known each other at Yale, where Polier's husband had been a professor of Bolin's.

5. Sol Rubin and Irving J. Sloan, *Juvenile Offenders and the Juvenile Justice System* (New York: Oceana Publications, Inc., 1986), 14; Patricia McFall Torbet, "Juvenile Probation: the Workhorse of the Juvenile System," *Juvenile Justice Bulletin* (March 1996): 1–5.

6. Interview with Jean Rudd, 10, Bolin Papers, Box 1; Klemesrud, "For a Remarkable Judge."

7. Interview with Jean Rudd, 31, Bolin Papers, Box 1.

8. As quoted in J. Clay Smith Jr., *Emancipation: The Making of the Black Lawyer, 1844–1944* (Philadelphia: University of Pennsylvania Press, 1993), 403; see also Gilbert Osofsky, *Harlem: The Making of a Ghetto, Negro New York, 1890–1930* (New York: Harper & Row, 1966), and Irma Watkins-Owens, *Blood Relations: Caribbean Immigrants and the Harlem Community, 1900–1930* (Bloomington: Indiana University Press, 1996).

9. Thomas Kessner, *Fiorello H. La Guardia and the Making of Modern New York* (New York: McGraw-Hill, 1989), 368–71, 373–74.

10. Judge Jane Bolin to Maceo Thomas, Chairman of the Colored Orphan Asylum, 18 February 1943; interview with Jean Rudd 30, Bolin Papers, Box 1.

11. Interview with Jean Rudd 30, Bolin Papers, Box 1.

12. Ibid.; "Wiltwyck School for Boys," Teaching Eleanor Roosevelt, Eleanor Roosevelt National Historic Site, online at http://www.nps.gov/archive/elro/glossary/wiltwyck-school-for-boys .htm (accessed 30 August 2010).

13. The amendment was sponsored by Earl Brown and Stanley Isaacs, two New York City councilmen with whom Bolin had had repeated talks about the disgrace of using public funds to prop up private agencies that refused to accept the city's African American and Puerto Rican children. Earl Brown was the first African American councilman for New York City, and Stanley Isaacs, who was also borough president of Manhattan, had a reputation as a civil rights advocate. Interview with Jean Rudd, 10, Bolin Papers, Box 1; see also Martha Biondi, *To Stand and Fight: The Struggle for Civil Rights in Postwar New York City* (Cambridge, MA: Harvard University Press, 2003), especially chap. 6.

14. Madelyn E. Turner to Mrs. James Nicely, 23 December 1950, Bolin Papers, Box 3.

15. Judge Bolin to the Honorable Henry McCarthy, 1 March 1955, Bolin Papers, Box 3.

16. Ibid.

17. Jane Bolin to John A. Wallace, 31 July 1963, Bolin Papers, Box 3.

18. Jane M. Bolin to Maceo Thomas, 18 February 1943, Bolin Papers, Box 3.

19. Ibid.

20. "Medicine: Harlem Shuffle," *Time Magazine,* 20 November 1944.

21. In 1929 there were seven black doctors to the institution's fifty-seven white doctors, though there was no overall shortage of African American physicians in the city. Roi Ottley and William J. Weatherby, ed., *The Negro in New York: An Informal Social History, 1626–1940* (New York: Praeger Publishers, 1969), 271–73.

22. Jane Bolin to Reverend Robinson, 20 December 1943, Bolin Papers, Box 3.

23. Ibid.

24. Ibid.

25. Ibid.

26. "First Annual Report of the Trustees of Sydenham Hospital to the Organization Committee for an Interracial Voluntary Hospital in the Harlem Area," *Journal of the National Medical Association* 37, no. 2 (March 1945): 73.

27. "Medicine: Harlem Shuffle."

28. Ernest Pugmire to Jane Bolin, 17 January 1947, Bolin Papers, Box 3.

29. Jane Bolin to Ernest Pugmire, 4 February 1947, Bolin Papers, Box 3.

30. Ibid.

31. Ibid.

32. Ernest Pugmire to Jane Bolin, 17 January 1947, Bolin Papers, Box 3.

33. Jane Bolin to Ernest Pugmire, 4 February 1947, Bolin Papers, Box 3.

34. Steven Lawson, *Running for Freedom: Civil Rights and Black Politics in America Since 1941* (New York: McGraw-Hill, 1991), 6–7.

35. Ibid.

36. Jane Bolin to Colby M. Chester, 25 February 1943, Bolin Papers, Box 3.

37. Lawson, *Running for Freedom,* 5–7.

38. Jane Bolin to Colby M. Chester, 25 February 1943, Bolin Papers, Box 3.

39. "A Standard to Which the Wise and Honest Can Repair," Commencement Speech at Cheyney State Teachers College, 1946, Bolin Papers, Box 3.

40. Ibid.

41. Jane Bolin to Justine Wise Polier, 24 October 1978, Bolin Papers, Box 3.

42. Jane Bolin to Frank Ortiz, 6 December 1962, Bolin Papers, Box 3.

43. Interview with Jean Rudd, 64, Bolin Papers, Box 1.

44. In Bruce McM. Wright, "A Black Brood on Black Judges," *Judicature* 57, no. 1 (June–July 1973), 23.

45. "Memorandum to Metropolitan Press," with letter from Peyton F. Anderson, chairman of the Harlem Branch of the YMCA, to all committee members, 6 April 1943, Bolin Papers, Box 3. Other committee members included Samuel Battle, parole commissioner of the City of New York; Lester Granger, executive secretary of the National Urban League (NUL); Austin R. McCormack, former commissioner of correction of the City of New York; Walter White, executive secretary of the NAACP; and others from varying offices of the YWCA, YMCA, and NUL.

46. Ibid.

47. Ibid.

48. Justine Wise Polier to Jane Bolin, 24 October 1978, Bolin Papers, Box 3. This was reminiscent of a similar protest waged by a fifteen-year-old Bolin against a local Poughkeepsie newspaper.

49. Biondi, *To Stand and Fight,* 70–74.

50. "Memorandum to Metropolitan Press."

51. The federal Harlem River Houses project was stepped up in the aftermath of the riot. However, as late as 1935, investigators reported that 84 percent of the housing lacked central heating and more than half of the apartments did not have private bathrooms. See Kessner, *La Guardia,* 372.

52. Ronald H. Bayor, *Fiorello La Guardia: Ethnicity and Reform* (Arlington Heights, IL: Harlan Davidson, 1993), 170–73.

53. Kessner, *La Guardia,* 134.

54. Jane Bolin to the Honorable Joseph T. Sharkey, 18 December 1950, Bolin Papers, Box 3.

55. Ibid.

56. Biondi, *To Stand and Fight,* 229–41; Bayor, *La Guardia,* 165–70.

57. Jane Bolin to Honorable Robert F. Wagner, 9 September 1957; Jane Bolin to Honorable Robert E. Barnes, 9 September 1957, Bolin Papers, Box 3.

58. Jane Bolin to Honorable Robert E. Barnes, 9 September 1957, Bolin Papers, Box 3.

59. In Sidney Fields, "Only Human," Clipping File, Bolin Papers, Box 3.

60. Biondi, *To Stand and Fight,* 240.

61. *Poughkeepsie New Yorker,* 17 February 1944, Bolin Papers, Box 3, Clipping File.

62. A sense of what Jane Bolin experienced and what she was aware of growing up in Poughkeepsie are discussed in chapter 1.

63. *Poughkeepsie New Yorker,* 23 February 1944, Bolin Papers, Box 3, Clipping File.

64. Ibid.

65. Lawrence H. Mamiya and Patricia A. Kaurouma, ed., *For Their Courage and For Their Struggles: The Black Oral History Project of Poughkeepsie, New York* (Poughkeepsie, NY: Urban Center for Africana Studies, Vassar College, 1978), 9–10.

66. Editorial, *The Advocate,* Cleveland, OH, 1 May 1920, as reprinted in Gerda Lerner, ed., *Black Women in White America: A Documentary History* (New York: Vintage Books, 1973), 484.

67. *Poughkeepsie New Yorker,* 23 February 1944.

68. *New York Herald Tribune* 20 February 1945, Bolin Papers, Box 3, Clipping File.

69. Ibid.

70. The ruling in *Plessy v. Ferguson,* 163 U.S. 537 (1896), provided legal precedent for racial segregation in American society. The NAACP became involved in a protracted fight and won in 1954 with the *Brown v. Board of Education of Topeka, Kansas,* 347 U.S. 483 (1954), decision that essentially said the "separate but equal" is inherently unequal and therefore unconstitutional.

Chapter 6. Persona Non Grata

1. These women included Jane Addams, founder of the Hull House settlement in Chicago; Florence Kelley, founder of the National Consumer's League; Mary White Ovington, leader in the National Consumer's League, New York Social Reform Club, and founder of Greenpoint Settlement; Sophinisba Breckinridge, Edith Abbott, and Grace Abbott, social service activists; Ellen Gates Starr, cofounder of Hull House; and Alice Hamilton, public health crusader. See Dorothy Salem, *To Better Our World: Black Women in Organized Reform, 1890–1920* (Brooklyn, NY: Carlson Publishing, Inc., 1990).

2. Both were active in interracial organizations. Terrell was a participant and speaker in the New York Social Reform Club and the National American Woman Suffrage Association and was one of the charter members of the Constitution League founded by John Milholland, a white reformer and philanthropist, to protect the constitutional rights of black Americans. Wells-Barnett worked closely with the likes of Jane Addams and Sophinisba Breckinridge in the Frederick Douglass Center and participated in the National American Woman Suffrage Association, all while on her antilynching crusade. See Dorothy Salem, "Black Women and

the NAACP, 1909–1922: An Encounter With Race, Class, and Gender," in Kim Marie Vaz, ed., *Black Women in America* (Thousand Oaks, CA: SAGE Publications, 1995), 56–57.

3. Salem, *To Better Our World*.

4. Salem, "Black Women and the NAACP," 54–70.

5. Thomas C. Holt, "The Lonely Warrior: Ida B. Wells-Barnett and the Struggle for Black Leadership," in John Hope Franklin and August Meier, ed., *Black Leaders of the Twentieth Century* (Urbana: University of Illinois Press, 1982), 50.

6. With the names of Amy Spingarn, Mary White Ovington, Lillian Alexander, and Marion Cuthbert listed among the members of the board of directors from New York City for 1948 and earlier, perhaps the executive office only intended to allow one woman at a time to be nominated from the New York Branch to the national board. Though less restrictive than allowing only one woman from the New York Branch on the board, the provision still limited the participation of women, and especially African American women, in the policy-making body of the NAACP. Memorandum to Nominating Committee, 29 December 1943, NAACP Papers, Board of Directors Folder, Library of Congress, Manuscript Division, Washington, D.C.

7. Ibid.

8. Mary McLeod Bethune to Sadie Alexander, 25 November 1939, University of Pennsylvania Transcripts 50, A374S, Box 6, Folder 13.

9. A total of sixty-one people came from Poughkeepsie, Clinton Corners, Salt Point, and two other nearby communities. NAACP Branch Files, Poughkeepsie, New York Folder, 1932–1934, NAACP Papers.

10. Director of Branches to Gaius C. Bolin, 14 April, 1931, NAACP Branch Files, Poughkeepsie. Lawrence H. Mamiya and Patricia A. Kaurouma found that a very small elite group of people, composed mainly of longtime Poughkeepsie residents and the professional class of doctors, lawyers, dentists, teachers, and ministers were perceived as the "leaders" of the black community both by themselves and others. Included in this group were the Bolins, the Morgans, the Lowes, the Paynes, and the Andersons, who were signatories and officers of the Dutchess County Branch of the NAACP. Mamiya and Kaurouma, ed., *For Their Courage and For Their Struggles: The Black Oral History Project of Poughkeepsie, New York* (Poughkeepsie, NY: Urban Center for Africana Studies, Vassar College, 1978), 18–154.

11. By July 1937 an application for charter of Poughkeepsie Youth Council Branch was approved by the national office of the NAACP. NAACP Branch Files, Poughkeepsie.

12. Gaius Bolin Jr. to William Pickens, Esq., 20 August 1931, NAACP Branch Files, Poughkeepsie.

13. Ibid. Mamiya and Kaurouma's oral history project reveals that the black leaders in Poughkeepsie, like in neighboring towns, believed in a "quiet way" of working by negotiating for jobs for blacks at local hospitals and factories. Social change occurred from the top down during their leadership, as no attempt was made to mobilize mass support in the form of protests, demonstrations, or picketing. Their effectiveness lasted from before the 1920s until after World War II when the largest influx of black migration to Poughkeepsie began. See Mamiya and Kaurouma, *For Their Courage*, 5–6.

14. The Scottsboro case rested on the conviction of nine innocent black youths; nevertheless, it produced important decisions that reaffirmed black people's right to basic constitutional

protections. Gaius Bolin to *The Crisis,* 7 August 1931.See generally, Dan Carter, *Scottsboro: A Tragedy of the American South* (Baton Rouge: Louisiana State University Press, 1969).

15. Transcript of Speech in Honor of Du Bois, Speeches Folder, Bolin Papers, Box 3.

16. Memorandum to Mr. Wilkins from Mr. Current, 28 October 1949, NAACP Branch Files, New York City Branch Folder, 1949, NAACP Papers. Art. V, sec. 7 provided that the "entire net proceeds of any fund-raising effort for exclusively national purposes shall be transmitted to the National Office."

17. Jane Bolin to Arthur Spingarn, 9 March 1950, Bolin Papers, Box 3.

18. Ibid. Also see Joanne Grant, *Ella Baker: Freedom Bound* (New York: John Wiley & Sons, Inc., 1998), especially chaps. 3, 4, and 5; Barbara Ransby, *Ella Baker and the Black Freedom Movement: A Radical Democratic Vision* (Chapel Hill: University of North Carolina Press, 2003), especially chap. 4.

19. Frequent controversy ensued over the division of funds often intended for the New York Branch but received by the New York National Office, and vice versa. Another financial incident involved a request by the New York Branch for permission to withhold funds from the national office. The national board granted the request but problems arose when the branch sought an extension of the withholding period. The particular latitude for retaining funds granted to the New York Branch by the national office in September 1948 created additional problems. The association's constitution and bylaws for branches, Article V, Section 7, state that all funds raised by branches are to be shared equally between the national office and the branch. In accordance with the request of the New York Branch, however, the national board on September 13, 1948, agreed to the following: "That the New York City Branch be granted permission to use such reasonable means as it may devise to defray the operating expenses of the local branch, the National Office to waive its share of the funds exclusive of membership receipts in this particular instance, with the understanding that this permission is granted through December 31, 1948 only, and the Branch must make a financial report of all funds raised to the Branch, the National Office, and the public." Hubert Delany to Roy Wilkins, 9 November 1949; Roy Wilkins to Hubert Delany, 17 November 1949; Roy Wilkins to Lindsay White, 20 January 1949, NAACP Branch Files, New York Folder, NAACP Papers.

20. Gloster B. Current to Roy Wilkins, 28 October 1949, NAACP Branch Files, New York City Branch Folder, 1949, NAACP Papers. The particular incident concerning Walter White stemmed from a controversy that raged over the political nature of the articles he wrote in the *New York Herald Tribune* favoring Harry Truman during the 1948 presidential campaign. At the time, Harlem had gone Democratic, but the articles were offensive to many Republicans. The New York Branch, though unique in its proximity to the national office, was not the only branch that suffered such experiences. Christopher Reed notes that almost every year seemed to bring some political contest in Chicago, and with each one, the number of volunteers, fundraising activities, and memberships decreased. *New York Amsterdam News,* 5 November 1949, 3, 39. See Christopher Robert Reed, *The Chicago NAACP and the Rise of Black Professional Leadership, 1910–1966* (Bloomington: Indiana University Press, 1997), 88.

21. Memorandum to National Board of Directors, October 1949, NAACP Branch Files, New York City Branch Folder, 1949, NAACP Papers. The New York Branch also charged that Du Bois's dismissal adversely affected their membership and fundraising campaign (Du Bois was dismissed between September and December 1948). Current reported to Wilkins that there was no adverse effect but blamed low membership on the branch's own lack of suc-

cessful campaigning. Gloster B. Current to Roy Wilkins, 28 October 1949, NAACP Branch Files, New York City Branch Folder, 1949, NAACP Papers.

22. The matter of the independent petition to nominate Bolin will be dealt with later in the chapter, but suffice it to say at this point that Roy Wilkins was wholly against Bolin's renomination. Hubert Delany to Roy Wilkins, 9 November 1949, NAACP Branch Files, New York, New York Folder, NAACP Papers.

23. Ibid.

24. Roy Wilkins to Hubert Delany, 18 November 1949, NAACP Branch Files, New York Folder, NAACP Papers.

25. Wilkins also resented what he saw as Delany's inaction when it came to the derelictions of the New York Branch and their failure to cooperate in carrying out the national program, campaigning for memberships, and in raising money for national projects. Roy Wilkins to Hubert Delany, 1 November 1949, NAACP Branch Files, New York City Folder, 1949, NAACP Papers.

26. Hubert Delany to Wilkins, 9 November 1949, NAACP Branch Files, New York, New York Folder, NAACP Papers.

27. Jane Bolin to Arthur Spingarn, 9 March 1950, NAACP Branch Files, New York Folder, NAACP Papers.

28. The increasing tension that erupted after Bolin's name was removed from the ballot motivated the branch's request for a conference and the national office's ignoring the request. *New York Amsterdam News,* 5 November 1949, 3, 39; Delany to Wilkins, 9 November 1949, NAACP Branch Files, New York, New York Folder, NAACP Papers.

29. Jane Bolin to Arthur Spingarn, 9 March 1950, Bolin Papers, Box 3.

30. This reference to "Hague attitude" is no doubt evoking the "I Am the Law" speech given by Frank Hague (Democratic Party boss and mayor of Jersey City, NJ, 1917–47) on city government. See "'I Am the Law,' Mayor Hague Tells 1,000 In Speech on Jersey City Government," *New York Times,* 11 November 1937. Bolin's concerns were reminiscent of those that hastened Ella Baker's resignation from the NAACP, and of those that permitted Walter White to reprimand Baker for her independent thinking that he felt defied his leadership. At a 1944 Administrative Committee meeting she abstained from a vote to endorse his letter to the mayor of New York City regarding a controversy at Harlem's Sydenham Hospital, which had recently added a number of African Americans to its directorate and staff and proclaimed itself as the first "interracial" voluntary hospital. Ransby, *Ella Baker,* 143. Also, "Medicine: Harlem Shuffle," *Time,* 20 November 1944. Not everyone in the NAACP celebrated Sydenham's model of integration, which for many fell short of that which was practiced at the city-owned Harlem Hospital. Furthermore, some in the NAACP leadership thought that the Sydenham model might siphon support from Harlem Hospital.

31. Hubert Delany to Roy Wilkins, 9 November 1949, NAACP Branch Files, New York Folder, NAACP Papers.

32. Ibid.; Jane Bolin to Arthur Spingarn, 9 March 1950, Bolin Papers, Box 3. Historian Patricia Sullivan reasons that a long overdue hike in membership fees to $2 was the primary cause for the 50 percent drop in membership to 250,000 in 1949, but agreed that the drop in membership also pointed to deeper weaknesses. Patricia Sullivan, *Lift Every Voice: The NAACP and the Making of the Civil Rights Movement* (New York: New Press, 2009), 373.

33. Wilkins also attributed the decrease to other factors affecting certain localities, such

as a shipping strike in San Francisco, a coal strike that affected the coal-producing states, a steel strike in Cleveland, and shutdowns and talks of strikes in Detroit. Wilkins to Delany, 18 November 1949, NAACP Branch Files, New York, New York Folder, NAACP Papers.

34. Wilkins to Gibson, 17 March 1950, NAACP Branch Files, New York Folder, NAACP Papers.

35. Bolin to Spingarn, 9 March 1950, Bolin Papers, Box 3. By the 1940s the association's Legal Defense Fund under the leadership of Charles Hamilton Houston and his social engineers had begun to seriously chip away at segregation in higher education and was poised for a frontal attack on *Plessy's* "separate but equal" doctrine. The NAACP Legal Defense Fund had indeed done a superb job on many fronts of the civil rights struggle, such as in *Gaines v. Canada,* 305 U.S. 337 (1938), *Pearson v. Murray,* 182 A. 590, 169 Md. 478, 103 A.L.R. 706 (1936), and *Sipuel v. Oklahoma State Board of Regents,* 332 U.S. 631 (1948) in education; *Shelley v. Kraemer,* 334 U.S. 1 (1948) in housing; and *Smith v. Allwright,* 321 U.S. 649 (1944) in voting.

36. Bolin to Spingarn, 9 March 1950, Bolin Papers, Box 3.

37. Reed, *The Chicago NAACP,* 68.

38. Carol Mueller, "Ella Baker and the Origins of Participatory Democracy," in Vicki L. Crawford, Jacqueline Anne Rouse, and Barbara Woods, ed., *Women in the Civil Rights Movement: Trailblazers and Torchbearers, 1941–1965* (Bloomington: Indiana University Press, 1993). Also see Grant, *Ella Baker,* especially chap. 3, 4, and 5.

39. In this capacity Bolin was better situated to garner the support of fellow board members such as Judge Hubert Delany. As will be discussed later, her philosophical conviction endeared many within the national office to the fight.

40. Delany to Wilkins, 9 November 1949, NAACP Branch Files, New York, New York Folder, NAACP Papers.

41. Bolin's second term as board member would expire in December 1949. The members of the Nominating Committee (elected by the conference) were Dr. J. L. Leach (Flint, Michigan), Mrs. Rosa B. Johnson (Marshalltown, Iowa), W. K. Saxon, (Asheville, North Carolina), Joshua Thompson (Amber, Pennsylvania) and (elected by the board) Judge Hubert T. Delany (New York City), Mrs. D. E. Lampkin (Pittsburgh), and Alfred Baker Lewis (Greenwich, Connecticut). Dr. Leach and Daisy Lampkin to Branch Officer, 14 November 1949, NAACP Branch Files, New York Folder, NAACP Papers; Thurgood Marshall to Bernard Young, Publisher of *Journal and Guide,* 18 October 1949, NAACP Board of Directors Files, Jane Bolin Folder, NAACP Papers; *The Afro-American,* 8 October 1949, 1, 2.

42. Bolin and Delany to Wilkins, 22 November 1949, NAACP Board of Directors Files, Jane Bolin Folder, NAACP Papers.

43. It is appropriate at this time to differentiate between the "staff," so often referenced by Bolin, and the "board." "Staff" is synonymous with the "paid staff" as in the chief administrative officers such as the executive secretary and assistant/acting executive secretary, unlike the volunteer members of the board of directors. The "national office" includes both staff and board members. *The Afro-American,* 8 October 1949, 1.

44. According to Article II, Section 3, as amended by the National Board of Directors at its meeting on 13 September 1948, "the said Association shall have a Nominating Committee consisting of seven (7) members of the Association; four (4) to be elected by the delegates to the annual convention; three (3) to be elected annually by the Board of Directors from its

own members." "Amendments to National Constitution," NAACP Branch Files, New York City Folder, New York, NAACP Papers.

45. During the period of this dissension, Walter White was executive secretary and Roy Wilkins was assistant secretary and, for some time, acting secretary. Bolin to Spingarn, 9 March 1950, Bolin Papers, Box 3; Delany to Wilkins, 9 November 1949, NAACP Branch Files, New York Folder, NAACP Papers; *The Afro-American,* 8 October 1949.

46. Bolin to Spingarn, 9 March 1949; Delany to Wilkins, 9 November 1949, NAACP Branch Files, New York Folder, NAACP Papers.

47. Minutes of Board of Directors Meeting, 10 October 1949, NAACP Branch Files, New York Folder, NAACP Papers.

48. Ibid. Bolin was no doubt referring to the 1934 incident surrounding an editorial Du Bois wrote that appeared in *The Crisis* without the prior approval of the Crisis Committee. The editorial criticized the association's policy and philosophy regarding segregation. Du Bois denounced the association's historic stand, contending that "the Association is an organization that never had taken and never could take an absolute stand against race segregation." When the board voted that no salaried officer could criticize its policy, work, or officers in *The Crisis,* that action was more than Du Bois was willing to concede, so he submitted, and the board accepted, his resignation in 1934. However, Bolin might have been referring to the much older Du Bois who, in 1948, was summarily dismissed from the association for basic policy differences. His dismissal came months after the presentation of "An Appeal to the World" petition on the denial of human rights to minorities and an appeal to the United Nations for redress. See Minnie Finch, *The NAACP: Its Fight For Justice* (Metuchen, NJ: Scarecrow Press, 1981), 102, 119–20; Charles Kellogg, *NAACP: A History of the National Association for the Advancement of Colored People* (Baltimore: Johns Hopkins Press, 1967); B. Joyce Ross, *J. E. Spingarn and the Rise of the NAACP* (New York: Athenaeum, 1972.)

49. Remarks by Judge Bolin at Board of Directors Meeting, 10 October 1949, NAACP Board of Directors File, Jane Bolin Folder, NAACP Papers.

50. Ibid. Walter White was instrumental in bringing Bolin into the fold of the national office, yet from the beginning she exhibited only contempt for him as executive secretary.

51. Board of Directors Meeting, 10 October 1949, NAACP Board of Directors Files, Jane Bolin Folder, NAACP Papers.

52. Minutes of Meeting of the Board of Directors, 14 November 1949, NAACP Board of Director Files, Jane Bolin Folder, NAACP Papers. It is interesting that Wilkins was now willing to consider the effects of bad publicity on the operations of the association as well as branch and national offices, when not too long before he dismissed similar concerns raised by the New York Branch.

53. "Both Regarded As 'Persona Non Grata,'" *Atlanta Daily World,* 23 November 1949.

54. NAACP Board of Directors Files, Jane Bolin Folder, NAACP Papers; *The Afro-American,* 8 October 1949, Bolin Papers, Box 3, Clipping File.

55. See generally, Ransby, *Ella Baker,* especially chap. 4.

56. NAACP Branch Files, New York Branch Folder, NAACP Papers.

57. Nominating Petition, NAACP Branch Files, New York Branch Folder, NAACP Papers.

58. Hubert Delany to Roy Wilkins, 22 November 1949, NAACP Branch Files, New York Folder, NAACP Papers.

59. Wilkins to Lindsay White, 1 November 1949, NAACP Branch Files, New York Branch Folder, NAACP Papers.

60. Ibid.; Bolin to Louis Wright, 6 December 1949, NAACP Board of Directors Files, Jane Bolin Folder, NAACP Papers.

61. Bolin to Louis Wright, 6 December 1949, NAACP Board of Directors Files, Jane Bolin Folder, NAACP Papers.

62. Lindsay White to Wilkins, 3 November 1949, NAACP Branch Files, New York Branch Folder, NAACP Papers.

63. The committee recommended the following individuals for election to the board: Kelly M. Alexander, Charlotte, NC; Dr. W. Montague Cobb, Washington, D.C.; Wesley W. Law, Savannah, GA; Dr. Harry J. Greene, Philadelphia, PA; Carl R. Johnson, Kansas City, MO. The list of incumbent board members recommended for reelection were Dr. Allan Knight Chalmers, Boston, MA; Dr. Nathan K. Christopher, Cleveland, OH; Earl B. Dickerson, Chicago, IL; Dr. George D. Flemmings, Fort Worth, TX; Dr. Allen F. Jackson, Baltimore, MD; Dr. O. Clay Maxwell, New York, NY; Philip Murray, Washington, D.C.; Theodore Spaulding, Philadelphia, PA; the Honorable Charles E. Toney, New York, NY; Dr. Louis T. Wright, New York, NY. Dr. Leach and Daisy Lampkin to Branch Officers, 28 October 1949 and 14 November 1949, NAACP Branch Files, New York Branch Folder, NAACP Papers.

64. These officers were the Reverend William Lloyd Imes, vice president, National Board of Directors; the Honorable Hubert Delany, member, Nominating Committee, National Board of Directors, chairman, National Board Committee on Branches; Earl B. Dickerson, member, National Board of Directors; James E. Allen, president, New York State Conference of NAACP Branches; Lindsay H. White, president, New York Branch of NAACP. NAACP Branch Files, New York Branch Folder, NAACP Papers.

65. Delany, Imes, Dickerson, Allen, and White to Branch Presidents, 16 November 1949, NAACP Board of Directors Files, Jane Bolin Folder, NAACP Papers. Hereinafter referenced as New York Branch to Branch Presidents.

66. Ibid. At first glance the sentence conjures up images of the antidemocratic. As authorized as this correspondence was, it intended, as did Dr. Leach's letter, to influence the outcome of the board election.

67. Ibid.

68. New York Branch to Branch Presidents.

69. The letter was addressed to Hurley simply because months prior she had visited the Williamsport and Lewisburg branches on Youth Division business. Rev. Madison A. Bowe to Ruby Hurley, 25 November 1949, NAACP Board of Directors Files, Jane Bolin Folder, NAACP Papers.

70. Everett Lawrence to Chairman of the Nominating Committee, 21 November 1949, NAACP Branch Files, New York Branch Folder, NAACP Papers.

71. Ibid.

72. Wilkins to Everett Lawrence, 23 November 1949, NAACP Branch Files, New York Branch Folder, NAACP Papers.

73. Wilkins to Reverend Bowe, 30 November 1949, NAACP Board of Directors Files, Jane Bolin Folder, NAACP Papers. Delany's statement has no bearing on whether Judge Bolin wanted to "fight" for reelection. After all, Delany's statement was made moments after the committee voted to remove her.

74. Delany to Wilkins, 30 November 1949, NAACP Branch Files, New York Branch Folder, NAACP Papers.

75. Ibid. Of course Wilkins's explanation stated that after Delany left the meeting, the committee continued its deliberations and unanimously agreed—in the light of Delany's statement to "personally fight" its action regarding Judge Bolin—to designate Lampkin as secretary and to authorize the chairman and the secretary to issue "such communications in the name of the committee as was deemed necessary by developing events. See Wilkins to Delany, November 29, 1949, NAACP Board of Directors Files, Jane Bolin Folder, NAACP Papers.

76. The balloting of the branches for members of the board of directors was done at the association's 3 January 1950 annual meeting.

77. Wilkins to Bolin, 10 January 1950, NAACP Board of Directors Files, Jane Bolin Folder, NAACP Papers.

78. Bolin to Wilkins, 11 January 1950, NAACP Board of Directors Files, Jane Bolin Folder, NAACP Papers.

79. New York Branch to Branch Presidents.

80. Memorandum to Self from Miss Jackson, Secretary, 20 January 1950, NAACP Board of Directors Filers, Jane Bolin Folder, NAACP Papers.

81. New York Branch to Branch Presidents.

82. Bolin to Wright, 8 February 1950, Bolin Papers, Box 3. As copied, the letter was sent to the following vice presidents: Mrs. Mary McLeod Bethune, Miss Nannie H. Burroughs, Mr. Godfrey L. Cabot, Hon. Arthur Capper, Miss Marion Cuthbert, Hon. Harry E. Davis, Mr. Douglas P. Falconer, Dr. Buell G. Gallagher, Bishop John A. Gregg, Dr. John Haynes Holmes, Dr. William Lloyd Imes, Hon. Hubert Humphrey, Hon. Irs W. Jayne, Mr. Isadore Martin, Mr. H. L. Mitchell, Miss L. Pearl Mitchell, Mr. T. G. Nutter, Miss Mary White Ovington, Dr. A. Clayton Powell Sr., Mr. A Philip Randolph, Rev. James H. Robinson, Mr. Ike Smalls, Mr. Willard S. Townsend, Bishop W. J. Walls.

83. Bolin to Spingarn, 9 March 1950, Bolin Papers, Box 3.

84. Marshall's memorandum said in part:

> In most corporations there are two bodies of officers—(1) directors who are elected by the stockholders or membership and (2) administrative officers, such as president, treasurer, secretary etc. (13 Am. Jur., Sec. 867). The appointment or election of the latter group is usually entrusted to the Board of Directors, although they may be elected by the stock-holders or the membership. (13 Am. Jur. Sec. 867). In this Association, the Directors are elected by the membership. The administrative officers are appointed by the Board. These administrative officers perform purely administrative duties and have only such powers and perform only such duties as are delegated to them by their appointing authority. (13 Am. Jur. Sec. 889). Generally, the administrative officers of a corporation are not simultane-ously directors of a corporation. As a matter of fact they are usually a distinct and separate body of officers, *Shriver v. Carlin,* 155 Md. 51, 141 A.434; *Stott v. Stott Realty Co.,* 246 Mich. 267, 224 N.W. 623; Uniform Business Corporation Act, section 32. However, officers may be simultaneously directors of a corporation unless the bylaws specifically prohibit this. The Membership Corporation Law of New York, section 45, specifically provides that the directors of a membership corporation shall be elected by the members and that

the officers shall be chosen as provided by the bylaws. The Constitution also by Article II limits the number of directors to 48. To allow the officers elected by the Directors to vote would be in effect adding to the number of directors contrary to the express provisions of our Constitution. Minutes of Board of Directors Meeting, 14 February 1950, NAACP Board of Directors Files, Jane Bolin Folder, NAACP Papers.

85. Minutes of Board of Directors Meeting, 14 February 1950, NAACP Board of Directors Files, Jane Bolin Folder, NAACP Papers.

86. William Lloyd Imes to Bolin, 17 February 1950, Bolin Papers, Box 3.

87. Bishop W. J. Walls to Bolin, 1 March 1950, Bolin Papers, Box 3.

88. Minutes of Board of Directors Meeting, 10 April 1950, NAACP Board of Directors Files, Jane Bolin Folder, NAACP Papers.

89. Ibid.

90. Bolin to Spingarn, 9 March 1950, NAACP Board of Directors Files, Jane Bolin Folder, NAACP Papers.

91. Wilkins to Louis Wright, 15 March 1950, NAACP Board of Directors Files, Jane Bolin Folder, NAACP Papers; Telegrams from *Norfolk Journal and Guide* and *Carolina Times* to the National Office, March 13, 1950, Bolin Papers, Box 3.

92. Bolin to Spingarn, 9 March 1950, Bolin Papers, Box 3.

93. Judge Charles E. Toney, Dr. Channing H. Tobias, and Dr. Louis T. Wright were appointed to serve on the committee. There was some division in reaching the decision to ask Bolin to withdraw her resignation. Minutes of Board of Directors Meeting, 13 March 1950, NAACP Board of Directors Files, Jane Bolin Folder, NAACP Papers.

94. "For Immediate Release," NAACP Board of Directors Files, Jane Bolin Folder, NAACP Papers.

95. Spingarn saw a lack of good faith in Bolin's release of the news of her resignation to the press and in her belief that vice presidents could vote. He essentially argued that Bolin knew or should have known that vice presidents did not vote, since he knew the duties of the office of president and that no one had told him what they were. In essence he imputed the responsibility to the officer to find out what his or her duties are. Minutes of Board of Directors Meeting, 13 March 1950, NAACP Board of Directors Files, Jane Bolin Folder, NAACP Papers.

96. "For Immediate Release," NAACP Board of Directors Files, Jane Bolin Folder, NAACP Papers.

97. Editorial, 18 March 1950, *Baltimore Afro-American.*

98. "Justice Bolin Rips Officers And Quits Job," 18 March 1950, *New York Amsterdam News.*

99. "Justice Jane Bolin Quits NAACP: Blasts 'Contemptuous Attitude,'" 18 March 1950, *New York Age.*

100. Wilkins to Wright, 15 March 1950, NAACP Board of Directors Files, Jane Bolin Folder, NAACP Papers.

101. Wright's statement was supplemented with four detailed sections of examples in support of the charge that Judge Bolin's actions were not in good faith. Wilkins attached a cover letter with his own comments to a desk copy of Wright's comment for William Gibson, editor of the *Afro-American.* Not realizing or not caring that Wilkins's comments were intended to be "off the record," Gibson printed them, thereby bringing yet another dimension to the controversy. "Statement on Judge Jane M. Bolin's Letter," by Dr. Louis T. Wright, Chairman

of the Board of the NAACP, 15 March 1950, NAACP Board of Directors Files, Jane Bolin Folder, NAACP Papers. See also Wilkins to William Gibson, 17 March 1950 and 22 March 1950, NAACP Board of Directors Files, Jane Bolin Folder, NAACP Papers.

102. Wilkins to Bernard Young, 22 March 1950, NAACP Board of Directors Files, Jane Bolin Folder, NAACP Papers.

103. As mentioned earlier, the *New York Amsterdam News* and the *New York Age* were aware of the ongoing struggle of Bolin and the New York Branch, and kept the issues in the news with or without confirmation from the national office.

104. Wilkins to William O. Walker, 20 April 1950, NAACP Board of Directors Files, Jane Bolin Folder, NAACP Papers.

105. Ibid.

106. Denton J. Brooks Jr. to Wright, 23 March 1950, NAACP Board of Directors Files, Jane Bolin Folder, NAACP Papers. The idea of administrative anonymity seems to have had great currency with the NAACP leadership and quite a few of its members. But is this endemic to the NAACP, all civil rights organizations, or all organizations? And does political time and place impact the desire for such anonymity? These are not questions that will be given close attention here, but are questions that elicit further inquiry.

107. Charles H. White to the Editor, *Pittsburg Courier,* Wilkins, and Charles A. Levy, 20 March 1950, NAACP Board of Directors Files, Jane Bolin Folder, NAACP Papers.

108. "For Immediate Release," NAACP Board of Directors Files, Jane Bolin Folder, NAACP Papers.

109. Bolin to Wright, 14 February 1951, NAACP Board of Directors Files, Jane Bolin Folder, NAACP Papers.

110. Thomas Kessner, *Fiorello H. La Guardia and the Making of Modern New York* (New York: McGraw-Hill, 1989), 570–72.

Epilogue

1. Organized by the Association of Family Court Judges in New York City, the program was sponsored by deputy mayors Herman Badillo and Basil Paterson; the chief judge of New York State Court of Appeals, Charles D. Breitel; and civil rights luminaries such as Kenneth B. Clark, Dorothy I. Height, Benjamin Hooks, Vernon D. Jordan, and Pauli Murray. It was held at Vanderbilt Auditorium of New York University School of Law.

2. Russell Wheeler, "The Political Function of Court Systems," *Judicature* 57 (1984): 296.

3. Political scientist Jewel Prestage uses this phrase to capture the political vulnerability of African American women in the judiciary. See Jewel Prestage, "Black Women Judges: An Examination of Their Socio-Economic, Educational and Political Backgrounds and Judicial Placement," in Franklin D. Jones and Michael O. Adams, ed., *Readings in American Political Issues,* (Dubuque, IA: Kendall/Hunt Publishing, 1987), 324–44.

4. Ann Firor Scott, "On Seeing and Not Seeing: A Case of Historical Invisibility," *Journal of American History* 71 (June 1984): 7–21.

5. Armistead S. Pride and Clint C. Wilson II, *A History of the Black Press* (Washington, D.C.: Howard University Press, 1997), 222–23.

6. The author is aware that much of what is said or not said in an interview is often directly related to the format of an interview and the type of questions asked. Yet, even as Bolin spoke

about her association with the NAACP, she never fully addressed the incident surrounding her resignation.

7. Deborah Gray White, "Mining the Forgotten: Manuscript Sources for Black Women's History," *Journal of American History* 74 (1997).

8. Darlene Clark Hine, "Rape and the Inner Lives of Black Women: Thoughts on the Culture of Dissemblance," in Virginia Bernhard, Betty Brandon, Elizabeth Fox-Genovese and Theda Perdue, ed. *Southern Women: Histories and Identities* (Columbia: University of Missouri Press, 1992), 177–89.

9. Interview with Jean Rudd, 1990; letter from Jane Bolin to Mary Paitoo, 6 June 1962; both in Bolin Papers, Box 1, Schomburg Center, New York City Public Library.

10. Letter from Donny to Jane, 14 June 1956, Bolin Papers, Box 1.

11. Letter from Jane Bolin to Mrs. Alexander, 25 April 1939, Bolin Papers, Box 1.

12. Millery Polyné, *From Douglass to Duvalier: U.S. African Americans, Haiti, and Pan Americanism, 1870–1964* (Gainesville: University Press of Florida, 2010), 92, 103.

Index

JACQUELINE A. McLEOD is an associate professor of history and African & African American studies at Metropolitan State College of Denver and coeditor of *Crossing Boundaries: Comparative History of Blacks in Diaspora*.

The University of Illinois Press
is a founding member of the
Association of American University Presses.

––––––––––––––––––––––––––––––––

Composed in 11/13 Perpetua
by Celia Shapland
at the University of Illinois Press
Manufactured by Sheridan Books, Inc.

University of Illinois Press
1325 South Oak Street
Champaign, IL 61820-6903
www.press.uillinois.edu